Doubting Thomas

DOUBTING THOMAS

Glenn W. Most

HARVARD UNIVERSITY PRESS
Cambridge, Massachusetts
London, England
2005

Frontispiece: The holy finger of St. Thomas Apostle.
Basilica of Santa Croce in Gerusalemme, Rome.

Designed by Gwen Nefsky Frankfeldt

Library of Congress Cataloging-in-Publication Data

Most, Glenn W.
Doubting Thomas / Glenn W. Most.
p.   cm.
Includes bibliographical references and index.
ISBN 0-674-01914-8 (alk. paper)
1. Thomas, Apostle, Saint, 1st cent.   I. Title.

BS2520.T45M67   2005
226'.092—dc22   2005046080

His hands sought to touch an impalpable and unreal body.
It was such a painful effort that this thing which was
moving away from him and trying to draw him
along as it went seemed the same to him
as that which was approaching
unspeakably.

—Maurice Blanchot,
THOMAS THE
OBSCURE

❧

❧

Contents

❧

Preface

The figure of Doubting Thomas gives us an excellent opportunity to put our finger upon central questions of faith and doubt, skepticism and persuasion, along two dimensions: through a variety of media and along a number of millennial traditions. Hence the organization of this book into two parts. In its first, shorter half, it considers the starting point of these traditions: the closing sections of the synoptic Gospels, which serve as background for what is to come in the conclusion of the Gospel of John, and then John's own extraordinary narrative, which forms the ultimate textual basis for the later versions of the story of Doubting Thomas. Then the book goes on, in a longer second half, to examine three of the most important traditions in which this starting point was received and transformed: various narrative elaborations upon the stories of Thomas in the New Testament Apocrypha and a few later texts; the traditions of the exegesis of John's account, from the church fathers through the Counter-Reformation; and finally the iconography of visual representations of this episode, from late antiquity through the beginning of the seventeenth century. The book begins and ends with two concerted acts of close interpretation, one devoted to John's account, the other to Caravaggio's painting of Doubting Thomas; in between, considerations of space, propriety, balance, and ignorance have all compelled a more exploratory approach, navigating by generalizations and suggestions among a large range of paradigmatic instances.

The orientation toward various media permits us to explore some of the ways in which fundamental issues of belief and disbelief, faith and doubt, are worked out within the constraints of different forms of communication ranging from the verbal, in narrative and exegesis, to the visual, in painting and sculpture. The focus upon the traditions lets us examine the contradiction between, on the one hand, a short and famous foundational text, and, on the other, the numerous instances of commentary and elaboration that justify themselves precisely by their claim to fidelity to that single text and yet manage in certain regards decisively to misunderstand it. For the one thing that most people think they know about Doubting Thomas, namely that he stuck his finger into Jesus' wounds, turns out upon inspection not only to receive no support at all from the source of this story, the Gospel of John, but indeed to be contradicted by it. Tracing some of the paths by which this evident but no doubt ineradicable mistake has wandered through almost two millennia of literature and art offers ample material for reflection upon the inextricable complicity of understanding and misunderstanding in enabling and complicating human communication.

The fact that the texts and issues explored here are mostly central ones within the Christian tradition is certainly convenient—it means that the interpretative traditions involved are well represented, both quantitatively and qualitatively. But this circumstance is not at all indispensable, for the methods used here can be applied to many other kinds of texts and issues. Nothing, in any case, is further from my intention than to defend or attack faith in Christianity or to justify or condemn Thomas's doubt: I am merely trying to reconstruct the conception and organization of certain textual and pictorial documents that have played a significant role in European culture over the past twenty centuries.

The story of Doubting Thomas is a particularly striking example that allows us to recognize with unusual clarity the degree to which cultural history is constituted by an incessant practice of recycling inherited models, retained by collective memory beyond the immediate situation for which they were first devised, into new contexts for which they must be adapted if they are to remain serviceable. That adaptation is always, to some degree at least, a falsification, for the original author or artist could not possibly have foreseen all the uses to which his creation would someday be put. But the model's vitality, and its only chance for survival, resides in its capacity to lend itself to that process of unceasing falsification without renouncing altogether its fundamental identity—it is not only for human beings, but also for their cultural products, that the notion of resurrection raises thorny problems of the continuation of personal identity. The task of cultural history, insofar as it studies such cases of reception and transmission, is neither to deplore such errors nor to attempt once and for all to correct them, but to uncover and to seek to understand them.

I am by profession a textual interpreter and a specialist in hermeneutics, interested above all in the workings of literary and philosophical texts and in the exegetical traditions they generate, and trained especially in classics and comparative literature. The fact that I have ventured here to explore a set of issues which might be thought to belong more properly to such scholarly disciplines as theology, New Testament studies, church history, and the history of art may be explained, but is of course not adequately justified, by appeal to the intrinsic fascination of this subject.

The justification for this systematic trespass, rather, lies in the very nature of the study of cultural reception. Precisely because authors, artists, and their audiences have always tended to feel themselves free of disciplinary constraints, study of such processes of cultural transmission as are exemplified in this book must necessarily transgress the boundaries that academic disciplines have, wisely or not, seen fit to draw around themselves. Interdisciplinarity is the necessary burden—and at the same time the irresistible fascination and the great opportunity—for any serious study of cultural reception. The question is therefore not whether interdisciplinarity is to be accepted—no other procedure is fitted to this object—but to what extent its risks can be minimized. I have no doubt that, despite all my efforts, I have not succeeded in learning as much as I should have about the many fields required for the purposes of this book. But I hope that my readers will forgive any omissions and distortions that remain.

Beyond these general questions of method, it may also be helpful if I clarify a few technical points. (1) For the sake of convenience and consistency I cite the Hebrew Bible and the New Testament from *The New Oxford Annotated Bible: The Holy Bible, Revised Standard Version Containing the Old and New Testaments*, edited by Herbert G. May and Bruce M. Metzger (New York, 1962, 1973). All other translations are my own, unless otherwise indicated. (2) The Greek text of the New Testament I cite from *The Greek New Testament*, edited by Kurt Aland, Matthew Black, Carlo M. Martini, Bruce M. Metzger, and Allen Wikgren, in cooperation with the Institute for New Testament Textual Research, Münster/Westphalia, 3rd ed. (New York, 1975). (3) In order to keep this book relatively slim and to make it accessible to nonspecialists but at the same time useful for students and scholars, I have chosen not to burden the presentation of my argument with a rebarbative apparatus of scholarly references, but instead to put all bibliographical references, indications of the most important secondary literature on these issues, and suggestions for further reading into a series of bibliographical essays which appear at the end.

❧

Even slender books can accumulate massive debts. In the present case, the length of the gestation of this study and the variety of fields into which it has ventured have increased my indebtedness beyond even my customary limits.

The idea for this book first came to me during the winter semester of 1996–97, when, in the course of a regular interdisciplinary seminar at Heidelberg University devoted to patristic texts, I worked through parts of Nonnus' *Metaphrasis* of the Gospel of John together with colleagues and students from classics, theology, papyrology, and other disciplines, and for the first time in years I had the opportunity to study that Gospel and its reception with particular care. The close philological analysis of the Greek text of the New Testament and the detailed comparison with Nonnus' poetic version set me onto a path which, at first, was signposted only by dim memories of apocryphal gospels and by a distinct visual impression of a painting by Caravaggio; many pleasantly spent hours later, that path has led to this book. Certainly, without the years of friendly and stimulating discussions in the Heidelberg "Kirchenväter" seminar, I would have had far less confidence in setting out on such a line of research.

In its final form this book reflects as well the new opportunities and stimulation that I have found since moving to the Scuola Normale Superiore at Pisa—just as the project has also been profoundly shaped, in its conception and elaboration, by friends, students, and colleagues at the Committee on Social Thought at the University of Chicago. The fact that, to a certain extent, this book has ended up, unexpectedly, to be in part a story about the historical relations between Italian culture and German culture (as these are viewed, and experienced, by an American) may well be anchored ultimately in the idiosyncrasies of my own life; to what extent it also might reflect authentically the issues I discuss, I must leave my readers to judge.

I am deeply grateful to a large number of friends, acquaintances, and family members, who for years have borne, relatively uncomplainingly, with my obstinate questions and requests. Here I can only offer thanks by name to those friends and colleagues who have read and commented on various chapters of this work in draft. They include, in Germany, Martin Baumbach, Christoph Burchard, Albrecht Dihle, William Furley, Luca Giuliani, Enno Rudolph, Claudia Wassmann, and the members of my Heidelberg Leibniz seminar; in the United States, Ewa Atanassow, Susan Bielstein, Arnold Davidson, Michael Fried, Charles Larmore, Josh Scodel, and Aaron Tugendhaft;

in England, Susanna Morton Braund, Alan Griffiths, and Anna Mastrogianni. In Heidelberg, Nicola Hoemke, with considerable energy and care, helped me to put together a repertory of pictorial images of Saint Thomas.

Early versions of individual chapters of this book were presented to helpfully critical discussion at various conferences and lectures: at the Max-Planck Institut für Wissenschaftsgeschichte in Berlin in June 1998, at Cambridge University in November 1998, in Iphofen (Bavaria) in May 1999, at Loyola University in Chicago in March 2000, at the Scuola Normale Superiore in Pisa in March 2000 and June 2002, at the Einstein Forum in Potsdam in November 2001, at Colle di Val d'Elsa in July 2003 and July 2004, and at the Leibniz-Kolleg in Tübingen in June 2004. The whole book, in a preliminary version, benefited greatly from an intense interdisciplinary seminar at Dartmouth University in February 1999; the participants were Sarah Allen, Jonathan Crewe, Pamela K. Crossley, Dale F. Eickelman, Robert Fogelin, Gene R. Garthwaite, Margaret Graber, and Adrian Randolph. Through the kindness of Professor Marc Fumaroli, I was able to present an abridged version of four chapters in a series of lectures at the Collège de France in Paris in June 2003.

Finally, I owe a special debt of gratitude to the two anonymous readers for Harvard University Press, and to a small number of friends who were willing to shoulder the burden of reading through the whole manuscript of the penultimate version of this book and who not only enriched it with their contributions but also saved me from more errors than I like to recall: Luigi Battezzato (Pisa), Brooke Hopkins (Salt Lake City), Katia Mitova (Chicago), Filippomaria Pontani (Pisa), Lucia Prauscello (Pisa), Adolf Martin Ritter (Heidelberg), Mario Telò (Pisa), and Isabelle Wienand (Fribourg). At a very late stage, when I imagined that no further changes were necessary, Elizabeth Gilbert, an extraordinary manuscript editor at the Press, improved not only its form but also its substance in many ways; working with her was a great pleasure.

My thanks to all those who, in one way or another, wittingly and unwittingly, by their faith and by their doubts, have touched this book and helped it, and its author, to learn and to grow.

❧

This book is dedicated to my students. It is intended for them, as an expression of my gratitude for all they have taught me, as a demonstration by example of one way in which texts and other cultural documents can be read, and above all as an encouragement to explore, and to take risks.

❧

Abbreviations

New Testament Apocrypha

E = J. K. Elliott, ed., *The Apocryphal New Testament: A Collection of Apocryphal Christian Literature in an English Translation based on M. R. James* (Oxford, 1993)
S-W = Wilhelm Schneemelcher, ed., *New Testament Apocrypha*, rev. ed., English trans. by R. McL. Wilson, 2 vols. (Cambridge, 1991–92)
Acts of Thomas = *The Acts of Thomas* (E 439–511; S-W 2.322–411)
Apocalypse = *The Apocalypse of Thomas* (E 645–51; S-W 2.748–52)
Contender = *The Book of Thomas the Contender* (S-W 1.232–47 under the title *The Book of Thomas*; not in E)
Gospel = *The Gospel of Thomas* (E 123–47; S-W 1.110–33)
Infancy = *The Infancy Gospel of Thomas* (E 68–83; S-W 1.439–52)

Church Fathers

CChr SL = *Corpus Christianorum, Series Latina* (Turnhout, 1952ff.)
CSEL = *Corpus scriptorum ecclesiasticorum Latinorum* (Vienna, 1866ff.)
GrChrSchr = *Die griechischen christlichen Schriftsteller der ersten drei Jahrhunderte* (Berlin, 1897ff.)
PG = *Patrologiae cursus completa, accurante J. P. Migne, Series Graeca* (Paris, 1857ff.)
PL = *Patrologiae cursus completa, accurante J. P. Migne, Series Latina* (Paris, 1841ff.)
SC = *Sources Chrétiennes* (Paris, 1941ff.)

I

THE TEXTUAL BASIS

Seeing and Believing

"Seeing," as the one-eyed man said to his blind friend, "is believing." Just what did he mean?

At first sight, we might think that his point was merely the difference in the reliability of the information that our various sense organs provide us about the world we live in. The other four senses require that we establish contact with their objects or even internalize them to a greater or lesser extent: taste presupposes ingestion, smell and hearing require that some physical aspect of the object perceived crosses the boundary into cavities within our head, touch is impossible without direct contact. Only sight objectifies what it perceives by setting it outside and before us: we cannot see something placed directly upon the surface of our eye any more than we can really taste or touch something held up at any distance in front of us.

Visual objectification means that whatever is seen is not altered by the mere fact of being seen. Since seeing something does not change the object perceived, we might well suppose this kind of sensory knowledge to be the most secure one available. For the information provided by the other senses is far more likely to be modified by the very process of perception. *"De gustibus non est disputandum"* (there is no point in disputing judgments of taste)—in part, at least, because one cannot taste something without consuming it, so that no two people can taste exactly the same thing and any one person's report about what he has tasted must be taken at face value. But you and I can readily compare our impressions upon seeing exactly the same object (or almost exactly, for in fact we cannot ever both see something from precisely the same vantage point at precisely the same moment). And yet by the same token, might we not prefer to make the opposite choice, taking the very primitiveness of the other senses, the fact that they involve us so much more viscerally and immediately in our world, as proof that the information they supply must be truer than that furnished by sight, less amenable to distortion, more reliable? After all, optical illusions are a familiar phenomenon, tactile illusions much less so.

If we wished, we could certainly travel farther along the strictly epistemological road opened up by these considerations. But to do so would doubtless mean to miss the point of the proverb with which we began: for the tacit comparison it asserts is surely not between sight and all four of the other senses, but rather between sight and hearing in particular. What the one-eyed man is really suggesting to his friend is that we tend to believe, or ought to believe, what we see and not what we merely hear. When we say "Seeing is believing," it is usually as a response to our hearing someone tell us about something that he says has happened or will happen but about which we are declaring that we shall remain skeptical so long as we have not witnessed it ourselves. Apparently, what we only hear does not provide as solid a foundation for belief as what we see.

Why not? No doubt the most important reason is that what we see we see for ourselves, while what we hear we hear from other people who tell us about it. This suggests a series of underlying assumptions that all seem to be presupposed by the proverb we are considering: that all true knowledge is ultimately based upon an act of direct and immediate vision; that under ideal circumstances the person who wants to know about something and the person who has seen it are one and the same; that unfortunately these ideal circumstances are not always the case; that when they are not, a chain of communication must connect at one end the person who has actually seen something, through a series of merely auditory links of increasing distance and misinformation, to the person at the other end who only hears about it; and that in consequence the person at the auditory end of that chain can only attain a smaller degree of certainty than his visual counterpart at the other end can. A social history of truth could demonstrate the ways in which trust in what other people tell us about the world is channeled and institutionalized so as to provide something approaching the degree of certainty we would ideally like. Such certainty is no doubt less than some philosophers might wish for, but it is usually, we like to think, enough to get by with in our rough and ready practical engagement with our world.

But in fact experience teaches us that it is far from certain to what extent we can trust our fellows to be reliable informants about the world we share with them. As Proverbs puts it, "The simple believes everything, but the prudent looks where he is going" (14:15); and so the prudent Queen of Sheba, who chose not to believe on the basis of mere hearsay the reports that had come to her ears concerning Solomon, decided to come and see with her own eyes whether or not they were true (1 Kings 10:7, 2 Chron. 9:6).

The problem is not just that other people can make mistakes or be misled: after all, so can we. That is bad enough; but what is worse, they may intentionally mislead us. If we could really believe that our fellow man had our own best interests at heart and wished our good not less than his own, then we would be more willing to entrust what matters most to us, the lives and happiness of ourselves and of those we love, to what he tells us. But we know full well that, in a crisis, most of us would not hesitate to sacrifice another person and his family in order to save ourselves and ours, and so we assume the same of him, particularly because our daily experience so often confirms other people's casual inconsiderateness and cheerful brutality.

The opening of Euripides' *Medea* stages this truth strikingly: when Medea's nurse cannot believe her ears when she hears—but does not see for herself—that the Greek hero Jason, who has brought her mistress to Corinth, has treacherously decided to marry the local princess, her fellow slave contemptuously asks her (and us), "Have you only now learned that everyone loves himself more than his neighbor?" (85–86). That is why we believe what we can see ourselves more readily than what others report to us: our trust in our eyes is not so much trust in our *eyes* as rather trust in *our* eyes, and in fact is founded upon our distrust in our fellows. Herodotus tells us that Candaules, the king of Sardis, who suffered the rare misfortune of falling in love with his very own wife, tried to convince his bodyguard Gyges of her surpassing beauty by telling him about it, but in vain; hence he arranged matters so that Gyges could see her naked, "since ears are less persuasive for human beings than eyes" (1.85.10). But Candaules' wife happened to see Gyges watching her and ended up betraying her husband in his turn and compelling Gyges to murder him: eyes are never innocent, and they rarely see exactly what we want them to, but instead less, or more.

These problems are ones with which we are familiar from ordinary life. But do the same rules apply in extraordinary situations? Suppose that the "good news" (which is what the word "Gospel" means etymologically) that someone asks us to believe upon hearing it is not some ordinary piece of gossip, about beautiful wives or fatuous husbands, but instead is a matter of life or death—and not only for us and for those we love but for all mankind, indeed for all creation. Suppose, what is more, that this news is so at odds with our usual lived experience that it is far harder to believe than even the most enthusiastic reports of a woman's extraordinary beauty—indeed, that it strains belief to, and in fact far beyond, the very breaking point. Suppose, then, that if we can manage to believe it, we shall not die ourselves but shall live forever—and that if we cannot believe it, nothing else will ever be able to save us. And suppose, finally, that we ourselves cannot see with our own eyes the person who has proclaimed this news and apparently demonstrated its truth, but that we must rely instead upon our ears, hearing the report that is told to us by other persons who claim to have seen this miracle themselves—or who claim to have heard it from others who claim that they saw it themselves, or heard about it from yet others who claim—and so on. Can we believe them?

From a theological point of view, the primary interest in the questions of belief I shall be considering resides in the general question of the nature of religious faith as compared with other kinds of belief and in the specific contents of the various religious doctrines involved; for the interpretations presented here, however, this theological dimension is not central. Instead, my purpose in Part I is to examine the concluding chapters of the synoptic Gospels and then, against the background they form, the structure and meaning of the story of Doubting Thomas as it appears toward the end of the Gospel of John. This exploration provides a basis for Part II, which considers various literary, exegetical, and artistic traditions arising from that story. It is not my aim in this first part to provide an objective and definitive account of what should count as the only true meaning of John's text, which would then have been distorted and misunderstood by subsequent appropriations. On the contrary, even if such a goal were practicable, my purpose would not be to pursue it here, but rather to emphasize a plurality of potential dimensions of meaning that his story opens up.

My own approach in dealing with these texts is not theological, but rhetorical, literary, and psychological. A word of explanation may be helpful to indicate what is, and what is not, involved in my use of all three terms.

Insofar as it is *rhetorical*, this interpretation is focused upon the authors' anticipation that their work will have readers and upon the traces of this expectation within the text, and examines those textual mechanisms designed to produce specific effects, particularly the effect of belief, upon such readers. For this approach, such a result depends upon the response of readers to determinate textual strategies that seek to produce belief by means of techniques that careful interpretation can identify. After all, every text, whatever else it attempts to do, must also seek to procure for itself its recipients' belief in it. Whether what is involved is a lyric poem or a declaration of love, instructions for escaping from a hotel room in case of fire or a message of religious salvation, nothing else can be achieved by a text if it does not in the first instance inspire the readers' trust in it—the "willing suspension of disbelief" of which Coleridge spoke is a premise required not only by literary works of art but by all means of communication. Thus if a text chooses to concentrate upon issues of belief, as all four Gospels do, especially at their ends, it thereby is choosing to emphasize questions that lie in some way or another at the basis of all texts whatsoever. It is this focus upon readers and upon the textual strategies for bringing them into a certain state of belief which a rhetorical interpretation of the sort attempted here seeks to identify; the term "rhetorical" as I am using it here is not at all intended to connote anything like dissimulation, deception, or hypocrisy.

Insofar as it is *literary*, this interpretation focuses in the first instance, as its fundamental datum, upon the written texts in which these questions of belief are articulated, and inquires into the ways in which these texts are structured and configured. It considers meaning to be produced not only by direct propositional assertions, but also by the ways in which individual parts of the text are set into relation with one another by such familiar structuring devices as parallelism, analogy, repetition, contradiction, heightening, diminution, irony, and implication. For it should be evident that no act of communication is restricted to the mere sum of its propositional contents: instead, much of the meaning that communication succeeds in transmitting (indeed, in certain kinds of texts, almost all of it) is located between the lines, in the tacit but conspicuously marked relations between its various explicit assertions. A literary interpretation of the kind undertaken here aims to uncover the unstated messages within the text under consideration by setting into meaningful relation with one another the explicit statements it makes, and to relate them systematically to the merely implicit ones; the term "literary" as I am using it is not at all intended to connote anything like fictionality, nonreferentiality, or mere aestheticism.

Finally, insofar as it is *psychological* this interpretation focuses upon the lacunae that are so evident a feature of the narrative style of these Gospels, and it attempts to set the explicit statements on either side of these gaps into relation with one another by introjecting into them, in as economical and as historically plausible a way as possible, what seem to be appropriate kinds of explanatory material, above all psychological hypotheses referring to the cognitive, emotional, and intentional states that may reasonably be conjectured to apply to the various characters involved in the situations described. The narrative style of the Hebrew Bible is notoriously thrifty: it suppresses irrelevant details, mentions only the most crucial actions, omits narrative links between these actions, and often leaves the decisive motivations and reactions of even the most important characters unstated. Unsurprisingly, the New Testament continues this Jewish narrative tradition, presumably not only because of the high degree of general religious and cultural continuity (despite their many evident differences) between these two sets of texts and between the communities that generated and studied them, but also because, more generally, any text that serves as the canonical reference point around whose unquestioned status an entire religious community organizes its identity will do well to be less explicit rather than more so. For in that way the sheer mass of the texts upon which the community's sense of self is founded will not become onerously extensive, and ample room will remain for the kind of disagreement and discussion about the implications, scope, and meaning of those texts that permits social differentiation but does not jeopardize the community's cohesion.

The result is that very often the Gospels not only report successive actions or events without indicating precisely how these are related, but that they also permit apparently divergent, discrepant, or even incompatible versions or incidents to stand next to one another in the same narrative without providing the reader with any explicit help in understanding how to relate them to one another. The venerable tradition of *Quellenforschung* ("source criticism"), in the hands of Rudolf Bultmann and many other great scholars, tended to take such gaps and discrepancies as evidence for compilation from earlier sources and to attempt to break down apparently unsatisfactory existing versions into what they took to be more satisfactory lost ones. But this seems all too often to be looking for the wrong answer to the right question, focusing exegetical attention quite properly upon a discourse's aporetic or contradictory nodes but then pursuing the chimera of a thoroughly nonaporetic discourse in a futile attempt to make them disappear once and for all. Instead, a literary approach that adapts some of the methods of traditional *Quellenforschung* to a different set of issues can recognize the virtues of this lacunary style, which succeeds remarkably well in posing a set of fascinating challenges for readers and may even have been designed for this very purpose. Given that the actions and reactions described by these biblical and apocryphal narratives are attributed to human and superhuman beings, and not to billiard balls, it is not enough, if we are to understand them, simply to catalogue the physical movements that accompany them: we must risk ascribing to them conjecturally a set of psychological motivations and reactions that have not been made explicit fully or, in some cases, at all. Any such hypothetical ascription inevitably requires that readers participate directly and intimately in the construction of the text's meaning, thereby providing gratifying possibilities for identification and engagement; but at the same time, readers can never be entirely certain that the particular ascription they happen to favor themselves will also strike other readers as being appropriate, and they must attempt to devise corroborative strategies to render their hypotheses more plausible. This concern for the views of the wider community is doubtless more urgent for those who are professionally engaged in reading in universities and other institutions, but even nonprofessional readers usually like to share and compare their literary experiences with others who have read the same books.

Just as on the pages of the Hebrew Bible only the consonants are written out and the words cannot be understood unless readers supply the vowels by infusing the written characters with the life of their own breath, so too the lacunary and discontinuous actions and events these Gospel narratives recount can only be understood if they are brought to life by their readers' introjection into them of the kinds of motivations and reactions, including above all psychological ones, that seem plausible to them on the basis of their own experience of literature and life. As the experiences of a text's readers gradually drift away, over the course of centuries, from the historical setting in which and for which the text was originally composed, such introjection will become increasingly difficult and more liable to arbitrariness; yet at the same time it is only by inviting readers to risk proposing fallible interpretive hypotheses that the text continues to attract new readers over time, so that it is precisely in the risk of the text's falsification that the latent chance of its survival will always reside. Certainly any particular psychological interpretation, such as the ones offered here, can only be tentative and incomplete; but it is impossible to imagine any act of interpretative reading of texts like these that could do without any kind of psychologization whatsoever. A psychological interpretation of the kind I undertake aims to link actions and incidents by ascribing to narrative agents plausible motivations and reactions; the term "psychological" as I am using it is not at all intended to connote anything like sentimentalism, banalization, or a doctrinaire form of Freudian (or any other) psychoanalysis.

But enough of preliminaries. Let us turn to the New Testament accounts themselves. Seeing, after all, is believing.

❧

Before Thomas:
The Synoptic Gospels

The three synoptic Evangelists all narrate the miracles following Jesus' crucifixion in terms of a simple and powerful antithesis between seeing and hearing, believing and disbelieving. Unsurprisingly, it is at their very conclusion that these texts articulate the issues of doubt and belief most urgently. For not only is the last event recounted, the resurrection of Jesus after his death, by far the hardest to believe and at the same time the only really decisive one for Jesus' message of salvation ("if Christ has not been raised, then our preaching is in vain and your faith is in vain," 1 Cor. 15:14). What is more, at the end of any text its author takes his leave from his readers and does what he can to ensure the persistence, even after they have laid his book down, of the persuasive effects he has hoped to have upon them. That is why, whatever the intertextual relations between the four Evangelists' stories, they all focus in their concluding sections upon the same central problem of persuasion: namely, to what degree seeing is, or is only almost, or is really not at all, believing. As their attempts to resolve this issue gradually become more and more refined, the problem seems to become more and more intractable. Perhaps the very difficulty of the problem increases not so much in spite of the ever more sophisticated strategies proposed to resolve it, as rather in consequence of them.

❧

Most modern New Testament scholars agree that Mark's is the earliest of the three synoptic Gospels. In any case, it is certainly simpler and more linear than Matthew's and Luke's—but, at least with regard to these issues of doubt and belief, no less disturbing in its implications.

Mark's narrative of the events following Jesus' burial confines us within the perspective of women for its entire length: everything we see, we see through their eyes. What they fail to understand we are given no information to enable us to understand better; when they are frightened we seem to be left with no other recourse than to share their fear. Doubtless, the fact that more than one woman is involved lends a somewhat greater degree of credibility to their reports concerning their experience; but the greater emotional and intuitive capacity that seems here to be attributed to women in comparison to men must be balanced against their uncontestedly low status as legal witnesses in first-century Palestine. Presumably, unless the women receive authoritative corroboration from some other source, we would do well not to believe too quickly what they report to their listeners and hence to us.

By telling us in the preceding chapter that two women see where Jesus is buried (15:47), Mark provides a transition to the following scene, in which the world of men and their established secular and religious authority is left entirely behind. For it is three women who go to Jesus' tomb after the Sabbath is past in order to anoint his dead body (16:1). Their worried question, who will roll the heavy stone away from the tomb's entrance (16:3), reminds us of their bodily weakness and prepares us for a typical miracle, a feat of superhuman strength that will surpass their own limited physical and mental capacities (16:4). Yet what they see within the tomb is nothing out of the ordinary: merely a youth sitting down on the right side (presumably the auspicious one), dressed in white (16:5)—they see no corpse there, but also no angel or any proof of resurrection. In spite of (or, perhaps, precisely because of) this matter-of-factness, the three women are terrified by what they see: the tomb is open rather than closed, Jesus is absent rather than present, a living youth confronts them rather than a dead man. Like a courteous servant explaining to unexpected visitors that his master has woken up from a nap and gone out for a stroll, the youth calmly reports that Jesus has awakened and is not there, and demonstrates the truth of the statement they have heard with their ears, by inviting them to look with their own eyes at the place where Jesus' body was laid out but which now is empty (16:6). He tells them to report to the disciples what they have seen and to tell them that, as Jesus promised (14:28), he will see them in Galilee (16:7). But far from being consoled by the youth's words, the women flee the tomb, beside themselves with terror; instead of reporting to the disciples, they say not a word to anyone out of fear (16:8).

And that is that. Mark's Gospel ends here; in the oldest manuscripts, the story breaks off at this point, and there is no evidence that Mark himself ever composed any continuation of it. As a conclusion for this Gospel narrative, however, such an abrupt close is perplexing in at least two ways.

On the one hand, some of the elements in this final passage seem to point beyond themselves to future events which are not narrated here but the narration of which the reader might reasonably expect to find somewhere later. For example, according to the youth, Jesus will meet the disciples in Galilee: well, did he? And if the women were too terrified to tell anyone, how did the disciples know to go there? In the absence of any confirmatory narrative, we have only the youth's prediction to go on: can we believe him? Again, how did the narrator—let us call him Mark—learn of the events recounted in this chapter? After all, these seem to have been witnessed by no one except the three women and the mysterious youth; but apparently the women told no one, and it is not indicated what became of the youth. Did the women in fact end up telling someone who told Mark, or did they tell Mark directly—but in that case, how did they manage to overcome their fear, and why does Mark not tell us about this? Or did Mark have some other source of information—but then whom (surely not the youth in the tomb), and why does he not tell us?

But on the other hand, other elements, which various earlier predictions have led us to expect to find in this section, are missing here, and it is not made clear to the reader how their absence is to be explained or interpreted. Above all, there have been four prophecies in this Gospel that Jesus would be resurrected after his death (8:31; 9:9, 31; 10:34). But in Mark's text we do not hear of anyone who sees Jesus resurrected, to say nothing of our seeing him resurrected ourselves; instead we merely hear of the women, who hear from the youth, that he has been awakened and is not there. But even if we think we can believe *them*, why should we believe *him*? How do we know that he is not a grave robber who has simply stolen the body and quick-wittedly invents this story when the women suddenly show up? Mark supplies no evidence to convince us that Jesus has risen and that we should believe his text's central message of salvation—a message that we might surely expect to be demonstrated in Jesus' case before we would be willing to believe it in ours.

At the close of any merely fictional narrative, such perplexities would be most unwelcome; here, at the conclusion of a text proposing its readers' salvation, they are quite intolerable. Whether Mark intended his narrative to end here, or whether he never completed it for some contingent reason, or whether he originally continued it beyond this point with a passage that was somehow lost is not known and remains controversial. But there are only two alternatives: either the ending of his narrative at this point was intentional or it was unintentional; and against the former alternative speaks the sheer, inexplicable bizarreness of this moment as a planned ending. Hence it seems likelier that an originally intended conclusion either was not written (that is, that Mark's act of composing the Gospel was interrupted) or was indeed written but was subsequently lost (the beginnings and ends of manuscripts are especially liable to mechanical damage or loss). Even if we assume that in the early Christian community for which the original text was presumably composed, there may have been far less need to commemorate in writing (and perhaps even a greater need to keep secret and hence entrusted only to oral communication) the central event of Christian faith, Jesus' resurrection, than the many lesser details of his life, this can hardly justify such an abrupt ending at the moment of greatest fear, bewilderment, and despair; and why, on this account, should a number of explicit forecasts of Jesus' resurrection have been made and retained in the part of the text committed to writing? In any case, for later readers such a narrative must certainly have seemed radically incomplete. The text as it stands is so disturbing that we will not be surprised to learn that in most manuscripts Mark's account has been supplemented by at least two inauthentic attempts to complete its message.

The so-called Shorter Ending (16:9–10) is transmitted in some manuscripts as a preface or alternative to a larger and more complex supplement, the so-called Longer Ending (16:9–20). The Shorter Ending simply corrects the two most obvious deficiencies of Mark's narrative, reporting that the women did after all tell Peter and the other disciples what the youth had told them to say (thereby clearing up the narratological problem of how Mark learned of the events he recounts), and that Jesus himself rose to send the disciples on their apostolic mission (thereby providing both narrative and theological closure for the earlier announcements that Jesus would indeed be resurrected). But this ending adds nothing beyond these minimal remedies for an obviously defective narrative.

Of greater interest is the Longer Ending. The second-century author of this passage (who was probably influenced by John's account of Jesus' resurrection, which we shall consider in the following chapter) immediately supplies what is most disturbingly lacking in the authentic text of Mark: a visible appearance of the risen Jesus to a named character, here Mary Magdalene (16:9, compare Luke 8:2), who can finally go and tell the disciples what has happened, as she was told to do (16:10).

But the fear and disobedience that Mary had displayed toward the youth in Mark's own account, far from being banished from the interpolator's supplement, stubbornly persist into this latter text and must be dealt with progressively in a climactically organized three-stage narrative. In the first stage, Mary speaks to the disciples, who are weeping and in mourning, for they are convinced that Jesus is dead. But she fails entirely to persuade them by her good news that

Jesus has indeed risen, and instead encounters only disbelief: "But when they heard that he was alive and had been seen by her, they would not believe it" (16:11). In one regard, matters have become even worse than they were in Mark's own account, for now it is not only two women who do not believe, but the whole group of male disciples; but in another regard things have improved somewhat, for the person whom they do not believe is only a woman, Mary Magdalene, so that the narrative can move on to a next, higher step of validation. In this second stage, for the very first time in this whole episode, we are lifted out of a limited female perspective. Mary is entirely forgotten, for she has fulfilled her narrative purpose. Jesus himself appears to male witnesses, but he does so to only two of the disciples, who have separated themselves off from the main body (16:12). Yet when they tell the others what they have seen, this time too mere words are not believed, even though they are pronounced by men and not women: "And they went back and told the rest, but they did not believe them" (16:13). So in the third stage Jesus makes a final appearance, this time to all the eleven disciples together, and explicitly rebukes them for their disbelief: "Afterward he appeared to the eleven themselves as they sat at table; and he upbraided them for their unbelief and hardness of heart, because they had not believed those who saw him after he had risen" (16:14). Presumably this time Jesus succeeds with the disciples: the very last sentence of the Gospel in this version confirms that they did indeed set out to fulfill their apostolic mission (16:20). But just to make sure that the point is not lost on the reader, the author adds to Jesus' final discourse a general sentence on the vital importance of belief: "He who believes and is baptized will be saved; but he who does not believe will be condemned" (16:16).

The anonymous author of the supplement to Mark's narrative evidently recognized that any complete and satisfactory version of the events after Jesus' burial had to find a balance between two sets of interdependent miracles: those inside the tomb, involving the absence of Jesus' dead body where it was expected to be; and those outside the tomb, involving the presence of Jesus' living body where it was not expected to be. Whatever the reasons for the rupture in Mark's own narrative, the last chapter of the Gospel that circulated under his name after the second century A.D. is divided in a simple and linear fashion into two parts, one inside (16:1–7) and the other outside (16:8–20); and its emphasis is placed not upon the first, terrified, unredeemed, frustrating part, but rather upon the second, joyous, redemptive, fulfilling one. By means of this supplement, the story as a whole does manage to achieve a high degree of closure, by deploying an alternating rhythm of verbal announcement and visual confirmation. But its narrative dynamic is generated not by belief (which can evidently not engender a narrative of this sort, but can only conclude one) but instead by the obsessively repeated mechanism of a reaction of disbelief to mere words. In the end, this thematization of disbelief requires the explicit intervention of Jesus himself to dispel that doubt. Yet the very excessiveness of the means of conviction that the interpolator's Jesus is compelled to deploy— his repeated appearances, his angry rebuke of the doubters, and his explicit linkage between disbelief and damnation—suggests just how virulent the malady of skepticism is that he must combat.

Mark's prematurely aborted account is troubling for its enigmatic inconclusiveness: but so too is the longer continuator's attempt to harness disbelief in the service of a belief upon which his narrative closure depends. For the doubt he introduces seeps beyond its apparent intended function and goes on to infect a story that must be cleansed of it repeatedly, and by ever more drastic means.

❧

Luke's version is very close to Mark's. A great believer in the power of names and an enthusiastic multiplier of characters, an author with a policeman's sense of verification by protocoled accumulation of witnesses, Luke adds various kinds of elaboration and circumstantial detail but adopts the same fundamental narrative strategy of alternating disbelief and confirmation, here structured by a marked emphasis upon the asserted fulfillment of earlier verbal predictions by later events.

Like the Longer Ending of the Gospel of Mark, but far more elabo-
rately, Luke's account of the events surrounding Jesus' resurrection is
organized as a series of six climactic steps. In the first step, the narrative begins not with just one youth, but with two men, who tell not
just three women that Jesus is risen, but more than three (24:4, 10),
and who remind them explicitly of words that he had once spoken
and that now have apparently been fulfilled (24:6–7). The women
recall these words of Jesus' (24:8) and hence can easily draw the
conclusion that he and the angels confirm one another reciprocally.
Yet in the second step, when the women report what they have seen
to the eleven disciples (and, with a multiplication characteristic of
Luke, to the others too, 24:9), "these words seemed to them an idle
tale, and they did not believe them" (24:11). So as a third step Peter,
a male of considerable authority within the group, must be sent to
the tomb in order to check the women's report and if possible to confirm it; but he remains in perplexity, for what he finds there is not
people, who could speak words to him that would convey a reliable
account of the events in question, but only voiceless objects, whose
interpretation is difficult and ambiguous (24:12; not in all manuscripts). We need another, fourth, step: Jesus himself must appear in-
cognito to two members of his group (so too he appears in a changed
form to two disciples at Mark 16:12). In a highly elaborated dramatic
scene, they tell him what they have heard (24:13–24) and he rebukes
them (24:25–26: in direct quotation, not in indirect discourse as at
Mark 16:14), confirming the meaning of present events by referring
back, as the angel had already done, to earlier verbal predictions that
have now been fulfilled (24:27). But up to this point, the two disciples cannot see properly ("but their eyes were kept from recognizing
him," 24:16). Hence we require a fifth step, a further persuasive climax. This is provided by the disciples' final recognition that the person with whom they have been speaking is in fact Jesus (24:31); this
is stimulated, appropriately enough at this Passover time, by his
breaking bread with them (24:30). In a sixth and final step, this discovery motivates them to return to Jerusalem so that they can report
what they have seen to the other disciples (and to the other people

who are together with them: another characteristic multiplication, 24:33–35). At this point we have been trained by Luke's narrative structure to know just what to expect: the disciples should refuse to believe the true words that have been reported to them and should give voice to a doubt that can only be dispelled by another miraculous vision; this time a satisfactory closure would finally be achieved by granting the vision of Jesus to all the disciples (and no doubt, given Luke's fondness for multiplication, to other people as well). But Luke surprises us: he chooses to avoid presenting us with yet another embarrassing scene of incredulity, and instead introduces Jesus at once into the meeting between the two who have seen him and the others who have not, before the latter have any opportunity to express their doubt (24:36).

The two disciples need only mention the name of Jesus, and their word is immediately made flesh: he suddenly appears in their midst and says to them, "Peace be with you" (24:36; not in all manuscripts). Surely this ought to settle matters once and for all. And yet Jesus' premature appearance, far from resolving the disciples' doubts, compounds them. Evidently they are sure that they are indeed seeing something: but their instinct is to believe that what they see is not the living Jesus but a ghost, presumably that of the dead Jesus. Hence their first reaction is, understandably, pure terror (24:37). How can Jesus persuade them that he is not a ghost? The sole strategy available to him is to speak, and to convince them of the materiality of his body. The logic of the exchange between Jesus and the disciples suggests that the only categories of beings to which, when he appears before them, they think they can possibly assign him are (a) living persons, (b) dead persons, and (c) ghosts; but since living persons have material bodies and speak, dead persons have material bodies but do not speak, and ghosts speak but do not have material bodies, they can easily conclude by a process of elimination that if he speaks and has a material body he can only be a living person.

Jesus' demonstration of his materiality is so constructed as to create the expectation that it will involve several steps. For first he offers his wounds for visual inspection ("See my hands and my feet, that it is I myself," 24:39); then he goes on to offer himself for tactile inspection as the next, higher stage of proof ("handle me, and see; for a spirit has not flesh and bones as you see that I have," 24:39). But in fact this tactile proof remains a mere offer that is not actually performed: despite suggesting the disciples touch him, Jesus returns to a merely optical demonstration, permitting the disciples to inspect his wounds visually ("And when he had said this, he showed them his hands and his feet" 24:40; not in all manuscripts). Apparently, in the end, none of the disciples actually touches him. Why not? Luke does not tell us, but reports merely that the disciples "still disbelieved for joy, and wondered" (24:41). So in a final step, Jesus must convince them of his materiality by an even more irrefutable proof, namely by eating fish before their very eyes (24:42–43; most manuscripts supplement this exquisitely banal foodstuff, a staple of life in contemporary Palestine, with something more richly symbolic, honey, the ointment of immortality). At this Passover season eating offers a weighty proof. Only thereafter can Jesus confirm one final time the truth of what they have seen, by reference to the verbal predictions that were uttered in the past and have now been actually fulfilled (24:44–46). In the end, it is the ears that validate the eyes: the disciples' memory of what they have read in the Bible and heard from Jesus' own lips provides the final, decisive proof of what they see before them, allowing them to interpret Jesus' return as promised and then fulfilled, and hence they believe in its reality.

According to Luke, when Jesus offered himself to the disciples to be touched, "they still disbelieved for joy, and wondered" (24:41). What precisely does this mean? The first point to notice is that there is a very similar passage at Acts 12:14, written by the same author: here Luke recounts that Peter, who has been miraculously released from prison, knocks at the door of Mary, the mother of John, and is answered by the maid Rhoda: "Recognizing Peter's voice, in her joy she did not open the gate but ran in and told that Peter was standing at the gate." In both passages, where we might expect joy to derive from recognition and to motivate an action intended to confirm it, the joy seems instead to block the appropriate action: the joy is so great, because it is so unexpected, that it becomes almost indistinguishable from a paralyzing astonishment. The parallel suggests a complex but intuitively plausible psychological explanation for this passage in the Gospel. Presumably the disciples have been hoping that it is indeed the living Jesus who is standing before them, and hence they are filled with joy when they become convinced that it really is he. But at the same time they are so afraid that what they have been desiring so ardently might not in fact have happened that, for fear of disappointment, they do not dare to allow themselves to believe fully that these hopes have really been fulfilled. Such a confused mixture of overwhelming joy and partial disbelief is not only familiar to us from our own experience but is also attested to by a number of ancient pagan and Christian texts (for example, Chariton 8.5.5–7; Libanius, *Orations* 38.3.10; Pseudo-John Chrysostom, *On the Widow's Son*, PG 61.793.25–26; Theodoret, *Epistles* II, SC 98.181.6–7).

Nonetheless, Luke's expression remains stylistically awkward and somewhat odd. So too, it is not made clear why, although Jesus explicitly offers his body to the disciples' touch, in point of fact they neither touch it nor refuse to do so. It seems that Luke has trapped himself here by his simultaneous allegiance to two conflicting narrative obligations. On the one hand, Jesus' extraordinary offer serves to indicate the depth of his compassion for the disciples and the importance he attaches to convincing them of his material resurrection; so Luke can certainly not permit them to refuse outright Jesus' offer by not touching him, for to do so would set at naught his miraculous generosity. But on the other hand, ever since Jesus sat with the two disciples at Emmaus and broke bread with them but vanished out of their sight instead of eating with them (24:30–31), Luke's whole narrative has evidently been directed toward an eventual climax that must consist in Jesus' finally eating together with the disciples, and not with only one or two of them but with all of them, and then explaining to all of them the true meaning of the scripture that they had failed to understand. So Luke can just as certainly not permit the disciples to accept Jesus' offer at this point by touching him, for if they were indeed to convince themselves by touching him first before he actually ate with them and explained the scripture, then that climactic and definitive act of shared communion and authoritative exegesis would completely lose its point.

Hence in Luke's text the possibility of touching Jesus' body is raised but not fulfilled. A gap thereby opens up within the narrative, one that could have been filled, if at all, only by a divine touch productive of a blissful faith. Perhaps the disciples' incredulous joy can be read as a compensatory symptom which covers up an incredulous despair underlying Luke's text as an unnamed and systematically repressed anxiety—one which, once it is evoked, his very efforts to suppress cannot help but suggest all the more insistently.

If so, then perhaps we may go on to interpret as Luke's final attempt to provide a pious camouflage for this deeply unsettling effect the fact that the very last vision of the disciples that he affords us in the closing words of his Gospel is one of an overwhelming, permanent, superhuman happiness: "And they returned to Jerusalem with great joy, and were continually in the temple blessing God" (24:52–53). But even this may not have seemed to some ancient readers a sufficiently unambiguous statement that in the end all the disciples' doubts were completely overcome: for a slightly fuller version is also transmitted, which interpolates the words "they worshiped him and" before indicating that the disciples "returned to Jerusalem with great joy." Viewed in the light of the doubts that Luke has invoked repeatedly throughout the course of his narrative only so that they can be overcome, but that cannot ever be entirely suppressed again once they have been summoned up, the very persistence with which this conclusion emphasizes the disciples' pious, reverent, thoroughly unquestioning joy can come to seem a bit suspect.

❧

Matthew, unlike Mark and Luke, unmistakably lifts the events within the tomb entirely into the realm of the supernatural. He recounts as marvelous events the visit of the two Marys to the sepulchre, the earthquake, and the angel's descent, appearance, and speech (28:1–7), and even the lengthy and detailed alternative explanation for the disappearance of Jesus' body that he provides (28:11–15), a banal, rationalizing account in terms of bribery and deceit, seems designed, precisely by being rejected, not only to confirm his own version against competitors as the only true one but also to enhance its miraculous quality all the more. In comparison with the other accounts of the events in the tomb, Matthew's is far more spectacular—it is not a youth or two men whom the women see this time, but an angel of the Lord, whose miraculous exploits we witness and whose dazzling appearance astonishes us. What is more, Matthew takes great care to recast the psychological effect of these events upon those who witness them. Matthew removes from the women the terror felt by the ones in Mark's account (the women in Matthew are evidently far too positive as characters to have such a craven reaction attributed to them) and projects it instead onto his guards (28:4; though they are living, they become "like dead men" when the angel arrives to signal that the dead Jesus has come to life again), so that this time the women react not only with fear but also with great joy (28:8). So too, it is not the cowardly guards, but the courageous women who evidently first establish verbal contact with the angel (28:5). The angel's final words to the women impose upon them a mission to tell the disciples what they have seen and promise them that they will see Jesus not in the tomb, where they expected to find him, but in Galilee, where seeing him will confirm the angel's report (28:7). Then the women rush out immediately to perform the angel's command (28:8; Matthew may be implicitly correcting Mark here). The remaining sentences tell of the miracles outside the tomb: on their way to tell the disciples that Jesus is risen, the two Marys do indeed meet Jesus immediately, confirming the angel's prediction, and now it is Jesus himself who bids them a second time to tell the disciples to go to Galilee, where they will see him (28:8–10). After the interposed refutation of the alternative version of the disappearance of Jesus' body, Matthew continues with a series of external miracles: the eleven disciples obey the women and go to Galilee, where Jesus meets them and assigns them their apostolic mission (28:16–20).

Matthew's account is not without some minor difficulties. For example, the disciples encounter Jesus at a mountain in Galilee where, it is said, he has arranged to meet with them (28:16), but Matthew nowhere explains how, when, or where Jesus made any such appointment. But this is a minor problem: the real crux lies elsewhere. For in its fundamental design Matthew's narrative is constructed as a series of verbal encounters that point ahead to later visual encounters that retroactively confirm and verify the verbal ones. First the angel says the women will see Jesus (28:7), and then they do in fact see Jesus (28:9); then Jesus says to the women that the disciples will see him in Galilee (28:10), and then they do in fact see Jesus there (28:17). Nothing could be simpler, and more effective, than such a narrative rhythm, which alternates a verbal prediction of an event which is to take place at some future time, and then the visual confirmation at that future time which retrospectively validates the prediction made at the earlier time. What is more, the repetition of this same pattern a second time at a higher level of authority (the first time the prediction is made only by an angel, splendid as he is, the second time by Jesus himself) makes us expect the effect to be all the more overwhelming. After all, the first time, when the two Marys had indeed seen Jesus, they had not been able to refrain from joyously expressing their veneration of him: "And they came up and took hold of his feet and worshiped him" (28:9).

But the second time around, something goes wrong. For what happens when the eleven disciples meet Jesus on the appointed mountain in Galilee? "And when they saw him they worshiped him; but some doubted" (28:17). Matthew says not a single word more about these doubters: he never tells us just who it was who doubted, nor how many they were (beyond the fact that there was more than one), nor whether they themselves failed to see Jesus and doubted for that reason (but if so, why could they not see him when the others could?), nor why if they did in fact see Jesus they doubted even so (for then why did these disbelieve, when on the very same basis the others believed?), nor how they expressed their doubt, nor what alternative explanation they offered for Jesus' appearance if they did see him, nor what the reaction of the believers was to the doubters, nor what the reaction of Jesus was to them. Indeed, the only thing Matthew tells us is that Jesus came and spoke to the disciples, announcing his omnipotence and defining their apostolic mission (28:18–20). Perhaps Matthew wants to suggest to us that Jesus' words succeeded where his mere appearance had failed, and if so we may wish to conclude that this last speech must somehow have finally managed to convince the doubters. But even if we do adopt this line of interpretation, we should not forget two things: first, that Matthew himself nowhere explicitly asserts that the doubters were ever convinced in the end (his account ends with the end of Jesus' speech), so that there is no reason to believe they were; and second, that, given the fundamental structure of his narrative, which provides confirmation for mere words by means of a fulfilling vision, it is entirely unclear how any mere words on the part of Jesus (or of anyone else) could possibly succeed in convincing the doubters when their vision of him with their own eyes had not sufficed.

The words "but some doubted" tear open a wound of disbelief in the body of a text whose whole aim is to induce belief in its readers. If Matthew had left them out altogether, no hint of a worrisome shadow would have fallen upon the triumphant tone of his conclusion. Why then did he choose to add them? Perhaps Matthew wanted to suggest that doubt is all too human, that even among Jesus' own disciples, who had the least cause of anyone to doubt him, there were nonetheless some who were not convinced by the visual evidence of his physical resurrection. But if so, he was taking an enormous risk for a small benefit: for such a suggestion would inevitably provide an exculpatory precedent for any future reader's possible disbelief. Perhaps, too, Matthew wished his readers to be provoked into reflection upon the general question of the relation between doubt and belief without his providing them any simple means to resolve that question. But Matthew's rather heavy-handed didacticism and mechanical narrative do not suggest that he had great confidence in his readers' ability to work out such complicated questions for themselves or much inclination to let them try to do so on their own.

Perhaps, in the end, we can imagine no more plausible reason for

Matthew's statement that some doubted than that he felt obliged to make mention of a tradition of which he had heard and according to which this was indeed what had happened. Had some of Jesus' own disciples circulated alternative, skeptical versions of the events? Did Q, the other postulated source for Matthew's and Luke's Gospels next to Mark, report so emphatically the doubt of some of Jesus' disciples that Matthew could not afford to ignore it? But even this hypothesis is not really satisfactory: for surely Matthew cannot have supposed that he could succeed in discrediting the doubters merely by mentioning them, without going on to indicate how they were finally convinced.

On any account, therefore, the rhetorical effect of the words "but some doubted" is potentially unsettling. For if some of Jesus' own disciples doubted, might not we ourselves feel permitted or even encouraged to do so as well? And if Matthew nowhere says that the doubters were ever persuaded, what in the world (or outside of it) could possibly succeed in persuading us? After all, we ourselves have no visions of Jesus available to us, but only words, the words of Matthew and of those other authors who write or tell stories like his: and if seeing was not believing for some of Jesus' own disciples, why should mere hearing—what is more, hearing about their disbelief—be enough for us?

All three of the synoptic Gospels make great efforts to leave us with faith. But the very means they employ cannot help but leave us with questions.

Believing and Touching:
The Gospel of John

In the Gospel of John, all the issues of doubt and belief that, in different ways, haunt the three synoptic Gospels converge to form an unsettling climax. Whether or not John made use of the Synoptics when he wrote his own Gospel several decades later, the strategies and anxieties that organize them are repeated, and indeed are greatly intensified, in his account. For John's Gospel is pervaded by an obsessive need to instill belief in its readers and by a corresponding anxiety lest he fail to convince them. No doubt that is why various forms of the Greek verb "to believe" ($\pi\iota\sigma\tau\epsilon\acute{\upsilon}\epsilon\iota\nu$) occur more than ninety times in the Gospel of John—as compared with only nine times in Mark (plus another four times in the two spurious endings), seven times in Luke, and nine times in Matthew. John's version of the miracles after Jesus' burial is only slightly longer than Luke's—fifty-six verses, compared with fifty-three for Luke, and only twenty each for Mark and Matthew—but it is by far the most complex and literarily sophisticated of the four Gospel accounts. Moreover, John chooses to concentrate the whole complex issue of belief in Jesus into the relation between seeing and believing: chapter 20 of his Gospel is only thirty-one verses long, but it contains thirteen verbs for seeing ($\beta\lambda\acute{\epsilon}\pi\epsilon\iota$ "[she] saw," 1; $\beta\lambda\acute{\epsilon}\pi\epsilon\iota$ "he saw," 5; $\theta\epsilon\omega\rho\epsilon\hat{\iota}$ "he saw," 6; $\epsilon\hat{\iota}\delta\epsilon\nu$ "he saw," 8; $\theta\epsilon\omega\rho\epsilon\hat{\iota}$ "she saw," 12; $\theta\epsilon\omega\rho\epsilon\hat{\iota}$ "[she] saw," 14; $\dot{\mathrm{E}}\acute{\omega}\rho\alpha\kappa\alpha$ "I have seen," 18; $\dot{\iota}\delta\acute{o}\nu\tau\epsilon\varsigma$ "they saw," 20; $\dot{\mathrm{E}}\omega\rho\acute{\alpha}\kappa\alpha\mu\epsilon\nu$ "We have seen,"

25; ἴδω "I see," 25; ἴδε "see," 27; ἑώρακας "you have seen," 29; οἱ μὴ ἰδόντες "those who have not seen," 29; although the words "to look" appear in verse 11 of the Revised Standard Version, nothing corresponds in the Greek text; and compare also ἔδειξεν "he showed," 20) and eight words for believing (ἐπίστευσεν "[he] believed," 8; οὐ μὴ πιστεύσω "I will not believe," 25; ἄπιστος "faithless," 27; πιστός "believing," 27; πεπίστευκας "Have you believed," 29; πιστεύσαντες "[those who] believe," 29; ἵνα πιστεύσητε "that you may believe," 31; πιστεύοντες "believing," 31).

Above all, in the Gospel of John the various strands of the whole discourse of doubt and conviction are intertwined into the texture of a single character in whom every one of these issues can be explored in depth. Enter Thomas, one of us but not one of us, into a text to which we do, and do not, belong.

⚜

Like a *symbolon*, the early Christian tokens which were broken in half and could then be fitted together as a proof of identity, chapter 20 of the Gospel of John is divided into two closely corresponding halves, each of which must be understood in terms of the other if either of them is to be understood at all.

The fact that John's story of the events surrounding Jesus' resurrection is intended to be taken as a relatively autonomous narrative unit, whatever its thematic interconnections with other parts of his Gospel, is already signaled by the opening to this chapter, "Now on the first day of the week Mary Magdalene came to the tomb early, while it was still dark" (20:1). For these words naturalize the opening of this narrative segment by the convention, familiar from many forms of literature, of allowing the beginning of the story to coincide with the opening of a natural unit of time, the day; here this naturalization is further reinforced by identifying the day in question as the first day of the week.

As in the Synoptic Gospels, it is a woman, Mary Magdalene, who, precisely because she is merely a humble female, is alone capable of setting in motion the mechanism of a narrative designed to supersede her. But this time she is the lone woman involved and is carefully placed in a hierarchical relation with two highly authoritative men, Simon Peter, the "rock" upon whom Jesus would build his church (Matt. 16:18), and the disciple John, "the one whom Jesus loved" (John 20:2). For Mary, it is enough to see that the stone has been removed from the tomb (20:1) to know that matters have gotten beyond her own competence and that she needs male help; she immediately runs to Simon Peter and John and tells them that Jesus' body has been removed (20:2). Indeed, if he is dead (and she believes she knows that) but his body is not there (and she believes this, although we are not told that she has in fact seen that it is missing), what other explanation is conceivable? In fact, of course, we know that she is the victim of a false inference, for she has not actually seen that the body has been stolen but only deduced it from the perceived removal of the stone and the supposed absence of the body. John runs faster than Simon Peter does, so that he arrives first; he sees the linen cloths used to wrap the body but does not enter (20:5). The narrator allows John to see more than Mary Magdalene had seen up to this point, but not to enter the tomb at first himself, so that that climactic privilege can be reserved for Simon Peter—but only temporarily: after Simon Peter, John too will enter the tomb, while Mary remains outside. Evidently an event of this degree of importance and implausibility must be witnessed not just by a woman, but by men, and by more than one man, if it is to be believed. It is probably no coincidence that rabbinic law requires in most cases the testimony of two adult male witnesses.

It is easy enough to explain this sequence of events in terms of the personalities involved. If John runs faster than Simon Peter, it is probably because John is the younger of the two (and perhaps also because he loves Jesus more); if he waits for Simon Peter to enter the tomb before going in himself, it is because Simon Peter has a position of authority within the group of disciples to which John must defer (compare 21:15–17). But the separation and distribution of the various actions and reactions among these characters also create a powerful narrative effect of suspense. John's haste is a bodily condensation of our own psychological anxiety to find out just what happened in the tomb; so too, his decision to wait outside the tomb, until Simon Peter finally arrives, frustrates our desire to know and thereby heightens it.

But the account of just what John and Simon Peter saw in the tomb, and what conclusions they drew from what they witnessed there, is complicated and obscure. For we are told only what Simon Peter saw when he entered the tomb, the napkin and the wrappings (20:6–7), but not what John saw once he entered (the only indication of what John saw comes earlier, when he is said to have stooped down outside the tomb: at that point he saw nothing but the linen cloths, 20:5). On the other hand, we learn of John's reaction, namely that "he saw and believed" (20:8), but we are not told how Simon Peter reacted. Yet the singular verbs applied to John ("he saw and believed," καὶ εἶδεν καὶ ἐπίστευσεν) are justified by means of an explanatory clause ("for": γάρ) referring to a state of ignorance described by verbs in the plural ("for as yet they did not know the scripture, that he must rise from the dead," οὐδέπω γὰρ ᾔδεισαν τὴν γραφήν, ὅτι δεῖ αὐτὸν ἐκ νεκρῶν ἀναστῆναι, 20:9). How is this odd switch between the third person singular and plural, marked in the Greek by the tiniest of differences in vocalization, to be explained? In a different author, we might be tempted to postulate an elegant rhetorical device (termed *apo koinou* in handbooks of rhetoric), which would apply both actions to both characters, so that we could understand that both Simon Peter and John saw the napkin and the linen wrappings inside the tomb, and that both Simon Peter and John saw and believed; but such a highly refined stylistic device would be quite anomalous in the context of the author John's usual prose style, and it is hard to see what its point would be here. Instead the strange contrast between the singular verbs "he [John] saw" (εἶδεν) and "he [John] believed" (ἐπίστευσεν) in 20:8 and the plural "they [Simon Peter and John] knew" (ᾔδεισαν) in 20:9 inevitably makes us wonder just what it was, in comparison to John, that Simon Peter did see and how he reacted to what he saw.

If so, the relevant point of comparison is surely not what they saw (napkin and linen cloths in the one case, at first only cloths in the other: but what difference should the napkin make?), but instead what their reaction was to what they saw. John saw and believed. What about Simon Peter? He saw: did he believe? John does not indicate his reaction: why not? Only four possibilities can be imagined: either Simon Peter's reaction was not important enough to be worth John's mentioning it (but this is most implausible, for if so why has John chosen to introduce him at all, and in such an authoritative role?); or John never found out what Simon Peter's reaction had been (but this is no less implausible, for could not John have simply inquired?); or Peter too believed, just as John did (but this is virtually impossible, for in that case why did John not use the plural verbs "they saw and believed" rather than the singular ones?); or Simon Peter did not believe, only John did (this must be right, for it is the only remaining possibility). In other words, neither Simon Peter nor John yet understood the scripture according to which Jesus would rise from the dead; John saw the linen wrappings and believed, but Simon Peter saw the napkin and wrappings and did not believe.

There can be little doubt about just what it was that John believed when he saw. For although the verb "he believed" (ἐπίστευσεν, 20:8) is used here in a grammatically ambiguous way without any explicit direct object, nonetheless the verb "to believe" (πιστεύειν) is a theologically loaded term in the Gospels and usually refers not to ordinary situations of belief concerning empirical states of affairs, but rather to religious faith in Jesus and, more specifically, to faith that he has risen from the dead. In a text as concerned as the Gospel of John is with belief in Jesus, we should therefore have little difficulty in understanding him to mean here that the disciple John believed what the author John would always have us believe to be the truth, namely that Jesus was risen.

On this view, the following verse (20:9) makes clear that, because John did not yet understand the scripture, it was only because he saw that he believed this. But it must be admitted that the logical connection which the causal connective particle "for" (γάρ) establishes in this way between verses 8 and 9 is very strained indeed. Not understanding the scripture seems a reason for not believing, rather than for believing. This is true for Simon Peter, who must have believed not that Jesus was risen, but instead what Mary Magdalene had told them, namely that Jesus was dead and that someone had stolen and hidden his body (20:2). To be sure, John does not assert explicitly that Simon Peter drew the wrong conclusion and chose to believe Mary; but it seems impossible to understand John's use of the singular and plural verb forms in any other way, and such an implicit sideswipe at Simon Peter would be typical of the attitude of slightly jealous rivalry that John displays with regard to him throughout his account (compare John 13:6–11, 36–38, 18:10–11, 15–17, 25–27, 21:21–22).

When Simon Peter and John go back to their own home or homes (20:10), leaving Mary Magdalene weeping outside the tomb (20:11), we have finally arrived at the same point in the narrative at which the other three Gospel accounts begin: Mary Magdalene weeps outside Jesus' tomb. The only difference is that John's Mary is now entirely, desolately alone, whereas the synoptic Mary is always accompanied and supported by at least one other woman. But if, in terms of the sequence of events, nothing has been gained by this prelude of ten verses, which occupies a third of the chapter, nevertheless it has performed considerable preparatory work with regard to the fundamental themes of belief and disbelief, knowledge and ignorance. John's narrative strategy compels us as readers to reenact in our own imagination the process of cognition that has taken place in these characters, a process that is not only tentative and partial but also, in the cases of Mary and Simon Peter, quite erroneous. For of the two authoritative men who have gone home, both having the same (incomplete) knowledge of scripture and the same visual experience of the grave clothes, one believes that Mary was right and that the corpse has been stolen, while the other believes that she is wrong and that Jesus has risen. What is the relation between sight and belief? Is seeing in fact believing? John "saw and believed" (20:8); Simon Peter saw—and believed Mary. Thus this first section of the chapter has provided us with examples of strikingly different kinds of belief based upon the same experience of ordinary vision; the rest of the chapter will go on to explore other instances of belief, well founded and otherwise, and in fact the chapter as a whole can be read as an inquiry into the nature and limits of human belief and its relation to sensory knowledge.

The mistake that Mary Magdalene and Simon Peter make in this first section is all the more striking because John has taken care to describe it in such a way that we as readers can easily understand. Of course, we "know" for doctrinal reasons that they must be wrong; but John's narrative is structured to render plausible an interpretation of events we must know to be false, to make us believe in the possibility of disbelief. To be sure, Mary Magdalene, as a mere woman, might be supposed by some readers to be easily induced into error; but of the two male disciples, it is the authoritative Simon Peter himself who seems to have adopted her erroneous belief. And although the disciple John seems to have the correct belief, we are not provided any reason to believe that he is justified in it. We all—certainly Mary Magdalene and Simon Peter within the author John's text, possibly the disciple John within it too, and surely we readers outside of the text as well—need to be reinforced in what is the correct belief. John's text needs, urgently, to supply us all with a miracle, one capable of making us believe.

❈

In narrative terms, John's story has reached an impasse, a point of blockage from which it is not clear how it can possibly continue. The mystery of the empty tomb has still not been explained; the men who were summoned have both gone home, one of them apparently in blatant error, the other in what happens to be true belief but not on a manifestly adequate basis. Hence the story must begin anew; and it is only Mary who can perform this crucial function, for there is no other character left besides her.

When John's Mary Magdalene starts the whole story over again by stooping down and looking into the sepulchre (20:11), she sees what she always sees at the beginning of the Gospel accounts: one or more angels in the place of the missing Jesus (20:12). But this time she has been preceded in her visual inspection of the tomb by Simon Peter and John, who had both seen nothing whatsoever except for linen cloths and a napkin—as it were, the mere outer veils of the truth, not the truth itself. Indeed, we can probably go further. For on the one hand, neither Simon Peter nor John is granted a vision of angels; they only see grave clothes, the napkin and the linen wrappings at some distance from one another (20:6–7). But on the other hand, it is not said anywhere that Mary herself sees any grave clothes, but only that she sees two angels, sitting at some distance from one another (20:12). The most economic explanation is that what the two disciples had seen but thought to be nothing more than grave clothes, Mary has recognized as being in actuality two angels. Apparently all three of them have seen the very same things; but only Mary has understood them for what they really are.

In John's account, the two angels thereby acquire a miraculous character even beyond what they possess in the synoptic Gospels. This is due not so much to their glorious appearance and their comforting words, which they share with their counterparts in those other narratives (except for Mark's), but rather to the unique structure of this narrative, which allows one humble woman to see what two authoritative men, a few seconds before, had entirely failed to perceive. In a single moment, the whole hierarchy that has organized the action of the narrative up to this point is turned upside down.

In contrast to the synoptic Gospels, the two angels say nothing to console Mary and entrust her with no mission. Why then is she permitted to see them? What is their function in the story? Whatever the differences in culture and sex that distinguish Mary from the two disciples Simon Peter and John, there is one difference in her behavior that may provide an explanation. The two men had simply run and looked, and then had gone back to the other disciples. But Mary is depicted weeping, weeping inconsolably, standing immovably at the tomb and crying her heart out: "But Mary stood weeping outside the tomb, and as she wept she stooped to look into the tomb" (20:11). Is she weeping now because Jesus has died, or because his body is missing and has thereby been desecrated and cannot be mourned properly by her? No doubt both reasons apply—indeed, the inexplicable absence of Jesus' body brings home to her in an especially distressing way her irrevocable loss. It can only be this outpouring of heart-breaking grief on her part that privileges her and affords her alone the grace of an angelic visitation denied the two more self-controlled (or less profoundly moved) male disciples—it is to her tears, after all, that the first words of the angels refer: "They said to her, 'Woman, why are you weeping?' " (20:13). Thus it is her disconsolate, solitary grief that grants her alone a vision of the angels. But at the same time her sorrow proves too much for them: they cannot console her (for what could they possibly say to comfort this woman who is so exclusively and entirely focused upon Jesus?) nor can they tell her to go away and pass on the news to the disciples (for what could they possibly do to induce her to leave a place that has been rendered holy for her by the mere fact that Jesus' body has lain there?).

So the angels must yield to a higher authority: just as Mary was entrusted with the task of initiating the narrative mechanism at the beginning of this chapter but then had to defer to Simon Peter and John when she was faced with a situation beyond her understanding, so too now, by an inverse symmetry, the angels are allowed to enter into the text but only so that they can immediately vanish from it once again and be replaced by Jesus himself, who appears to Mary when she turns around (20:14). At this moment, nothing occupies her thoughts except her grief; yet so fixated is she upon the missing body of the Lord she reveres that she does not recognize the body of Jesus—even though he is standing right in front of her. He is not said to be in disguise, nor is there any indication that her vision has been impaired; instead, her obsessive grief has summoned Jesus to her but at the same time prevents her from recognizing him. Evidently, however positively her grief is valorized as a symptom of her attachment to Jesus, the text takes pains to emphasize that in fact she is grieving for the wrong reason, mourning a person who she mistakenly thinks has died and left her forever.

Hence, in an error that in another genre would be almost comical, she mistakes Jesus for the gardener, addressing him as such (20:15). Why a gardener rather than anyone else? In dramatic and psychological terms, the reason must be that Jesus, without his grave clothes, is almost naked, and so Mary thinks he must be a menial laborer, for example, given that they are in the cemetery, a gardener; but in figural and symbolic terms, her unwitting reference to the Garden of Eden is unmistakable.

At this point we might perhaps expect an extended masquerade, of the sort we find in Luke 24:15–31, in which Jesus keeps up the disguise, conversing with, and testing, his ignorant interlocutor while we watch from the comfortable vantage point of superior knowledge. But here as elsewhere in John's Gospel, a weeping Mary is a figure of transcendent pathos who summons up the deepest emotions of grief and sympathy on the part of Jesus (and, presumably, of the reader too). So too, in chapter 11 of this Gospel we encountered a Mary whose brother Lazarus had died of an illness; on that occasion, Jesus reacted to that Mary's sorrow by being deeply moved (11:33, 38) and weeping (11:35), two things he never does anywhere else in the whole of the Gospel of John, not even when he himself is being betrayed, tortured, and crucified. Whether or not these two mourning Marys are to be thought of as one and the same person—John does not explicitly equate the two figures, and most scholars today would deny their identity, but the Western church has tended to conflate them since Gregory the Great (*Homily on the Gospels* 33 = PL 76.1238–46)—at the very least the analogy between them is far too strong to permit Jesus in chapter 20 to respond any less deeply than he had in chapter 11.

But if that Mary was saddened by her brother's death, this Mary is overwhelmed now by Jesus': in retrospect, even the death of a beloved brother can serve to let us measure by contrast the depth of a loving attachment to Jesus. Mary's grief is far too devastating to be played with: Jesus immediately lays aside his unrecognizability and addresses her with, not the impersonal (and perhaps somewhat disparaging) "Woman" (the vocative Γύναι) that the angels (20:13) and he too himself had used at first (20:15), instead using, with sublime simplicity, nothing more and nothing less than her own name, "Mary" (20:16). So intimate is the bond of connection which this one word immediately establishes between the two of them—by his acknowledgment that he knows who she is, by his indication to her thereby that she knows who he is, by his definition of her identity by means of her name which disperses at once the mists of her confusion, perhaps too (who knows?) by a particularly gentle tone of voice—that she must turn around once more (20:16).

Although she has already turned to face him once (20:14), in the meantime she has evidently averted her gaze while she has been speaking with him, as any modest woman would do. Now she turns to him once again, but this time in a gesture not only of social salutation but also of spiritual recognition, and speaks in turn one word to him: not his name, nor "Lord" (the Greek vocative κύριε), his title of social respect and legal authority, which she had used twice earlier in this same chapter when she was speaking about him in the third person to others (20:2, 13), but instead a solemn "Hebrew" (that is, Aramaic) designation of religious wisdom and power, "Rabboni (which means Teacher)" (20:16). Thereby she creates a coordinating horizontal axis of fully human exchange and simultaneously a subordinating vertical axis of female deference before the male privilege of learning and Scriptural expertise.

It is only then that Jesus can exploit the privileged status she has accorded him in order to give her the verbal command to go and tell the disciples—but tell them what? This time, in contrast to all three synoptic Gospels, she is not to make an appointment for them with him by telling them that they will see him at some future time at some definite place on earth, but rather she must simply proclaim to them that he himself is going up to heaven (20:17). She is to function not as an appointments secretary, but as a glorious herald. This is not the first time, of course, that we have heard that Jesus came from his father and would return to him (compare 16:16, 28): but in this context Jesus' announcement leaves a number of questions open. Will the disciples ever see him again? For that matter, will he ever return to the earth? What is to become of them on that earth? Mary does not pause to wonder about these issues, but instead she obeys Jesus' instructions at once without hesitation or delay (as in Matthew's account, but not as in Mark's, which John may be implicitly correcting) and goes to deliver this message, incomplete and ambiguous as it is, to the disciples (20:18). What their reaction to her words is, we are not told.

Thus comes to an abrupt end this first, highly dramatic act.

※

If Mary dominates the first act of which John 20 is composed, Thomas is the central figure of its second act. The two characters, Mary and Thomas, correspond perfectly: the woman Jesus was particularly fond of balances the disciple who was particularly attached to him; the figure of grief (the emotional side of Mary's false belief that Jesus is dead), which is then transmuted into joy, is answered by the paradigm of disbelief (the cognitive side of Thomas's false belief that Jesus is dead), which is then transformed into belief; both characters are obsessed by the body of Jesus and seem to have little understanding of, or even interest in, his spiritual significance. The events in the two halves of the chapter are also constructed so as to correspond to each other: the miracle of Jesus' disappearance from the sealed sepulchre in the first half is inverted by his two appearances within the locked room where the disciples are assembled in the second half; and in every case the events take place on the first day of the week (20:1, 19, 26).

One further indication proves that the two halves of the chapter, the two characters, and the two sets of events were designed to correspond perfectly with one another. In the first half, Jesus responds to Mary's cry of recognition with the words "Do not touch me" (or perhaps "Do not take hold of me," Μή μου ἄπτου, or, in the familiar Latin version, *noli me tangere*, 20:17). Evidently Mary's joy at discovering his beloved body once more in front of her is so great that, with a deeply human and immediately understandable gesture, her first instinct is to touch it lovingly. Indeed, why should she not? After all,

Mary of Bethany caressed his living body at earlier moments in this very same Gospel without being reprimanded (11:2, 12:3). What is more, in the synoptic versions of the events following Jesus' crucifixion there is never any prohibition whatsoever against anyone's touching Jesus' risen body. In Matthew, when Jesus meets the two Marys on their way from the tomb to the disciples, "they came up and took hold of his feet and worshiped him" (28:9); in Luke, Jesus himself invites the disciples, "handle me, and see" (24:39). The contradiction between John's account and the synoptic Gospels in this regard is so flagrant that some translators seem to have tried to camouflage it by mistranslation—thus one standard Italian translation expands the lapidary Μή μου ἄπτου ("Do not touch me") into "Non continuare più ad abbracciarmi i piedi così" ("Do not continue any longer to embrace my feet in this way"); and even the Revised Standard Version, which translates the verb ἄπτομαι uniformly as "touch" in every single one of its other thirty-five occurrences in the New Testament, renders it here, and here alone, as "Do not hold me." To be sure, the grammatical form of Jesus' negative imperative is semantically ambiguous: it may prohibit an action that Mary has not yet begun actually to perform, or else ask her to desist from an action that she has already initiated. But the crucial point here is not which of these two grammatical alternatives we should prefer, but rather the fact that, in either case, Jesus is addressing to Mary a strict prohibition with regard to her making physical contact with him.

But why should Mary not touch Jesus? By calling him "Rabboni," Mary had offered Jesus a lovingly respectful deference for which her touching him would provide a bodily equivalent: why does Jesus refuse her? In John's account, Jesus explains the prohibition against her touching him by saying merely that he has not yet ascended to his father (20:17). How are we to understand this? Does he intend to suggest that he is still defiled by death and must be purified by his father before Mary, whom he wishes to protect, can touch him without thereby endangering herself? Or is his concern directed more toward himself than toward her, so that, for example, he wishes to reduce to a minimum any interchange with mere humans before hastening to his father? Neither John nor Jesus gives us any hint in either of these directions or indeed in any other: Jesus' words remain thoroughly obscure—in fact they seem to be nothing more than an ad hoc construction improvised so as to lend some appearance of legitimacy to his prohibition against Mary's touching him. This prohibition, which forms the culminating moment of the first half of the chapter, is so much at variance with the other accounts and so unexpected and unexplained in its immediate context that it seems to have been placed here primarily in order to prepare for the second half of this chapter, in which the question of touching Jesus' body will be the central issue—but in which, so far from prohibiting a woman from touching him, Jesus will invite a man to touch him. Of course, within the immediate dramatic situation of John's story, Jesus' words "Do not touch me" are spoken only to Mary Magdalene; but in fact we can only understand them fully if we take them as an anticipation of a later stage of the narrative and interpret them as looking forward to the only other person in this whole chapter with whom Jesus has an individual exchange, Thomas.

That is, Jesus' prohibition against Mary's touching him (20:17) and his invitation that Thomas touch him (20:27) must be understood together: these two utterances are the points at which the two halves of the *symbolon* of this chapter fit most precisely together.

❧

The second act of this chapter is divided into two symmetrical scenes: both take place in the same location, both occur on the first day of the week, both have exactly the same characters, with the single, decisive exception of Thomas, who turns out unexpectedly to have been missing the first time but is centrally present the second time.

In the opening of the first scene, we find the disciples gathered on the evening of the day of Mary's encounter with Jesus; they have secluded themselves behind locked doors (20:19). Questions might arise. Where have they been, and what have they been doing, during the time since Jesus' crucifixion? When Mary Magdalene ran to find

Simon Peter and John (20:2), were they with the other disciples? If so, why did only these two come? If not, where were they and why were they not together with the others? Again, have the disciples spent all this time together in fear and in mournful remembrance of Jesus, or have they only gathered together now on this very evening, the first day of the week, to commemorate and revere him? Did Simon Peter and John discuss with each other the fact that they had drawn opposite conclusions from the very same sight of the grave clothes in the otherwise empty tomb, and, if they had in fact attempted to reconcile their divergent views, how successful were they? We are not told the answers to any of these questions: for this text, what defines the disciples is not whatever they might happen to do on their own on a daily basis, but rather their solidarity as a single, cohesive group focused entirely upon Jesus. The internal unity of the community of the disciples is emphasized by the external menace said to be represented by the Jews, against whom they have locked the doors. So cohesive is the group that John's text does not give us the slightest reason to suspect that any one of the eleven disciples remaining after Judas's betrayal might be missing.

Jesus' sudden apparition, despite the locked doors, seems to be a miraculous response to the disciples' prayers. Just as Mary Magdalene's grief had summoned him in the first act, so now their pious commemoration summons him in the second one. The physical obstacles that succeed in keeping out human, unbelieving enemies have no power to prevent the appearance of the superhuman friend in whom the disciples have not ceased to believe. Jesus comes not to disperse their doubts—there is not the slightest indication that they might have felt any—but rather to reward their faith. Correspondingly, he does not rebuke them, but salutes them lovingly, "Peace be with you" (20:19). They react joyously to the sight he affords them of his wounded hands and side (20:20, compare Luke 24:41)—not, of course, because they are pleased to see the signs that testify to his sufferings, but because while the wounds he bears prove indeed that he has died, at the same time his presence among them confirms that he is really risen. Jesus' action of self-presentation condenses paradoxically into a single person the otherwise mutually exclusive antitheses of life (the subject of the action, the person who can show) and death (the object of the action, the mortal wounds, the dead person who is shown). We are used to a living victor pointing contemptuously down at his vanquished foe, or to a wounded survivor exhibiting proudly the injuries he has survived: but where have we ever seen a living person displaying himself as a dead one?

Jesus rewards the joy of his faithful disciples by delivering a speech paralleling their apostolic mission to his own (20:21), by breathing the divine inspiration of the Holy Spirit into them (20:22), and, climactically, by transferring to them his own capability of remitting or retaining the sins of others (20:23). The first of these three topics forms the conclusion of the Gospels of Mark (16:15–18) and Matthew (28:18–20), but nothing as grand as the latter two subjects is even hinted at in those other accounts. In Luke, Jesus says that he has sent "the promise of my Father upon you" (24:49) and has ordered "that repentance and forgiveness of sins should be preached in his name to all nations" (24:47); but it is a considerable leap from such lofty but not implausible assertions to the unique and anomalous acts of blowing the Holy Spirit itself into the disciples and transferring to them the right of divine judgment about people's sins.

Such hyperbole is typically climactic and conclusive. Nothing suggests that the Gospel of John will not come to an end right here: if it did, no reader would ever have suspected that anything might have been intended to follow upon so magnificent a conclusion (20:23).

❧

Hence nothing prepares us for the sentence that follows: "Now Thomas, one of the twelve, called the Twin, was not with them when Jesus came" (20:24). Once again, questions arise. Why was he not with the other ten disciples? Was his absence his choice or theirs? Had he wanted to come but not been able to, or had he not wanted to come, or had he not known about the meeting? And in any of these cases, what had the reason been? Where, in fact, was he?

Whatever could have drawn him away from the safety of the enclosed solidarity of his fellow disciples into the uncertainties and dangers of a city filled with menacing enemies? And above all, on the evening of the first day of the week after Jesus' crucifixion, what could he possibly have had to do more urgent than commemorating Jesus together with his fellows?

John does not provide us with the materials that would permit us to answer any of these questions. Thomas's absence cannot be explained from the immediate context alone, but only from a later one, retrospectively, in terms of the consequences it produces—above all, from the solitary encounter between Jesus and Thomas that it prepares and that otherwise would not have been possible. But at the present moment, it is the sheer surprise of this absence that most impresses the reader. As we saw above, when we heard of the first gathering of the disciples after Jesus' death, nothing led us to expect that any one of them might have been missing from this tightly cohesive group. Our astonishment at suddenly discovering that one of them, Thomas, had in fact been absent, focuses our attention upon the solitary enigma he embodies.

But John takes care not to leave Thomas alone for more than the time of a single sentence: he immediately associates him once again with the group of disciples and shows him in a dialogue with them, albeit an asymmetrical one: Thomas on the one hand, all the other disciples on the other. When John writes that "the other disciples told him, 'We have seen the Lord' " (20:25), what attitude are we to ascribe to them? It is improbable that they are merely reporting neutrally to him a recent event of no great import to them or to him; but at the same time it is not very likely, though not quite impossible, that they are simply wishing altruistically to pass on to him something they themselves consider a joyous piece of news, something remarkable which they have seen and at which they expect him too to rejoice. After all, unlike all the other Gospel characters whom Jesus or angels explicitly order to report the news of the risen Christ, the disciples in John's account have been told by no one to tell Thomas or anyone else that they have seen the Lord, or for that matter to report anything else; and in no other case is the whereabouts of one of the recipients of the verbal message from the scene of visual apparition left a mystery, let alone as pointedly as it is in the case of Thomas. Hence it is certainly plausible, and may even be preferable, to understand the disciples' words as an implicit reproach, almost as though they were gloating over the miracle that had been made available to them but denied to Thomas. "Why weren't you here with us?" they seem to be chiding him. "See what you missed?"

Obviously the context preceding this sentence does not compel so antagonistic an understanding of the disciples' intention. But the lines immediately following become difficult to make sense of unless we attribute some such view of their motivation to Thomas himself. For otherwise the sudden, drastic violence of his reply to the disciples seems inexplicable: "But he said to them, 'Unless I see in his hands the print of the nails, and place my finger in the mark of the nails, and place my hand in his side, I will not believe'" (20:25). Thomas's doubt seems to be directed not only to the content of the message that has been transmitted to him (that is, he refuses to believe them *that Jesus is risen*) but also to the messengers who have brought it to him, his fellow disciples, whose word he does not trust (that is, he refuses to believe *them* that Jesus is risen). He seems to be angry with them because of his exclusion, jealous that they alone have participated in a miracle that has been denied only to him. As for Thomas's emphasis upon the wounds, we can infer (even if it is not explicitly asserted) that the other ten disciples must have said to him not just that they had seen Jesus, but also that he had shown them his wounds as proof that he had died and was now risen (see also Luke 24:39–40).

Thomas does not specify what exactly he will believe if his conditions are met, for the emphasis of the text is upon his refusal to believe rather than upon the contents of the belief he refuses to adopt—once again, as in 20:8, the grammatical object of the verb "I will not believe" (οὐ μὴ πιστεύσω, 20:25) is suppressed. But there can be little doubt that here, as in general, the object of "to believe" (πιστεύειν) is that Jesus has risen from the dead. Thomas is not doubting the identity of Jesus, as in a recognition scene in a Greek tragedy or romance, in which a person without the right name and a name without a person are brought together in an act of definitive personal identification: for here it is not a question of whether the man the disciples saw really was or was not Jesus. Instead, Thomas's fellow disciples have claimed both (A) that Jesus has died and (B) that they have seen him risen once again after his death. For Thomas to disbelieve their claim means either (A) to disbelieve that Jesus has died and/or (B) to disbelieve that he has risen again after death. But (A) to disbelieve that Jesus has died means to believe that he is still alive. If Jesus' wounds were real, this would prove that he had actually died; hence Thomas demands to be convinced of the reality of Jesus' wounds. And (B) to disbelieve that Jesus has risen again after death means to believe that he has not only really died but has stayed dead, so that anything the disciples had seen could not have been Jesus' risen body but only a ghost, a phantom. If Jesus' body could be touched and could offer to the exploring hand the resistance of materiality, this would prove that he was not a ghost but had actually risen again. Hence Thomas demands to touch Jesus' body. In precisely the same way, in the Gospel of Luke the disciples mistake the risen Jesus for a ghost ($\pi\nu\epsilon\hat{\upsilon}\mu\alpha$, "spirit," Luke 24:37, 39), and he convinces them that he is not one by concretely demonstrating his physical materiality (24:36–43).

In other words, Thomas believes either that Jesus is dead or that he is alive, but in either case that his fellow disciples are liars. As we saw earlier, distrust of one's ears usually turns out to be distrust of one's fellows. What will it take to convince Thomas of the truth of what the other disciples have told him?

❦

Thomas's outburst has two stages, which we may term (1) conventional doubt and (2) hyperbolic doubt.

In the first stage ("Unless I see in his hands the print of the nails"), Thomas asserts that he will only believe what the other disciples have reported to his ears if and when he can see its truth for himself with his own eyes. In terms of the social mechanism of cognitive distrust analyzed earlier, Thomas prefers seeing with his own eyes to merely hearing with his ears what other people claim to have seen with their eyes. We are operating here within the traditional scheme of "seeing is believing," the rhythm of alternating verbal pronouncements and visual confirmations that structures all three of the other Gospels (as well as so much of literature and ordinary life); the only unusual thing here is Thomas's concentration upon Jesus' wounds as the proof of his death (and hence of his resurrection). This first stage of doubt should really be enough, and for the other three Evangelists it seems to have sufficed. We expect a scene to follow in which Thomas will see the wounds and will thereby be fully convinced of Jesus' resurrection, so that John's narrative will be able to conclude with general rejoicing.

But instead, completely unexpectedly, John has Thomas go one step further. In a second stage of uniquely hyperbolic doubt ("and place my finger in the mark of the nails, and place my hand in his side"), Thomas declares that merely seeing Jesus' wounds will not be enough to make him believe that he is risen: he will have to touch him, to place his finger into one of the holes in Jesus' hands and his hand into the wound in Jesus' side. Thomas is granting a greater degree of epistemological validity to what he can touch with his hands than to what he can see with his eyes. And this second step is itself constructed as a two-part climax: first Thomas' single finger, then his whole hand; first the small hole left by a nail, then the broad wound made by a spear; first Jesus' hand, a relatively public part of his body, then his more intimate, private flank.

Why must full proof for Thomas be tactile rather than just visual? Why is Thomas dissatisfied with merely reading the visual signs of Jesus' wounds upon the white page of his body, so that he insists upon touching them too? For the Gospel of Luke, the proof furnished by seeing Jesus eat had sufficed, and not only once but twice (Luke 24:30–31, 41–43): why is it not enough for John?

We might envision various responses to this difficulty. We might be tempted to think of a Jewish tradition according to which angels too can actually eat and drink, or can at least give the appearance of eating and drinking without its being possible for humans to tell that they are not in fact doing so (compare Genesis 18.8, 19:3; Tobit 12:19; Testament of Abraham, Recension A, 4:9–11a). But if Thomas wanted to make sure that Jesus was not an angel, would it not have been enough for him to touch Jesus' body, without inserting his finger and hand into the wounds?

A more philosophical approach would refer to the doctrine, attested occasionally in ancient Greek epistemology, that the most secure form of human knowledge is that granted by touch, which admits of no error, while every other kind of sensory knowledge, including that gained by sight, is more fallible. Yet this doctrine is found in only a few Greek philosophical texts (for example, Theophrastus, *Metaphysics* 25.9b15)—most Greek philosophers much preferred sight to any of the other senses (for example, Heraclitus, Frg. 101a Diels-Kranz; Plato, *Phaedrus* 250D, *Rep.* 5.475E, *Timaeus* 47A–B; Aristotle, *Metaphysics* 1.1.980a24ff.)—and, although Thomas's words can be interpreted as having philosophically interesting implications, there can be little doubt that John's account is not designed to make us believe that Thomas is above all a serious philosopher.

Or might Thomas suspect that any wounds he might think he sees upon Jesus' body could have been merely painted illusionistically onto its surface, so that a solely visual inspection would not reveal their falsity? But even to raise such a possibility would run the risk of reducing the whole story to a sham—Jesus would not really have died, and his resurrection would be no miracle. Such an interpretation would trivialize the story intolerably.

Or finally, has Thomas, in a moment of passionate anger at his fellow disciples, conflated one demand, that he be allowed to look at the wounds (which, if granted, would prove that Jesus had really died), with another demand, that he be permitted to touch his body (which, if granted, would disprove that he is a ghost or an angel and hence prove that he is really still alive), thereby creating a confusing notion, that of *touching* the *wounds*, which combines elements of both quite different alternatives? On some psychological level, something like this may well be happening here. But to reduce Thomas's outburst to a simple mental lapse, a momentary category mistake, cannot explain its powerful effect upon the reader.

Within the immediate dramatic situation, the point of Thomas's hyperbolic demand must be a different one. Coming as it does a mere eight verses after Jesus had said "Do not touch me" to Mary Magdalene (20:17), Thomas's requirement bears the weight of a violation—a radical, though of course an unintentional one (Thomas had not heard Jesus' words to Mary)—of an express prohibition on the part of Jesus. We are struck by the contrast between the scenes in which people had been healed by the simple act of touching Jesus or the very fringe of his garment (Mark 5:21–34, Matt. 9:18–26, Luke 8:40–56) and this aggressive and skeptical demand on Thomas's part to touch Jesus' wounds. What is more, Thomas's demand not only violates an explicit religious taboo: it also arouses visceral sensations of revulsion and disgust. For few things are more loathsome than open wounds on human bodies. Even the thought of touching the outside surface of such injuries with a finger must make one's gorge rise— how much more so to imagine inserting a finger into a small wound, or putting one's hand all the way into a larger one.

And finally, Thomas's demand actually to touch Jesus' body creates what might well seem an insuperable problem for the logical coherence of John's narrative. For Jesus' passage through the locked doors behind which the disciples have barricaded themselves (20:19) must mean that he does not possess a fully material body in the ordinary sense. So if Thomas were to demand only visual proof of Jesus' identity, we could easily imagine such proof being furnished: then the risen Jesus would turn out to be a spirit or a ghost. But Thomas's demand for a tactile proof is a demand for incontrovertible evidence of Jesus' full physical materiality. Yet a body that can be touched cannot pass through locked doors. This seems to leave the continuation of John's story with only two options, neither satisfactory. If Thomas's wish is refused and he does not touch Jesus, Jesus will seem a mere wraith; but then what good will the resurrection be for us? If

Thomas's wish is granted and he does touch Jesus, the logic of John's story will break down into irremediable self-contradiction; and then how will it manage to convince us?

How can John rescue himself from this narrative aporia?

❧

Thomas's hyperbolic doubt violates both our religious sense of taboo, by committing a sacrilegious blasphemy, and our physical sense of well-being, by provoking a sense of disgust; and it poses a serious dilemma for the logical coherence of John's whole narrative. So startling are his words that John's narrative cannot continue beyond them: it seems suddenly to break off right here. Once again, questions arise. How did the disciples respond to Thomas's extraordinary outburst? What did they do for the next week? Did Thomas spend those days together with them, or apart? If the former, how did they all get along with one another for that period of time? If the latter, where was he? Again, John does not answer any of these questions. Instead, he takes up the story again exactly one week after the disciples' first vision. Once again it is the first day of the week, once again the disciples are locked into a room for fear of the Jews, once again they are commemorating Jesus; but this time Thomas is with them (20:26). Whatever the reason that had kept him apart from them the first time, they have all made very sure that he will be with them this second time, just in case Jesus should happen to come back on the corresponding day of the next week.

And he does, precisely as he did the first time, and with the very same words of greeting to all the disciples. As information, this is not news: it seems to be an exact repetition of what we already know. If the repetition is not to be pointless, then the point must derive from the only difference between the two situations, Thomas's absence the first time and his presence the second time. In other words, Jesus has come back this second time only because this time Thomas is there: Jesus has returned for no other reason than in order to convince him. Nowhere else in the Gospels does Jesus return for the sole purpose of convincing a single person: Thomas's sudden prominence is unique, and perhaps not entirely enviable.

At this crucial point of the narrative we might well wonder how Jesus will react to Thomas's profession of disbelief. Might he not be irritated? If, for example, Jesus were a pagan Greek god, that is, a being with superhuman capabilities but very human desires and defects, he would doubtless respond by making a brief but convincing demonstration of his superior physical power. Instantaneous incineration might well provide a highly persuasive argument (think of Zeus and Semele). But such a strategy suffers from overkill, as it were, for it does not allow the skeptic himself to survive his lesson long enough to change his mind, let alone his way of life; would not a somewhat less lethal demonstration make the point just as well? Moreover, what if the god in question is a new kind of god, gentler, sadder, more inclined to love humans than to lust after them, a god subject to every humiliation, pain, and death that humans suffer, one summoned not only to rule over humans, but also, and above all, to protect them, if only from themselves? And what if the humans to whom that god is sent are no longer thought to be exemplified above all by the sublimely tragic hero who stakes his life with ferocious obstinacy upon some single idea, be it mistaken or no, but rather by the small, frightened survivor, anxious to live on in this world and also willing to live on in the next one, especially if the price for doing so is not outward obedience to dietary rules or public sacrifice but the inner impulse of belief—someone capable of changing the direction of his life in midstream by the miracle of sudden, radical conversion? How can Jesus, a very different god from the kind most inhabitants of the ancient Mediterranean world were used to, one endowed not only with unlimited power but also with a capacity for unlimited suffering, convince Thomas that he really is divine?

❧

"Then he said to Thomas, 'Put your finger here, and see my hands; and put out your hand, and place it in my side; do not be faithless, but believing' " (20:27). The first, conventional stage of Thomas's doubt had been visual, and at first sight Jesus might seem, in inviting Thomas to "see" his hands, to be offering a purely optical demonstration to him in the same terms as those that Thomas himself had proposed. Yet in fact Jesus' first words, inviting Thomas to stretch out his finger and place it at some specific but undisclosed location, already discard this first stage as trivial and uninteresting. Instead, Jesus offers Thomas the same tactile demonstration which the disciple had said would alone suffice to dispel his second stage of hyperbolic doubt: Jesus' imperative that Thomas "see" his hands, following as it does upon the order that he "put" his finger "here," must mean that he is telling Thomas not merely to stick out his finger and then only look at Jesus' hands rather than touching them, but rather that it is by inserting his finger into the hole left by the nail that Thomas will be enabled to see Jesus' hands for what they really are, the hands of a man who has been killed by mortal wounds.

Thomas has asked for the impossible—and Jesus has granted it. Why has he done so? Is Jesus' gift to him solely an expression of kindness, of his gentleness toward human beings? Or might it be a seduction offered with the voice of the tempter, designed to destroy any mortal blind enough to submit to it? Consider Dionysus in Euripides' *Bacchae*, who leads another doubter, Pentheus, on to his destruction, step by tempting step, by offering to fulfill for him the very criteria of belief that Pentheus himself has sacrilegiously demanded. Might Jesus too be making Thomas an offer he dare not accept?

Such a suggestion might seem disconcerting, but it certainly fits well with the next verse: "Thomas answered him, 'My Lord and my God!' " (20:28). For there can be no doubt that Thomas's outcry is to be understood as an act of hyperbolic submission to Jesus' authority, one that follows, reverses, and redeems the act of hyperbolic doubt that Thomas has just committed. This is the first time in the whole of John's Gospel, or in fact in any of the New Testament Gospels, that anyone calls Jesus a god, let alone to his face; and Thomas calls him not simply "God" but "my God," asserting his personal acknowledgment of the validity for himself of Jesus' divine status. In speaking these words Thomas is not only virtually citing Psalm 35:23, "my God and my Lord" (the context is complaint about mistreatment by other men and a prayer to God for protection), but also adapting, and perhaps parodying, the salutation "Dominus et deus noster"

("Our Lord and God"), which the Roman emperor Domitian required of his subjects (Suetonius, *Domitian* 13.4; Martial 5.8.1). But above all, he is echoing the same words that Jesus himself had used at the end of his encounter with Mary, the counterpart to this scene, when he said to her that he was going to his father, "my God" (20:17). Of course the echo is unconscious, for Thomas was not a witness to the scene between Mary and Jesus; but just as earlier his desire to touch Jesus' body unknowingly violated the prohibition that Jesus had uttered to her, so too now his acknowledgment of Jesus as a God for him unknowingly but precisely quotes and applies to Jesus himself the very same words that Jesus had applied to his God.

Thomas's pious exclamation, following as it does upon his impious one, might seem to be merely a momentary outburst. Yet in fact it is carefully prepared for and functions as an essential part of a simple but highly effective narrative structure—it is merely the most superficial indication of a careful construction. Thomas's only two utterances in this entire scene are both passionate but complementary outbursts, one aggressive and the other pious, one violently demanding the satisfaction of conditions before belief will be accorded and the other expressing the fullest possible commitment to that very same belief. Thomas himself has demanded that certain criteria be fulfilled before he will recognize Jesus as risen, but in fact he only acquires the ability to recognize Jesus after Jesus has first recognized Thomas and publicly announced his own awareness of Thomas's desire to touch him. That is, it is God's recognition of man that is the prerequisite for man's recognition of God. Precisely the same sequence of steps—first a human being's incapacity to recognize Jesus, then Jesus' recognition of that human, and finally the human's joyous acknowledgment of Jesus—structures Mary's encounter with the risen Jesus, the counterpart earlier in this same chapter to the scene of Thomas: first Mary thinks mistakenly that Jesus is the gardener (20:14–15); then Jesus addresses her as Mary, identifying her as the person she really is (20:16); finally she acknowledges him as who he really is by calling him "Rabboni" (20:16). But what is perhaps even more remarkable is that we find precisely the same narrative structure in the very first miracle of Jesus' recounted in John's Gospel, the story of the otherwise entirely unknown disciple Nathanael (1:43–51), to which nothing corresponds in the synoptic Gospels. Here too we have first an expression of human doubt (when Nathanael hears that Jesus of Nazareth is the one whose coming Moses prophesied, he asks, "Can anything good come out of Nazareth?" 1:46); then Jesus recognizes Nathanael as "an Israelite indeed, in whom is no guile" (1:47) and says he saw him under the fig tree (1:48); and thereupon Nathanael acknowledges him, saying, "Rabbi, you are the Son of God! You are the King of Israel!" (1:49). It is perhaps significant that Nathanael only recurs in one other passage, in the continuation of the Gospel of John, thought by many scholars to be spurious, at 21:2; and that here he is associated with Thomas, and paired, perhaps significantly, with him.

These three episodes of divine recognition—of Nathanael, of Mary, and of Thomas—are parallel to one another and were most likely intended to be mutually illuminating; one suspects that John has devised the first story, that of Nathanael, so that it would prepare us here, at the very beginning of his Gospel, to understand better the scenes of Mary and Thomas later, at its very close. If so, then it is surely not only the similarities between the three stories that carry a semantic charge—man can only recognize God if God already recognizes him, human knowledge is inadequate unless it is supported by divine grace. By the same token, the differences among them will also be meaningful: for Thomas's doubt is the most radically aggressive of all three, just as his acknowledgment of Jesus as God is the most hyperbolically pious. And Jesus' recognition of Thomas is not limited to a name, as with Mary, or a characterization, as with Nathanael: instead, Jesus recognizes Thomas by recognizing what it is that Thomas most deeply wants to do, by quoting to Thomas's face the same words that Thomas had spoken some days earlier to the other disciples (only an incorrigibly skeptical reader might suggest that the reason Jesus knows what Thomas said is that in the meantime one of these disciples had reported those very words to him, and even that would surely suppose a living Jesus). But if so, then

Thomas no longer needs to touch Jesus in order to confirm his identity: Jesus' recognition of Thomas has superseded the criteria that Thomas initially required, and Thomas can now abandon them because they are no longer needed.

At the same time, John has brilliantly resolved the narrative aporia raised by Thomas's hyperbolic doubt. For Jesus has neither refused Thomas's demand nor has he actually fulfilled it. By offering his body to be touched, Jesus has suggested that it could be touched, without proving that in fact it can be. And Thomas, by withdrawing his requirement that he touch Jesus' body, has left the question of the materiality of that body entirely open. We are told that it can be seen (20:20, compare 29). But we shall never know whether it could have been touched. What kind and degree of materiality Jesus' risen body really has, John has been careful not to reveal.

❧

But if this is the objective meaning of Thomas's words, what is the psychological disposition that accompanies them? John tells us nothing about Thomas's feelings, yet the passionate intensity of Thomas's outburst seems to require that we supply it with some kind of emotional motivation, particularly since it comes immediately after the emotionally laden sentences that have preceded it. We can scarcely understand Thomas's words unless we ascribe some fairly specific dispositional state to him. But just what kind of state?

Many readers have seen in Thomas's reaction a movement of pious joy, and no doubt a man's reaction to divine recognition might well assume such a form. But at the same time there are other, darker readings of Thomas's emotional state that the text might also be interpreted as intending to suggest. For example, might not Thomas feel a profound sense of contrition and shame, before Jesus and the other disciples, for his having disbelieved their report of the resurrection, particularly now that he is faced with Jesus' generous offer that he inspect his wounds and is surrounded by the other disciples who had expressed no doubts? Yet shame, or contrition, seems too banal, and too mild, an emotion to be entirely plausible as a reaction to such an

extraordinary situation and as a motivation for Thomas's second outburst. Perhaps, instead, Thomas should be thought to be acting here
not out of exultation or shame, but instead out of terror. After all, Jesus' entrance through the locked doors, his recognition of Thomas in
terms not of his name alone, but of a desire about whose impiety
there can be little doubt, his citation of words spoken when he was
not present, and his free offering of what Thomas had angrily demanded might well provoke a feeling of abysmal dread. When Jesus
offers to Thomas precisely what he himself demanded in an instant
of blind irritation and exasperation but probably thought quite impossible, Thomas might well be recognizing, in terror, the overwhelming power of Jesus and therefore calling out self-defensively an
admission of Jesus' divinity.

On this view, what exactly is it that Thomas fears? We might at
first be tempted to think that he is merely afraid for his own personal
safety—for if Jesus can transform his own death into life (what no
one else had ever been able to do) then could he not easily transform
Thomas's life into death (what any roof tile could do in a moment)?
But it is unlikely that the same Thomas who had been eager to die together with Jesus in an earlier chapter of this same Gospel (11:16)
would suddenly now be so terrified that Jesus' power to revivify
might be used to annihilate him: anxiety about his personal safety
may well be a minor factor in his momentary emotional state, but it
surely cannot be the whole story. Instead, Thomas's terror, if it really
is terror, is above all a sacred terror: confronted with the reality of
what he previously excluded as impossible in terms of the laws of the
natural world, Thomas recognizes to his horror that what is standing
before him in the person of Jesus is a sublime religious *mysterium*, not
just the man whom he thought he knew but instead a site of such
transcendently superhuman power that merely to be anywhere in its
proximity—to say nothing of trying to touch it or, what is more, to
stick his hand into it—must fill him with overwhelming dread. Struck
by a terror that goes far deeper than the mere instinct of self-preser-
vation, Thomas cries out words that assert a complete recognition of
Jesus' divinity and a total submission to it, in the hope that such an

assertion of hyperbolic piety will cancel out and redeem his earlier assertion of hyperbolic impiety—and thereby save him.

❧

On either account, Thomas does not actually touch Jesus, either because he no longer needs to, or because he is too terrified to do so. If this is so, then the one thing that most people think that they know about Doubting Thomas, namely that he stuck his fingers into Jesus' wounds, is false, at least on the basis of the text of the Gospel of John (and there is no other ultimate source for the story).

This point bears examination in some detail. Let us reconsider the text of John for a moment:

> Then he said to Thomas, "Put your finger here, and see my hands; and put out your hand, and place it in my side; do not be faithless, but believing." Thomas answered him, "My Lord and my God!" (20:27–28)

What is it precisely that motivates Thomas's pious outcry? Those readers who believe that this exclamation is provoked by his touching Jesus' wounds must suppose that a narrative lacuna intervenes between Jesus' statement and Thomas's, one in which it would have been said that Thomas touched him and therefore believed. As it were, many readers seem to think that a sentence like "Then Thomas touched Jesus' wounds, and lo! he believed" is missing and must be supplied mentally by them. Of course the Gospel narratives are full of such lacunae, as we have often seen. But in supplying this kind of material here, such readers are overlooking a small but decisive textual fact. John does not say that Thomas "said" or "uttered" or "exclaimed" or "cried out" these words, but that he "answered him" (ἀπεκρίθη) with them. The grammar of the verb used here, ἀποκρίνεσθαι ("to answer"), is unambiguous: it occurs more than two hundred times in the New Testament, and whenever it introduces a quoted speech B spoken by one person that follows a quoted speech A spoken by someone else, then speech B is a direct and immediate response to speech A; speech B is caused directly by speech A, not by any other event intervening between the two speeches. In the present case, this can only mean one thing: there is no room between Jesus' speech and Thomas' speech in which something else could happen that might motivate Thomas's words. Thomas's outcry is caused by the words that Jesus addresses to him, and not by anything else.

Thus the very grammar of John's language means that it is not only superfluous but in fact mistaken to posit that Thomas touches Jesus even if the text does not say he did: Thomas's speech is motivated by Jesus' speech, not by any action on the part of Thomas. What is more, the whole structure of John's narrative precludes the possibility that Thomas did in fact convince himself by touching Jesus' wounds. Thomas did not need, or did not dare, to touch Jesus' wounds: his change of mind was due not to his having satisfied the very same criteria of belief that he had established earlier, but to his rejecting those criteria, either out of his joyous gratitude for the divine recognition of himself or out of his overwhelming terror at having violated a sacred prohibition. Thomas's attempt to found religious faith upon the empirical sense of touch fails utterly: to suppose that Thomas might actually have touched Jesus, and thereby have been brought to belief in his divinity, is to misunderstand not just some detail of John's account, but its deepest and most fundamental message.

Any possible doubts on this score are dispelled by Jesus' immediate reaction to Thomas' outcry: "Jesus said to him, 'Have you believed because you have seen me? Blessed are those who have not seen and yet believe'" (20:29). For Jesus does not say that Thomas has believed because he has touched him, but rather that he has believed because he has seen him; and what is more, Jesus goes on to set Thomas, who has only believed because he could see, into an unfavorable contrast with all those other people who are capable of believing even though they have not seen. This can only mean that Thomas saw, and did not touch; for otherwise Jesus would have had to say, "Have you believed because you have touched me?" With Jesus' actual words, which only mention sight, we abandon the level of hyperbolic doubt that can only be overcome by touch, and return to the familiar level of conventional doubt, for which visual proof is enough. Seeing, once again, has become believing: Jesus' words to Thomas, "Have you believed because you have seen me?" (20:29), echo the Evangelist's words earlier in the chapter about John, "he saw and believed" (20:8). Jesus seems, magnanimously, to have chosen to pretend that Thomas had never asked for the hyperbolic, tactile demonstration after all, and hence allows their interchange to return instead to the less sacrilegious and less disgusting medium of sight.

Yet even if seeing has once again become believing, it turns out that in the end sight does not provide the highest form of belief. Now Jesus asserts that this highest form belongs to those who can believe without seeing: once again, as earlier in this same Gospel (4:48, 6:30), the traditional requirement of needing to see in order to be able to believe is attributed to those of little faith, and a nobler status is reserved for those people who are capable of achieving faith without having been eye-witnesses themselves.

Jesus' disdain for those who can only believe if they see has good precedents in the Hebrew Bible, which in general privileges that faith which is based upon hearing God's word alone over any require- ment that belief be grounded upon the sight of miracles. In Exodus, for example, God only supplies Moses and Aaron with wonders after Moses has warned him that the Jews will refuse to believe that Moses has seen him until they see him perform miracles—whereupon they believe (4:1ff., 30–31). So too in the New Testament, where Mark shows the chief priests and the scribes mocking Jesus on the cross by inviting him to "come down now from the cross, that we may see and believe" (Mark 15:32); where it is above all the Pharisees and others like them who, mockingly or in earnest, demand a visual sign from Jesus (Mark 8:11–12; Luke 11:16, 29–32; Matt. 12:38–42, 16:1–4); and where the author of the Letter to the Hebrews defines true faith as "the assurance of things hoped for, the conviction of things not seen" (Heb. 11:1). And earlier in this same Gospel of John, Jesus him- self has already criticized those who cannot believe unless they have seen signs (4:48)—indeed, Thomas's demand "Unless I see . . . I will not believe" (ἐὰν μὴ ἴδω . . . οὐ μὴ πιστεύσω, 20:25) is a precise verbal echo of Jesus' reproof, "Unless you see . . . you will not believe" (ἐὰν μὴ . . . ἴδητε, οὐ μὴ πιστεύσητε, 4:48)—and the tendency of some people to ask to see signs so that they can believe has been implicitly criticized (2:18, 6:30).

But here the rejection of sight as a necessary criterion for belief takes on added weight, since the whole movement of the narrative of this chapter has been directed toward substituting Jesus' body, which can be touched and seen, with a verbal message, which can only be heard. Mary had gone to the tomb to seek Jesus' body; but what she found instead was a spoken message which she heard when it was delivered to her by the angels (20:13). It was only when her anguish had proved inconsolable that that verbal message was replaced by Jesus' body—not the dead one she had sought, but instead a very different one, his risen body (20:14ff.). Now, too, Thomas has sought to touch Jesus; but even though he has backed down from this demand and asserted belief on the basis of sight alone, Jesus dismisses such belief as second-rate in comparison with the faith of those people who only hear a verbal message but can nonetheless succeed in believing on that basis alone. The substitution of the risen body for the verbal message is thereby rescinded: we return to the level of verbal messages alone, and it is on the sole basis of these verbal messages that those people whom Jesus praises for believing will be able to do so.

Yet this tendency to privilege hearing over sight, or to criticize a faith that would insist upon being founded upon sight, is only one of the two fundamental strands both in John's Gospel and in the synoptic Gospels. At the same time these texts are no less committed to recounting the miracles that Jesus performed and numerous people witnessed, as a guarantee of Jesus' divinity and as a compelling reason to believe in him. Like the other three Gospels, the Gospel of John is filled with accounts of signs and wonders and with attestations of belief founded upon them (John 1:50–51; 2:11, 22, 23; 3:2; 4:29, 39, 53; 5:36; 6:2, 14, 26, 29; 7:3–5, 31; 9:3–4; 10:25, 38; 11:45; 12:11, 18; 13:19; 14:29). If, within the confines of the Gospels, such wonders lead to the assertion of belief on the part of those who view them, then why else should the Evangelists have recounted them in their narratives than to procure belief on the part of those who read about them? It would be rather self-defeating for an Evangelist to tell of faith consequent upon witnessing wonders, with the sole purpose of teaching his readers to disdain just such a faith and to prefer only one that did not need to be based upon sight. Indeed, is it possible even to imagine a Gospel that would be entirely free of such a purpose and of such episodes designed to help attain it? It is a central part of the rhetorical structure of these Gospels to play off both strands of this paradox against each other: on the one hand to privilege above all the faith of those who saw Jesus' wonders and believed (for otherwise it would have been far more difficult to found the new religion in the first place); and on the other to privilege above all the faith of those who believed in Jesus without ever having seen him (for otherwise it would have been impossible for the new religion to survive beyond its origin). So it will not surprise us to find that the Gospel of John seems to have been intended to conclude climactically with the following passage, whose authenticity has never been questioned: "Now Jesus did many other signs in the presence of the disciples, which are not written in this book; but these are written that you may believe that Jesus is the Christ, the Son of God, and that believing you may have life in his name" (20:30–31).

It is important to keep this distinction between faith based on sight and faith even without sight, which certainly plays a crucial role in John's story of Doubting Thomas, separate from another distinction which might be thought relevant to that story but most probably is not: namely, between belief *that* x, that is, belief that some proposition is true on the basis of adequate evidence and compelling arguments (let us call this "epistemic belief"), and belief *in* x, that is, belief in someone or something independent of any evidence whatsoever and sometimes against all evidence (let us call this "nonepistemic belief"). There can be little doubt that, by and large, the synoptic Gospels attempt to found a nonepistemic belief in Jesus upon the epistemic belief that, given the evidence they abundantly supply, it is reasonable to conclude that he possessed certain capabilities and performed certain actions and hence must have been divine.

But what of the Gospel of John? Might John's central message in his story of Doubting Thomas, who first establishes criteria for according an epistemic belief but then adopts what seems to be a nonepistemic belief without having satisfied those criteria, be the demonstration of the failure of just this synoptic project? Might John's intention be to demonstrate that the only true religious belief is nonepistemic, that any belief that demands evidence in its support is second-rate and ultimately irreligious?

This interpretation is tempting, but ultimately implausible. For the Greek terms for "to believe" ($\pi\iota\sigma\tau\epsilon\acute{\upsilon}\epsilon\iota\nu$) and "belief, faith" ($\pi\acute{\iota}\sigma\tau\iota\varsigma$) can apply to both categories of belief in the New Testament, while the systematic distinction between the two of the sort described here belongs to a much later period in the development of religious thought (especially to that of the Reformation, to Luther and Calvin, and then, later, to Pascal). Most important, against the notion that John's narrative is intended to recount Thomas's transformation from epistemic to nonepistemic belief it must be objected that this story does not in fact show Thomas coming to believe in Jesus without any evidence whatsoever, let alone against all evidence; instead it shows him abandoning the criterion of touching Jesus' wounds and accepting that of seeing his living body and above all hearing his words as the basis for his belief. Thomas's faith in Jesus would only be genuinely nonepistemic if he managed to believe in him without Jesus' returning at all or if Jesus said to him not, "Have you believed because you have seen me?" but rather words to the effect of "Have you believed even though you have not seen me?" But this would be a very different story from the one told by John; and in such a story as that one, which John has chosen not to tell, Jesus could not go on to say, "Blessed are those who have not seen and yet believe."

❧

When John's Jesus praises the people who are capable of believing without seeing, just whom does he have in mind? Surely it is we ourselves he is thinking of, the readers of his Gospel through the rest of human history, who will not have had the opportunity to see Jesus himself, as Thomas and the other characters in his text were able to do, and who will have to rely upon John's own Gospel and other oral and written texts—that is, upon hearsay—if we are to find out about Jesus' message of salvation, which we must believe if we are to be saved (compare also 17:20). *We* shall have to believe without seeing, but only on the basis of what we have heard or read (the Greek verb ἀκούω means both "to hear" and "to read"). Nothing is harder; nothing, given the nature of this particular message, is more important.

That is why John builds into his text the figure of Thomas, who doubts so that he may come to believe and who believes so that he may make us believe too. Thomas is like us, because he doubts but is then convinced; but he is unlike us, because he was able to see Jesus whereas we can only hear about him. Hence Thomas is greater than we are, for he was one of Jesus' disciples, was particularly attached to him, and was important enough for Jesus to return only in order to convince him; but we are potentially greater than Thomas, for he was only capable of believing what he saw, whereas we shall be able to believe even without seeing. In other words, Mary Magdalene is a foil for Thomas, setting up the theme of touching against which Thomas's demand for certainty will be measured; and Thomas is a foil for us, for his own change from disbelief to belief anticipates— and is potentially inferior to—our own.

Achieving this effect was so important that John has gone to considerable trouble, at the very end of his narrative, to introduce his Thomas and to devise a crucial function for him—a Thomas who can doubt and then come to believe so that we, in reading about him, can believe too. In this regard the Gospel of John is completely different from the other three canonical Gospels. In the synoptic Gospels, Thomas is merely one of the twelve disciples and appears in each Gospel only a single time, as one name among others in the various lists of the disciples (Mark 3:18, Luke 6:15, Matt. 10:3; so too Acts 1:13); he is not distinguished in any way from the other disciples. Only John lifts him out of the anonymity of the crowd by attributing to him a specific and unique identity.

John achieves this effect not only by entrusting to Thomas the mission of becoming convinced and convincing us at the end of his narrative, but also by carefully inserting episodes at two earlier points in which Thomas utters statements that express to a smaller degree his doubt or misunderstanding of Jesus' message and that thereby prepare us to accept him fully in this same role when we encounter him once again at the end of the Gospel. Neither of these other two utterances of Thomas's is transmitted by any other Gospel; whether John invented these details himself or heard about them from some source, he has narrated them in such a way that they supply a perfect preparation for the ending at which he was evidently aiming from the very beginning.

In the first episode, part of John's version of the story of Lazarus, Jesus announces that, in spite of the dangers he will incur from the Jews, he will travel to Bethany because Lazarus has died, whereupon Thomas says to the other disciples, "Let us also go, that we may die with him" (11:16). Thomas's wish to die together with Jesus expresses not only the depth of his love and dedication for Jesus but also his total misunderstanding of Jesus' message—especially as what is involved in this scene is Lazarus' resurrection, a harbinger of Jesus' own resurrection. If Thomas does not understand here that Jesus is going to Bethany, not in order to die, and not in order to visit a dead man, but in order to bring that dead man back to life, then we shall not be surprised later when Thomas doubts that Jesus himself has died and then is risen once again.

In the second episode, at the Last Supper, Thomas reacts to Jesus' words, "And you know the way where I am going" (14:4), by asking, "Lord, we do not know where you are going; how can we know the way?" (14:5); Jesus must then explain to him, "I am the way, and the truth, and the life; no one comes to the Father, but by me" (14:6). Once again, Thomas's complete perplexity is evident: he is deeply loyal to Jesus, he wants desperately to believe Jesus' message, but quite simply he just does not manage to understand it—until the very end. It is surely not accidental that both of these earlier passages refer by anticipation to the third and final one, 11:16 by mentioning Jesus' death and 14:5 by prompting Jesus' answer about coming to the Father (compare 20:17).

We may say of Thomas that he is Jesus' Crito, the disciple who loves his master with absolute dedication but does not really have the foggiest idea of what his message is all about. In Plato's *Phaedo*, Crito asks Socrates how they should bury him once he has died (115C)—and thereby shows, as Socrates gently and humorously points out (115C–D), that he has understood nothing of all that Socrates has been demonstrating at great length (and moreover during his whole life) about the eternity of the immortal soul and the unimportance of the mortal body. Crito tries to persuade Socrates to delay taking the poison as long as possible (117B–C), as though death were an evil; once Socrates does drink the poison, Crito leaves the company because he cannot contain the grief that, according to Socrates, is entirely inappropriate as a reaction to his death (117D); it is to Crito that Socrates addresses his very last words (118A); and it is Crito who closes his dead teacher's mouth and eyes (118A). Both Thomas and Crito are fascinated by their teacher's material body and cannot quite grasp that the real person, whom they love so much, will in fact not die together with that body, but will go on to live forever: both figures give us a model of love that we cannot surpass, but a model of understanding that we must, and easily can, outdo. That is why in both cases their teacher speaks what seem to be his final words to them, so that they can close off the boundary of the text on whose other side stand we, the text's readers, its living addressees.

It is unlikely, but perhaps not impossible, that John might have been inspired to invent his Thomas by acquaintance with the figure of Crito in Plato's *Phaedo*. On the one hand, if John had acquired any familiarity at all with Greek literature, then, however modest his education, he could scarcely have failed to come into some degree of contact with Plato's dialogues, above all with the *Phaedo*—papyri of the Platonic texts far outnumber those of any other pagan philosopher, or indeed of any other pagan prose author except Demosthenes. But on the other hand, two writers as astute as Plato and John could easily have both invented the device of the devoted but dimwitted disciple quite independently of each other, for they were certainly both perspicacious enough to be able to recognize its extraordinarily effective rhetorical impact. In any case, whether John was consciously imitating Plato or whether the affinities are merely structural and coincidental, the similarity between Thomas and Crito may later have helped to construct a bridge of communication between John's text and some pagan Greek readers, one over which not only understanding could pass, but also belief.

Thus Thomas was designed by John not to doubt, but instead to believe, and not just to believe, but to make us believe too. He seems to have been materialized by John as an anticipation of the risen Jesus' offering himself to his disciples' touch (as in Luke 24:39): projecting backward from this climactic moment of the tradition, John may well have invented Thomas as the perfectly suitable discile to whom such an offer could be made, and be neither frustrated nor fulfilled, for Thomas's edification and our own.

And yet a problem remains: for if Thomas was designed merely to program and valorize our own belief, which is a belief without seeing, would it not have been enough for John to have Thomas declare that he would only believe when he saw? After all, this is the language that John has Jesus use when he contrasts Thomas's behavior with that of the blessed; in the end Thomas's hyperbole turns out to be quite dispensable, at least in logical terms, for he finally adopts belief without satisfying the criteria he had enunciated as being indispensable for it. Thomas's hyperbolic doubt is not really necessary for John's own rhetorical purpose: it exceeds the role his author has allotted to him and creates a space of sacrilegious surplus, a theological and psychological lacuna as unsettling as the notion of inserting our own finger or hand into a dead man's unhealed wounds. There is an opaque residue in Thomas's excessiveness, a remainder not reducible to the actual requirements of the text, one which will go on to fascinate the whole of the Western tradition—and, do what it can to suppress or minimize that excess, that tradition will often end up doing nothing else than repeating and amplifying it.

❧

After Jesus' words to Thomas, John writes, "Now Jesus did many other signs in the presence of the disciples, which are not written in this book; but these are written that you may believe that Jesus is the Christ, the Son of God, and that believing you may have life in his name" (20:30–31). This is certainly the point at which we must expect John to finally end his Gospel, after the false conclusion at 20:23. The emphasis upon the importance of our believing draws the obvious moral from the story of Thomas (20:19–29), makes explicit the contrast we are meant to understand in Jesus' reference to the blessed (20:29), and by asserting the necessity of belief for salvation brings this Gospel to a climax that is very similar to what we find near the end of the spurious continuation of the Gospel of Mark (Mark 16:16).

Once again, if John's Gospel had ended here, no reader would ever have suspected that anything was missing. And yet the text goes on, to tell of Jesus' further miraculous appearances at the sea of Tiberias (21:1–14), to announce the primacy of Simon Peter (21:15–17), to foretell the future of Simon Peter and John (21:18–23), and to conclude with a signature (21:24) and an assertion of the infinity of Jesus' miracles as contrasted with the finitude of this text (21:25).

New Testament scholars are largely (though not unanimously) in agreement that these final sections were not composed at the same time that John wrote the rest of the Gospel but were added later, perhaps 21:1–23 by John himself, most likely 21:24–25 by some later editor. If so, then the closure that John seems once to have thought he had definitively established by means of the figure of Thomas evidently turned out not to be sufficient, at least for some of his readers, perhaps even for himself as well.

John had assigned Thomas the function of closing off his text and guaranteeing, once and for all, our belief in a story whose credibility causes various kinds of difficulties for the synoptic Evangelists. John uses Thomas, who creates doubt, only so that this doubt may be given a name and finally abolished: once Thomas has been convinced, the text has completed its mission and should now be capable of being brought to a definitive, absolute close.

Yet the questions raised by John's story of Doubting Thomas can seemingly not be answered so easily; instead of stopping once and for all they go on, incessantly raising new problems of their own. It is as though the hole that Thomas's hyperbolic doubt has opened up within the tissue of belief could not be closed again—as though every attempt to close it one last time only made it open anew—as though that hole had become not merely a textual lacuna but a painful and incurable wound.

❧

Touching a God

Not only does John not assert that Thomas touched Jesus' body: he has gone to considerable trouble to make it quite clear that Thomas did not do so. The textual evidence of John's authorial intention seems indisputable. Yet this unambiguous result of a straightforward narrative analysis of a brief and well-known text stands in a curious relation to an equally undeniable fact, namely that most people who claim to know anything at all about Doubting Thomas are convinced that he did in fact touch Jesus' wounds.

The tension between these two pieces of evidence can only mean that John did not manage to make such a misunderstanding completely impossible. Of course, as we shall see in Part II, this misunderstanding of John's narrative has been influenced by a number of external factors—not only by the weight of canonical misinterpretation and authoritative error but above all by the pictorial tradition that has interpreted this story for many generations of recipients who apparently found the written text more remote or more obscure than visual evidence. But nonetheless the error must in some way also be immanent within John's Gospel, for otherwise it could not have persisted to the degree it has at the same time that the text has been read, studied, and retold so often.

If we are driven to conclude that John himself has opened the door to this misunderstanding by the way in which he narrated his story, then at least two important questions are raised: what are the narrative mechanisms within John's text that lead readers to misunderstand this story in this particular way; and why did John choose to narrate the story in the way that he did.

What misleads so many readers are two interconnected facts. On the one hand John accords a peculiar emphasis to Thomas's desire to touch Jesus, but on the other hand he does not mention explicitly any actual act that would have fulfilled that wish. John has been careful to deploy a whole series of strategies for making Thomas's first outburst memorable: the surprise of Thomas's retrospectively declared absence from Jesus' first appearance; the split between all the other disciples, who have seen Jesus, and Thomas, who has not; the unexpectedness of Thomas's outcry; its climactic structure; its violation both of an explicit taboo announced to Mary Magdalene and of our own feelings of disgust and revulsion. But on the other hand, just at the very point in the narrative where we would expect the fulfillment or nonfulfillment of this scandalous desire to be emphatically reported, there is a gap: we are told about Jesus' verbal invitation, Thomas's verbal response, and Jesus' verbal reaction, but we are not told anything at all about any physical action on Thomas's part. The inevitable result is that readers who have been forcefully struck by Thomas's desire to touch Jesus do not notice as clearly the far less obvious fact that John does not go on to narrate what became of this desire in the world of action—it takes more effort to notice an absence than a presence, and not all readers will see spontaneously why they should make this effort. Hence most readers seem to assume unconsciously that Thomas's desire must have been fulfilled in action in the end.

Why, then, did John not simply tell his readers that Thomas did not touch Jesus after all? We can imagine a number of possible answers to this question. For one thing, to dwell at too great a length upon the fact that Thomas did not touch Jesus might well have seemed anticlimactic—after Thomas's passionate exclamation, a return to moderation and a failure to act could hardly have been narrated without seeming a bit of a letdown. But John could surely have added just a couple of words to the effect that "Thomas forbore to touch him and answered him, 'My Lord and my God!'"—yet even this he has refused to do. Why?

One answer might be that John's story is structured most authentically around the opposition between seeing and hearing, from the opening, in which the two disciples come to see for themselves about what Mary Magdalene has told them (20:2–3), to the conclusion, in which Jesus contrasts those who believe on the basis of sight to those who believe without seeing (20:29). In this light, touch may be interpreted as a drastic form of sight that exaggerates the relative proximity of perceiving subject and perceived object that are necessary for vision and stands in even starker contrast to hearing than seeing does: touch would be invoked momentarily by Thomas in his exasperation at not believing what he has heard from his fellow disciples, and Thomas's shift would be taken over by Jesus as a momentary offer to him that is soon superseded by a return to the fundamental contrast between seeing and hearing. John may have felt that insisting too much on the question of whether Thomas really touched Jesus might have focused readers' attention upon the wrong issue and rendered more awkward the transition he wished to make back to the contrast between eyes and ears.

But John may also have intended to indicate by his silence that the question of touching or not touching Jesus is not really the decisive point, that what matters is not whether his body can be touched but that his body, touchable or not, has risen again from the dead. John has chosen to place all his emphasis on the miracles of resurrection and of divine recognitions—not on the criteria of belief in the conditions of the material world, upon which Thomas had so passionately insisted. To tell us explicitly whether Thomas had touched Jesus after all would suggest that this mattered in some way—and to do so would reduce the level of awareness of the text to that embodied by Thomas at the beginning of this scene. The only way the text can rise to the far higher level embodied by Thomas at its end is to indicate that his demand for tactile criteria must be decisively transcended, and this the text accomplishes in two ways. First, transcendence is achieved within the *content* of the narrative, by John's entrusting to Jesus the (perhaps slightly disdainful) gesture of aristocratic magnanimity with which he offers to Thomas the very object, his martyred body, that this latter had so rudely demanded. Part of the point of this story is the reestablishment of the proper relation between master and disciple, and this is confirmed by the beginning of Thomas's second, pious outburst, "My Lord!" Second, within the *mode* of its narration, the text transcends Thomas's demand for physical confirmation by John's refusal to grant Thomas the satisfaction even of mentioning whether that demand was fulfilled or not. In the end, the outcome of Thomas's demand to touch Jesus is passed over in silence—in the end, John seems to be suggesting, that is all it deserves.

But if this reconstruction is right, then John seems to have been guilty of a slight but significant miscalculation. For he has made Thomas's expression of his desire to touch Jesus just a bit too striking, too disturbing, too unforgettable. No doubt that is why—despite the unmistakable structure of the narrative which moves swiftly from disbelief to belief, despite Jesus' request that Thomas be not disbelieving but believing, and despite Thomas's culminating outcry which is an expression of unqualified belief—it is not as "Believing Thomas" that Thomas has come to be remembered in all languages, but as "Doubting Thomas," "der ungläubige Thomas," "Thomas l'incrédule," "Tommaso l'incredulo." The idea of touching Jesus' wounded body seems to exert far too strong a fascination upon most readers when they encounter it for them to be able later simply to forget it, or dismiss it, or explain it away—especially since what is involved is touching it not with a loving caress, like Mary Magdalene, but with a skeptical thrust (though translators often say that Thomas wants to "place" his hand in Jesus' side, in fact the Greek verb used by John is much stronger and means basically to "throw" or "hurl").

John's narrative, like so many other ones in both Testaments, is filled with lacunae; but few are as compelling as this one. Here a gap opens up within the texture of his story, one delimited by a simple, unanswered question—just what transpired between Jesus and Thomas beyond the words spoken by the two that John reports?—and filled by an unforgettable yet intolerable image, that of Thomas's finger and hand entering into the wounds in Jesus' hands and side. Out of that gap will issue the many traditions of the story of Doubting Thomas.

II

RESPONSES
AND
DEVELOPMENTS

❦

Sources and Reflections

Whether or not the skeptical dimensions uncovered in these New Testament texts in Part I really correspond to their authors' likely intentions, we must bear in mind that authorial intentions never wholly succeed in delimiting the traditions of reaction and elaboration to which they give rise. Just as so many of our most ordinary actions give rise to consequences, and to consequences of those consequences, that go beyond, and against, our original motivation, so too the literary and artistic reception of texts is never bound by the original intentions of their authors yet is always in some way a response to them. A receptive tradition is unified solely by the structure, both manifest and latent, of its foundational texts, not by their author's intention (which of course lies at their origin but is usually unrecoverable except for the evidence deposited in them). The implications and tensions we have seen underlying the surface of John's story about Thomas recur throughout the later traditions of its reception; it is to these that we turn in this second part.

But first we must address a question raised by the investigation of these receptive traditions: what precisely is the founding text that lies at their beginning? For us, the account of Doubting Thomas in the Gospel of John is the earliest surviving version of the story: but can we be reasonably sure that John invented the story in the form in which he proposes it, or might it go back to earlier accounts that are no longer extant? The fact that Thomas is so perfectly adapted to John's authorial and doctrinal needs does not prove that John invented him from whole cloth, for an author as skilled as John can surely have taken over from earlier traditions an already existing figure and modified him to suit his own purposes—at least so long as those traditions were not so strong, so determinate, or so different as to place excessive constraints upon his authorial freedom.

In the end, we may not be able to decide this issue definitively, but the evidence, tenuous as it is, does point toward John's decisive role in creating the figure of Doubting Thomas as we know it. For John is not only the sole canonical Evangelist to tell us anything more about Thomas than that he was one of the disciples: he is also the only one who explains that Thomas's name has a meaning and tells us what it is. This he does by providing the Aramaic name, derived from the word *t'ōme*, meaning "twin," with a translation into its Greek equivalent, $\Delta i\delta\nu\mu\sigma s$ ("Didymos," or Twin), and thereby indicating that it corresponds in its meaning. Moreover, he does this not just once but twice, one time on Thomas's first appearance in the Gospel, at the death of Lazarus ("Thomas, called the Twin," 11:16), and a second time at the beginning of the key episode involving his doubt and subsequent belief ("Now Thomas, one of the twelve, called the Twin," 20:24).

Why does John take the trouble to provide this explanation, and not just once but twice? Is it simply an antiquarian's pedantic exactitude, or officious solicitude to help readers from other cultures? To dismiss John's repeated authorial gesture like this would mean to disregard the fact that whenever he cites an Aramaic term and provides a Greek translation for it, he does so not in order to supply useful but dispensable information but so as to lend greater significance to a particular moment of the narrative. That is, such translations are not only semantic but also emphatic in purpose: John uses them to indicate that the events involved are so important that even the names connected with them must be significant. Apart from these two explanations of Thomas's name (a third, parasitic one occurs in the spurious appendix, 21:2), John provides such translations only three times: twice for crucial places, where Pontius Pilate judged Jesus ("Pilate . . . sat down on the judgment seat at a place called The Pavement, and in Hebrew, Gabbatha," 19:13) and where Jesus was led out to be crucified ("he went out . . . to the place called the place of a skull, which is called in Hebrew Golgotha," 19:17); and once, as we saw earlier, at the climax of the exchange between Mary Magdalene and Jesus in the garden ("She turned and said to him in Hebrew, 'Rabboni!' [which means Teacher]," 20:16). It seems plausible to suppose that John's explanation of the significance of Thomas's name is similarly intended to lend emphasis to some important aspect of Thomas's character as it functions within the narrative. But if so, which one?

There are at least two regards in which Thomas's name is perfectly apt for him. The first is that, as a twin, Thomas is burdened by the negative associations that many cultures, not least those of ancient Palestine, have traditionally linked with the phenomenon of a twin birth. For such relatively infrequent occurrences raise perplexing questions of personal identity, since they bring to birth two beings who obviously differ from each other yet often can barely be distinguished; in many societies twins are thought to be produced either by the mother's adultery or by divine intervention (or both). That twins could be regarded with suspicion in Palestine in biblical times is made clear in the Hebrew Bible, which mentions twins only twice: once in the miraculous birth to Isaac and the sterile Rebecca of the twins Esau and Jacob, who contend bitterly with one another for primacy (Gen. 25:22ff.); and once in the birth of the twins Fares and Zerah (rivals in precedence at their birth) to Tamar after she has had incestuous intercourse with her father-in-law Judah (Gen. 38:27ff.). As it happens, there are good obstetric reasons for twins to be viewed negatively: in traditional cultures, and in modern ones until very recent times, the mortality and morbidity rates for both the mother and the children have always been much higher in twin births than in single ones.

We may speculate that the name Thomas ("Twin") was probably given most often to the second-born of a pair of twins, after the first-born son had received the sole name that his parents had chosen for what they had had every reason to believe would be their single offspring. If so, we may then further attach to John's Thomas all of the negative associations that are particularly reserved for the second-born of a pair of twins: being sinister, as opposed to auspicious, and being only secondary, rather than the real son. In many cultures, the second-born infant of a pair of twins is often thought to be weaker than the first-born (and in fact this is often the case); this weakness is sometimes explained by the supposition that he has a merely mortal father while his only slightly older sibling has an immortal one. Indeed, in some cultures the second-born twin may be exposed at birth; and even without such assistance, the incidence of mortality of the second-born twin in traditional cultures is considerably higher than that of the first-born one even today, and was surely so in the Palestine of New Testament times.

In all these respects, Thomas the Twin is predestined by his name to fulfill the role John assigns him. But there is also another regard in which Thomas's name suits him. For in the narrative John has devised, Thomas plays above all the role of a doubter, and in many languages (though not in all) the words for "doubt" and for "two" are etymologically related: in Greek διστάζειν ("distazein," to doubt: the word occurs in the New Testament at Matt. 28:17) and δίς, in Latin *dubitare* and *duo*, in German *zweifeln* and *zwei*, in English *doubt* and *double*, and in many other languages (though not, apparently, in Hebrew or Aramaic). This widespread usage suggests that doubt is being conceived above all as the response to a situation in which there are two alternatives, of which it is not certain which is the right one. As the twin, the second son who cannot easily be distinguished from the first one, Thomas is the perfect embodiment of doubt in general and of doubt about identity in particular. If we cannot ever be entirely sure exactly who he is (is he Thomas or rather his twin brother?), then we can understand all the more easily that he himself is uncertain about who Jesus is. Or, to put it differently, Thomas, in doubting Jesus, is simply living up to his name. As "Thomas," he had no choice but to doubt; in overcoming his doubt in the end, he ceased to be true to himself. Perhaps that is one reason why he is known as "Doubting Thomas."

Sometimes a *nomen*, or name, is an omen. Transparently semantic names in literary texts almost always convey a specific message, all the more so when their significance is explicitly pointed out by the author. Why should John have chosen to explain Thomas's name, and not once but twice, if not to emphasize the relevance of that name to Thomas's function in his narrative? And why should he have bothered to indicate that relevance, unless John's choice of Thomas for this function was either entirely his own invention, or was his profound reinterpretation of previous traditions? In either case, John's emphasis upon Thomas's name seems designed to provide a justification for the originality of his narrative strategy. For if John were merely taking over from earlier sources Thomas's role as the most prominent doubter of Jesus, why would he have needed to explain the significance of Thomas's name? My hypothesis is that John found the name of Thomas in such disciple lists as those contained in the synoptic Gospels, and that he recognized on the basis of its etymological meaning that it was Thomas alone who could be the ideal embodiment for all the issues of doubt and belief with which he had decided to conclude his Gospel.

If so, then Thomas's secondariness was an invention of John's originality, and it is John's version that we may take as the founding text for the Western traditions of Doubting Thomas. For either there were in fact no earlier versions, or else John diverged so radically from any there were that these can safely be ignored. Of course this does not mean that every detail of later versions of Thomas's story derives uniquely from John's narrative—a founding text is never the sole source for the interpretative traditions deriving from it, but only provides guiding signals, hints for development, and occasions for creative error. But it does mean that a certain set of basic motifs that recur throughout most of those later versions does indeed derive ultimately, directly or indirectly, from John's Gospel, and that the fundamental configuration of the character and behavior of Thomas as John imagined him has determined why certain thematic materials could later be attached to him while others were not. It is most likely in the Gospel of John that Thomas, not only as the Believer but already as the Doubter, was born.

Narrative Developments:
The Apocrypha and Beyond

When a text is a narrative, the text that interprets it is most likely to be a narrative too. Textual genres tend to generate interpretations congruent to themselves. Thus commentaries on precepts and rules are most often themselves admonitory and regulatory in character, as in the Mishnah and other ancient and modern commentaries on legal codes; exegeses of philosophical texts usually themselves adopt the form of argument, proof, and refutation, starting with Aristotle's explications of his predecessors and continuing into the disciplinary journals of our own day. So too, the likeliest form for interpretive texts aimed at elucidating narratives is itself narrative. For most readers of narratives have always been far more interested in the worlds the narratives depict, in the qualities, actions, and sufferings of the characters they contain, than in other features such as the specific textual mechanisms by which they portray those worlds. The attention and imagination of most readers (and listeners) are directed through the verbal medium toward the actions and characters the words represent: no wonder that this medium, real though it is, can tend to fade out of the recipient's consciousness and vanish in favor of the narrated events. We no longer see the letters d-o-g or hear the sound "dog" but envision a barking dog. Non-narrative interpretations of narratives are of course not at all impossible (professors of literature have been earning their living producing them at least since Hellenistic times); but, historically, they are the less probable case, and the less frequent one.

The exfoliation of secondary narratives from a primary one often obscures the fine line separating a "mere" interpretation aimed at extracting the significance of some earlier narrative by narrative means, and a "new" narrative aimed at telling the same story in a more plausible way. The second author—narrator and interpreter alike—discovers holes in the earlier text that he seeks to fill out by supplying additional information designed to clarify the chain of events. Or he will want to provide a different version of the same events, altering the point of view from which they are told or the psychological motivation that occasioned them or the moral judgments that are asserted or implied regarding them by the characters or the narrator. This is the fundamental mechanism by which narrative traditions have always flourished. It was in this way that Homer interpreted the versions of oral epic that he heard, penetrated through them to the general structure of the heroic traditions they embodied, and created a new version of the old stories that was both an interpretation of those traditions and a critique of his predecessors and competitors. Likewise, once a standard version of the heroic events had become relatively defined and the fluid oral tradition had begun to congeal, its stories could be entrusted to poets and painters to be interpreted and narrated anew by their own means. In Rome, the *res gestae* (heroic deeds) of the great patriotic ancestors were preserved in family chronicles precisely by being constantly retold and varied, until these became relatively professionalized, first in Republican historiography and finally in Livy's great Augustan synthesis. And in the Jewish tradition, the elliptical, ambiguous, and controversial narratives of the Torah were interpreted by further narratives, especially by the Haggadic Midrash, which sought to explain their meaning by recounting them yet again.

That even fictional narratives tend to generate narrative interpretations is suggested anecdotally by ordinary viewers' and readers' reactions to contemporary films and novels, for insofar as these go beyond just expressing likes and dislikes, they often do little more than narrate anew, with additions, subtractions, and other changes, the characters and actions represented. We may well suppose this tendency to be all the stronger for those narratives that claim any degree of historical accuracy: for the greater importance of the characters and actions over the construction of the text will certainly be increased when these characters and actions acquire all the pathos of reality, and seem no longer to be figments of their narrator's fancy but instead fragments of the very same reality we ourselves inhabit. What then of a narrative that claims to tell us not about just any historical incidents, but about those that, properly understood, are alone capable of rescuing us from eternal damnation and of saving us, at least in the next world and perhaps even in this one? What of the story of Thomas in the Gospel of John?

❧

To investigate the first narrative developments of Thomas's story means in essence to explore the New Testament Apocrypha. For, with the exceptions of the (no doubt spurious) chapter 21 of the Gospel of John—in which Jesus appears one last time, by the Sea of Tiberias, to Simon Peter, Thomas called the Twin (Didymos), Nathanael, the sons of Zebedee, and two other unnamed disciples (21:2) and a single mention in a list of Jesus' disciples at Acts 1:13— the Thomas whom John bequeathed to Western culture never recurs even once in the rest of the canonical writings of the Christian Testament. But he goes on to become one of the most prominent figures in the apocryphal texts associated with the New Testament, and the combination of these texts with John's narrative eventually makes him a familiar figure in medieval Christian legend, enshrined, for example, in such enormously popular collections as hagiographer Jacobus de Voragine's *Golden Legend* (*Legenda aurea*).

Before abandoning the relative solidity of the New Testament and wading into the murky swamps of the Apocrypha, however, a word of caution is in order. It would be a serious mistake to suppose that the New Testament and the Christian Apocrypha are two equally balanced bodies of textual material that can simply be compared with one another. For before the second half of the second century A.D. the canon of writings we recognize today as the New Testament was far from being defined as such; and the large group of writings nowadays termed "apocryphal" is in fact not a unified category of texts but a highly heterogeneous potpourri with little in common besides an affirmative attitude to some version of Christianity, a generic structure as narrative or revelatory text rather than as pure textual exegesis, and the fate of having been excluded, for one reason or another, from the New Testament as it eventually came to be defined. The consolidation and delimitation of the New Testament was a gradual and difficult process, one in which geographical and sociological factors are likely to have played at least as decisive a role as purely theological ones, and which was in part clarified and accelerated precisely by the exclusion of what came to be termed heresies. Thus the concept of Apocrypha certainly presupposes that of canonical writings (which the Apocrypha, most simply put, are not), but without what later came to be termed the Apocrypha there would not have been a canon of the New Testament as such in the first place. Many aspects of this complex dialectical process are still uncertain. These difficulties, however, need not worry us unduly here, since I am not making general claims about the development of the New Testament but focusing only on a small number of apocryphal texts.

Having circumvented one part of the quagmire of the New Testament Apocrypha, we must now venture into another, even more slippery part, namely their relation to the phenomenon designated by many modern scholars as Gnosticism. For if it is true that outside of the Gospel of John, Doubting Thomas is present as such only in the Apocrypha, it is also true that the texts involving Doubting Thomas are not evenly distributed throughout the Apocrypha: he plays very different roles within what scholars have characterized as the Gnostic apocryphal writings, on the one hand, and in non-Gnostic or anti-Gnostic ones, on the other.

There is perhaps no other region of the apocryphal swamp in which the footing is as uncertain as it is with regard to the bundle of religious and spiritual movements called Gnosticism. Just who (if anyone) the Gnostics were, what they believed in, to what extent they would have been prepared to use the term "Gnostic" in describing themselves, whether there was Gnosticism before there was Christianity and if so to what extent this Gnosticism influenced Christianity itself in its early phases, what the relations were in the first centuries of Christianity among the large variety of postulated Gnostic sects and between them and the various forms of contemporary Christianity, and what Christianity would have become if it had never chosen or felt itself obliged to define itself in contradistinction to something which it termed Gnosticism—these and many other questions continue to be hotly debated by scholars ever since (indeed all the more so since) the discovery of what seems to be a genuine Gnostic library at Nag Hammadi in Upper Egypt in 1945–46. This finding made it possible, for the first time since late antiquity, to judge the Gnostics on the basis of their own writings and not only on that of scattered fragments, all out of context and some forged, and hostile witnesses polemicizing against alleged heresies. Indeed, so vast are the uncertainties attached to the concept of Gnosticism that in recent years a few scholars have even proposed provocatively that we would do better to abandon the term altogether.

It is certainly beyond my ambitions here to attempt anything even approaching a definitive analysis of Gnosticism—but it is also not at all necessary. For present purposes, it is enough to indicate the minimal set of features of which the co-presence would probably suffice to characterize a text as Gnostic in the eyes of most scholars in the field: whether some other text that only manifested one or two of them could also properly be termed Gnostic is a question that need not concern us. For it will turn out that these minimal features are enough to demarcate a set of texts that scholars have almost universally claimed for Gnosticism, and in which Thomas's role is decisively different from the one he plays in all the others. My central thesis in this chapter is that the overlap between these texts and Thomas's role is not accidental, but that there is a coherent logic to Thomas's development into a central figure for the Gnostics. For the sake of the argument presented here we do not have to reify or absolutize Gnosticism, or indeed think of it as anything more substantial than as a general tendency of thought both alongside of and within a number of varieties of Christian belief, and not as a specific religion or as an exclusive community. For even a minimally defined Gnosticism is specific enough to capture a highly determinate variant of Doubting Thomas.

The three features whose co-presence will for us define an apocryphal text as being Gnostic are the following systematic preferences.

Knowledge over faith. As its very name suggests, Gnosticism is a doctrine that puts the highest priority upon knowledge, which is often known by its authorities from the beginning. Only the acceptance of a specific set of alleged truths about man and the world can procure salvation, and it is this knowledge that is most important. Belief without understanding is of no avail, for that kind of belief might well turn out to be belief in the wrong things or belief for the wrong reasons: only a faith that is founded upon true and secure knowledge can save us. No Gnostic could have declared with Tertullian, "It is certain because it is impossible" ("*certum est quia impossibile est,*" *De carne Christi* 5.4 = *CChr SL* 2.881).

Elite over masses. In consequence, Gnosticism addresses itself not to the whole of humanity, but only to that small portion of mankind which is intellectually and spiritually fitted to understand its message. The Gnostics see themselves as a saved, and saving, remnant: if they maintain that they are also Christians, they identify themselves as the highest and smallest elite, within the lower and larger elite of the Christian community as a whole, surrounded by the lowest and largest group of the condemned heathens. No Gnostic could have accepted the claim to universality asserted in the very name of the Catholic Church, for which Jesus' mission was to save all mankind (or even, in some versions, all creation).

Spirit over matter and body. For the Gnostics, only the spirit is ontologically real and hence worthy, and capable, of salvation. The material world we happen to inhabit is a dreadful mistake, the creation of a bungling or malevolent junior God; for us to be saved means to be rescued from out of this material world and to be restored to a purely spiritual domain, to that home to which we most properly belong. In the present world, it is our bodies that chain us most painfully to the condition of materiality: hence most Gnostics tend strongly to urge asceticism in such corporeal matters as food, drink, and sexuality, and, if they are Christians, to deny that Jesus was fully embodied in his incarnation or that he was resurrected in the same material body after his death.

To be sure, isolated traces of all three of these tendencies can be found in the canonical New Testament and in many other contemporary texts: evidently, Gnostic modes of thought offered a plausible interpretation of certain elements of Christianity (or should we say that Christianity offered a plausible interpretation of certain elements of Gnosticism?). But my argument is concerned not with the genesis of Gnosticism or of Christianity, with the large-scale interrelations of these two systems of belief, or even with the question of the historical existence of Gnosticism as a substantial and coherent religious movement independent of the polemics of certain early church fathers. Instead, my focus is on the intertextual relations between the Gospel of John and certain other texts written at the earliest at least half a century or so later. Hence the crucial fact is that all three of these fundamental features are prominently shared by all five of the apocryphal Gnostic writings that center on the figure of someone named Thomas (I shall leave open for the moment the question of whether this Thomas is the same Thomas as the Doubting Thomas of the Gospel of John):

1. *The Infancy Gospel of Thomas* (here referred to as *Infancy:* E 68–83; S-W 1.439–52): a list of miraculous acts and wise discourses of the child Jesus, performed between the ages of five and twelve, ascribed in different versions to "Thomas the Israelite philosopher" or to "the holy Apostle Thomas." It is uncertain whether the earliest version was Greek or Syriac, but the text was probably composed toward the end of the second century. A number of early church fathers rejected as Gnostic a "Gospel of Thomas"

that is likely to have been, if not identical with, at least closely related to, either this text or the following one.

2. *The Gospel of Thomas (Gospel:* E 123–47; S-W 1.110–33): a collection of 114 sayings attributed to "the living Jesus" and said to have been written down by "Didymos Judas Thomas," of which about half have close parallels in the canonical Gospels. The full version in Coptic, discovered at Nag Hammadi, differs in many details from several highly fragmentary Greek papyri. The original text probably goes back to the middle of the second century and may come from Edessa in Syria. The theologian and martyr Hippolyus of Rome, who died in 235, certainly refers to *Gospel,* but it is uncertain whether other references by the early church fathers to a "Gospel of Thomas" are to some version of *Gospel* or of *Infancy.*

3. *The Book of Thomas the Contender (Contender:* S-W 1.232–47 under the title *The Book of Thomas;* not in E): a brief collection of sayings and discourses spoken by Jesus to "Judas Thomas," particularly counseling sexual abstinence, mostly in answer to the latter's questions and said to have been written down by Matthew. The text is known only from a Coptic manuscript found at Nag Hammadi, but the original version is likely to have been written in Greek. It is uncertain whether it dates from the second or third century; there appear to be no references to *Contender* in any other extant texts.

4. *The Acts of Thomas* (E 439–511; S-W 2.322–411): a lengthy account, in fourteen "Acts," of the mission to India of the Apostle "Judas Thomas, also called Didymos," in which Thomas converts many heathens, performs numerous miracles, holds learned discourses, particularly counseling sexual abstinence, sings the celebrated "Hymn of the Pearl," and is finally martyred. The original version may have been written in Syriac, perhaps at Edessa, in the early third century; the text is transmitted, in slightly differ-

ent versions, in a large number of manuscripts in Greek and Syriac. The church fathers refer frequently to some version of this text, warning vigorously against its heretical nature.

5. *The Apocalypse of Thomas (Apocalypse:* E 645–51; S-W 2.748–52): a speech by Jesus to Thomas recounting what will happen at the end of the world, dependent at least partly upon the canonical Apocalypse of John. A longer version seems to contain allusions to historical events of the fifth century; a shorter version probably goes back to an earlier date. The original language was probably Latin. There seems to be no reference to this work before its condemnation by the Gelasian Decree (probably sixth century).

To these five texts the fate of Thomas as a Gnostic saint has been entrusted, and it is with these that we shall begin.

❧

The first point to be noted is that the very fact that Thomas appears so frequently in the New Testament Apocrypha is in itself remarkable. No other character figures as the protagonist or putative author in so many apocryphal writings; indeed, no other character is even mentioned in them by name as frequently as Thomas is, with the sole exceptions of Jesus himself and the disciples Peter and John (who are particularly significant for institutional and doctrinal reasons). It is almost as though the canonization of the New Testament was achieved, in part at least, by systematically excluding Thomas.

But is the apocryphal Thomas in fact at all related to the New Testament Thomas whom John elaborated into Doubting Thomas, or is he merely a homonym? Are we justified in linking this apocryphal Thomas with the disciple Thomas, and in particular with Doubting Thomas? After all, in the first centuries of the Christian era Palestine seems to have been subject to severe onomastic scarcity, so that there were far fewer names available than people to whom they were to be assigned; just as there are a multiplicity of distinguishable Marys, Jameses, and Johns, so too we cannot simply assume on principle that all these Thomases are the same person.

In my view the Thomases referred to in the Apocrypha are indeed intended to be understood by their readers as being identical with the disciple Thomas named in the canonical New Testament Gospels. If true, this claim can only mean that the stories about Thomas in the Apocrypha all derive ultimately either from the Gospel of John or from other narrative sources that are no longer extant. And given the early widespread diffusion of the Gospel of John (as far as we can tell, it was already accepted in Christian and Gnostic circles in Rome, Egypt, Syria, and the Middle East from the first years of the second century), all such other stories, in order to seem plausible to their recipients, must have been capable of entering into a meaningful intertextual relationship with that Gospel, either by developing it further in a plausible way or by correcting and revising it polemically. This does not mean that all the apocryphal stories about an individual named Thomas are narrative interpretations of the episode involving Doubting Thomas in the Gospel of John. For we cannot exclude the possibility that these stories go back, at least in part, to sources that are now lost—the geneaology of the story of Doubting Thomas must probably admit more than one ultimate source to explain all the variation in its many later versions. But it does mean that those authors and readers of the apocryphal stories who also had some degree of direct or indirect familiarity with the Gospel of John had to be able to regard the relation between these stories and that Gospel as being plausible.

In some cases, the relation between the apocryphal materials and the Gospel of John is particularly close. For example, in *Acts of Thomas*, Thomas's pious outcry from John 20:28 is quoted verbatim two or three times in highly prominent locations of the narrative: once near the beginning, in Thomas's very first apostolic adventure, at a wedding in Andrapolis, at the beginning of his lengthy climactic prayer (§10); a second time near the end, at the beginning of a lengthy conclusive prayer before his martyrdom (§144); and, in one version, a third time at the opening of his very last short prayer just before he is slain by the soldiers (§167). Several other passages in *Acts of Thomas* also allude, less precisely but no less unmistakably, to the same words (§§2, 26, 39). Moreover, at the very beginning of *Acts of Thomas* the apostolic missionary's name is indicated as "Judas Thomas, also called Didymos" (§1), and various combinations of these three names are used throughout the text; the link with John's repeated designation, "Thomas, also called Didymos" (John 11:16, 20:24), is evident.

In the other texts in this group of five, the relation to the Gospel of John is more indirect. We may take as a starting point the opening words of the *Gospel of Thomas:* "These are the secret words which the living Jesus spoke and Didymos Judas Thomas wrote down" (E 135). Why is Jesus called "living" here? If the reference is to Jesus before the crucifixion, the epithet seems otiose (at best one might expect something like "the eternally living Jesus" or "Jesus who was alive then and is still alive now," or something similar); hence scholars are agreed that this phrase in *Gospel* must refer to words spoken by Jesus after his resurrection, when he might be thought to be dead but is instead very much alive. How this scene is to be imagined is made clear several paragraphs later:

> Jesus said to his disciples, "Compare me to someone and tell whom I am like." Simon Peter said to him, "You are like a righteous angel." Matthew said to him, "You are like a wise philosopher." Thomas said to him, "Master, my mouth is incapable of saying whom you are like." Jesus said, "I am not your master. Because you drank, you are drunk from the bubbling spring which I measured out." And he took him and drew him aside and spoke three words to him. When Thomas returned to his companions they asked him, "What did Jesus say to you?" Thomas said to them, "If I tell you one of the words which he spoke to me, you will pick up stones and throw them at me. And fire will come from the stones and burn you up." (§13 = E 137)

Unlike the other disciples, who think they know what Jesus is like and imagine that they can capture his essence by comparing him to familiar religious or secular categories, Thomas knows that he does not know: his admission of incapacity and subordination, beginning as it does by calling Jesus his "Master," is at the very least compatible with, and may even be a development out of, his pious exclamation in John, "My Lord and my God!" (John 20:28). By acknowledging his ignorance, Thomas demonstrates that he has attained a higher level of understanding than either Simon Peter or Matthew (and thereby calls implicitly into question both the authority of the church that traces its legitimacy to the former and that of the synoptic Gospel attributed to the latter): Thomas has drunk from the spring of knowledge (compare John 4:14) and has thereby become a worthy interlocutor for Jesus. Hence Jesus can draw him aside from the other disciples and impart to him a secret wisdom that is denied to them. In other words, both Thomas's separation from the other disciples and his exclusive conversation with Jesus, which had fundamentally characterized John's account, here recur as the justification for supposing a privileged interaction between Jesus and this one disciple: Thomas becomes the repository for an esoteric wisdom that alone can save mankind but that is denied to all the other disciples, let alone to all other humans, except by his mediation.

The close situational and even verbal connection with the Gospel of John, combined with the name "Didymos Judas Thomas," suggests that *Gospel* is linked with the Gospel of John by some degree of affiliation (notwithstanding other sources to which it might also go back); and this helps us make a similar argument about *Contender* and *Apocalypse*. For the former text begins with the same situation of privileged communication between Jesus and Thomas, this time overheard and passed on to the rest of us by the Evangelist Matthew ("The secret words that the Saviour spoke to Judas Thomas and which I, Matthew, wrote down. I was passing by and heard them speak with one another."), and it quotes Jesus addressing Thomas as "Brother Thomas . . . my twin and my sole true friend" and praising him, just as in *Gospel*, for having begun on the path of knowledge ("And I know that you have begun to understand," S-W 1.241)—indeed, this effort to comprehend seems to have been so significant in the eyes of the author of this text that it is probably the reason why he chose to term Thomas "the Contender" (or, in other translations, "the Athlete") in its subscription.

Apocalypse begins with a direct address on the part of Jesus to Thomas ("Hear, Thomas, the things which must come to pass in the last times," E 646) and on the whole follows far more closely than any of the other apocryphal Apocalypses the Revelation of John, which was ascribed by most early readers to the same author as the Gospel of John. So too, the Gnostic text known as the *Pistis Sophia* (*Faith Wisdom*) shows Jesus declaring that he has delivered secret discourses to Philip, Thomas, and Matthew, ordering these three to write them down and transmit them to the world (§§42–43). In all these cases, the Thomas to whom this Gnostic Jesus imparts a secret wisdom bears a clear likeness to the Thomas of the Gospel of John.

❧

If, then, we may regard as probable some degree of genetic affiliation between the Gnostic Thomas and the Johannine Thomas (whatever other lost sources must also be postulated for these Gnostic texts), we must ask why it was Doubting Thomas to whom the role of Gnostic saint came to be assigned and not some other disciple. Of course this question does not arise for an approach that believes unquestioningly in the historical veracity of the texts at issue (for in that case Thomas is said to have done or said these things just because he really did do or say them) nor for one that assumes their purely arbitrary and fictional nature (for then there is no more reason why Thomas should have been assigned this role than any other figure). But if the former approach requires that we make a religious commitment to the truth of Gnosticism of a kind to which, I imagine, few of us would be inclined to subscribe, the latter one refuses to accord these texts the dignity and seriousness with which their authors and many ancient readers certainly invested them. Between the barren alternatives of absolute truth and absolute fiction there is at least one other category in which we can understand such texts, that of belief: for if the producers and recipients of these texts were familiar with the story of Doubting Thomas in the Gospel of John and at the same time found plausible these Gnostic accounts of the saint's words and actions, then there must have been conspicuous features in that Gospel that not only were not incompatible with the Gnostic writings, but could also be strongly and interestingly linked with them. Let us consider the features of John's Thomas that encouraged such a development, and the interpretation of John's story that it implies.

As we saw in Part I, Thomas, as John depicts him, displays a paradoxical combination of extreme intimacy with and devotion to Jesus, on the one hand, and no less extreme isolation from and skepticism toward him, on the other. On the one hand he is prepared, unlike the other disciples, to die with Jesus when he wants to go to the family of Lazarus (11:16); Jesus returns for him alone, to convince him of his resurrection (20:26); Jesus offers him alone his body for tactile inspection (20:27); and Thomas cries out "My Lord and my God!" (20:28), an expression of absolute subservience and the first explicit acknowledgment of Jesus' divinity in any of the canonical Gospels. On the other hand Thomas has no idea at all what Jesus means when he says at the Last Supper, "And you know the way where I am going" (14:4–5); he refuses to believe his fellow disciples' word that they have seen Jesus reappear until he has acquired his own proof, and he phrases with a disconcertingly harsh bluntness the criteria whose satisfaction he demands if he is to accord his belief (20:25); and Jesus' last words to him declare that his faith, because it was based upon seeing, is inferior to that of those who believe without seeing (20:29). On the one hand, Thomas seems to constitute a tiny elite within the larger elite of the circle of Jesus' disciples (elites always tend to form smaller elites within themselves), for Jesus reserves a set of highly significant actions and discourses for him alone, to the exclusion of the other disciples and of all other people; on the other, he seems to represent, within the very circle of those who are closest to Jesus, an element of doubt, of foreignness, of the skeptical attitude of those outsiders who do not believe in him at all.

One of the most peculiar aspects of the Gnostic Thomas is certainly far easier to understand if it is linked directly with this essential ambiguity of John's Thomas. For the attentive reader will have noticed that in *Acts of Thomas* the designation of Thomas as "Judas Thomas, also called Didymos" (§1) supplements the Johannine designation "Thomas, also called Didymos" with one further name lacking in the Gospel account, "Judas." So too, at the very opening of the Coptic version of *Gospel* we find the designation "Didymos Judas Thomas" (E 135), and at the beginning of *Contender*, "Judas Thomas" (S-W 1.241).

Why has the name "Judas" been added to "Thomas"? Our first temptation might be to point to the disciple Judas who betrayed Jesus. But before committing ourselves to this interpretation, we should note that *Contender* has Jesus address Thomas as "Brother Thomas . . . my twin" (S-W 1.241) and that *Acts of Thomas* expressly designates Thomas "also called Didymos" as the twin brother ($\delta\acute{\iota}\delta\upsilon\mu\sigma\varsigma$) of none other than Jesus himself. When the bridegroom at Andrapolis goes to fetch his bride,

> he saw the Lord Jesus talking with his bride. He had the appearance of Judas Thomas, the apostle, who shortly before had blessed them and departed; and he [the bridegroom] said to him [Jesus], "Did you not go out before them all? And how is it that you are here now?" And the Lord said to him, "I am not Judas Thomas, I am his brother." (*Acts of Thomas* §11)

So too, a serpent says to Thomas, "I know that you are the twin brother of Christ and always bring our race to naught" (§31); a colt of an ass addresses him as "Twin brother of Christ" (§39); and over and over again, people who see both Jesus and Thomas think they are seeing double (§§34, 43, 45, 56).

The Gnostic conviction that Thomas is Jesus' twin brother is an odd notion. How could it have come about? It is most likely that some role might have been played in the genesis of this notion by the occasional use of the term "brothers" in the Gospels to refer to Jesus' disciples—for example, in this very chapter of John, Jesus tells Mary to "go to my brethren" and tell them he is ascending to the Father (John 20:17): so some readers probably thought that if Thomas was his disciple, he may also have been his brother. And of course we cannot exclude the possibility that independent sources, now lost, might for whatever reason have described Thomas as Jesus' twin brother. But it also seems likely that certain readers of John's Gospel were struck by his assertions that Thomas was also called "Didymos" or "Twin" and wondered whose twin brother Thomas might be; casting about for a plausible candidate, they fell sooner or later upon Jesus (why, we shall see shortly). Two of the other Gospels report that Jesus had four brothers, James, Joses, Simon, and Judas (Mark 6:3, Matt. 13:55; and compare Eusebius, *Ecclesiastical History* 3.20); wondering just which of Jesus' reported brothers could have been his twin, these readers came up with Judas (again, we shall see shortly why). Often in mythology, the double birth of two brothers, one immortal and the other mortal, is explained by the mother's having been impregnated by two different fathers, one divine and the other human: so too, Jesus and his weaker brother Thomas, like Heracles and Iphicles, or Polydeuces and Castor, could perhaps be thought to share one mother, Mary, but two fathers, God for the former and Joseph for the latter.

It is perhaps this same identification that lets Thomas be described as a carpenter in *Acts of Thomas*—he goes to India because the king there needs someone to build him a palace (§2)—and thereafter to go on to become the patron saint of architects (his standard iconographical symbol is the architect's square): for the very same passages in the Gospels report that the husband of Mary, Joseph, was a carpenter himself (Mark 6:3, Matt. 13:55), and his mortal son Thomas is presumably continuing in his father's profession (his wife's divine son was destined to go on to greater things). This also lets us see how John's Thomas could come to have attributed to him a report of Jesus' childhood like *Infancy*: for who could possibly be a better witness to the miracles that Jesus performed as a young child, before any of the disciples had ever met him, than one of his very own brothers? For the very same reason, an apocryphal Gospel is ascribed to another attested brother of Jesus, James (§25 = E 66–67; S-W 1.421–38).

If this reasoning is correct, then the creative misunderstanding that the Gnostics applied to the textual data in the New Testament consisted in their construing John's statement that the name of Thomas means "Twin" to imply that he was the twin brother of Jesus. Such a leap is surely erroneous from the point of view of what we can infer to have been John's intentions; but it is not entirely devoid of logic. It presumes above all the economy of the text: why should John have mentioned this fact if it was not significant, and of whom could Thomas be the twin brother if not of someone mentioned prominently within the Gospels? Given these premises and given the mixture of extreme closeness and extreme distance between Jesus and Thomas in John, the identification of Thomas as Jesus' twin brother seems easy, if not inevitable. Hence it is not surprising that the medieval church came to celebrate Thomas's holy day as December 21—four days away from Jesus' birthday, to be sure, but perhaps still close enough for him to be able to be counted as his twin brother. Yet if December 25 occurs shortly after the winter solstice, when the days finally begin once again to grow longer, December 21 occurs just before it, and is the shortest day of the whole year. Even in his birthday, Thomas represents the more somber possibility: he is the dark twin.

For Thomas always remains, in some sense, a traitor. John reports that Jesus' own brothers did not believe in him (John 7:5), but it is remarkable that of all the four brothers of Jesus reported by the Gospels, the only one that Thomas is ever identified with is Judas, the homonym of the disciple who betrayed Jesus. After all, does Thomas not go on to divulge in many of these apocryphal texts the very secrets Jesus confides to him alone? In no surviving apocryphal text does Jesus ever entrust Thomas with the mission of reporting to the world the secrets he imparts to him, and yet all those secrets end up somehow being made more or less public. Who, more appropriately than Thomas, could possibly have enjoyed Jesus' confidence so fully as to have received from him this secret wisdom—and who could have betrayed it so thoroughly by passing it on to us? Of course such a betrayal need not be taken too seriously: it is in a certain sense a convenient device that permits these esoteric doctrines to remain secret yet at the same time to be disseminated. But the choice of Thomas as the figure who divulges them is surely not arbitrary. It is worth noting in this connection that at least one Gnostic Gospel circulated that was attributed to Judas Iscariot himself; later it was condemned as heretical and now is entirely lost (E 25; S-W 1.386–87).

Perhaps the most extraordinary expression of this mixture of nearness and farness in Thomas's relation to Jesus is the persistent tradition that identifies in him the apostle who converted to Christianity first Edessa, in eastern Syria, and then India. To this day, there are Christians in India who call themselves "Thomas Christians" and trace their faith back to the apostle Thomas himself. All three of the synoptic Gospels end with variously formulated expressions of a mission, imposed by Jesus upon his disciples, to convert the whole world (Mark 16:15, the Longer Ending; Luke 24:47; Matt. 28:19); the canonical Acts of the Apostles recounts the miracle of Pentecost, in which the apostles spoke in every human tongue, suggesting a universal apostolic mission (Acts 2:4–11). In similar fashion the apocryphal *Acts of Thomas* begins with a scene, found elsewhere as well, in which the apostles divide up the different parts of the world and assign to themselves by lot the one each of them is to convert (*Acts of Thomas* §1, compare S-W 2.18f.). Just which nations were assigned to Thomas varied from authority to authority—Edessa and India are the most widely reported, but some authors add the Parthians, the Medes, Ceylon, and the southern tip of the Arabian peninsula—but no one had any doubt that the region in question was located somewhere in the Far East. Thus Barhebraeus calls Thomas "primus Orientis pontifex" (the first pope of the East: *chronicon ecclesiast.* 111.4, ed. Lamy), while Isidore of Seville reports that he preached to the Parthians, the Medes, the Persians, the Hyrcanians, the Bactrians, and the Indians, and penetrated deep into the Orient (*On the Birth and Death of the Fathers Who Occur in the Holy Scripture* 74.132 = *PL* 83.152).

The logical connection whereby Thomas is assigned the eastern extremity of the Christian world—first Edessa, and then, once the eastern edge of Christianity moved farther east, India and other eastern peoples—can be reconstructed. After Thomas has entered centripetally into so extraordinary a degree of proximity with Jesus, he must be flung centrifugally outward to the farthest limit of the known world so as to win new converts to Christianity. But why the eastern limit? Perhaps the myth of Dionysus' proselytizing expedition to India played some role; it is worth noting that the fifth-century Egyptian poet Nonnus composed both an epic on this myth and a paraphrase of the Gospel of John. But the most likely reason is that, from the perspective of the Roman Empire, the western horizon (Spain, Gaul, Britain) had already become far too pacified and civilized to present a real test of Thomas's skills and commitment, while the desolate wastelands in the frozen North and desert South were thought to be uninhabited and hence could offer him no genuine opportunity. All that remained was the savage, bellicose, overpopulated East—the perfect challenge for a missionary, and perhaps also the perfect punishment for an erstwhile doubter.

And there Thomas must fulfill an apostolic mission of large-scale proselytization for which he above all others is consummately fitted. Having himself finally been freed of all doubts concerning Jesus' divinity after intense struggle, he has become the ideal candidate for converting others—indeed, the apocryphal *Acts of Thomas* consists largely of enthusiastic accounts of his enormously successful mass conversions. Evidently, if you can convince Thomas, he can convince (almost) anyone. The reader familiar with Greek literature may recall Teiresias' prophecy of the fate of Odysseus after his return to Ithaca: he must placate his old enemy Poseidon by traveling inland to a place where the sea is so little known that his oar is mistaken for a winnowing-fan, and there he must found a temple to the god of the sea, extending and strengthening the latter's cultic power (Homer, *Odyssey*, 11.119–34).

❧

If John's Thomas was capable of becoming a Gnostic saint, this is because many authors and readers could believe he perfectly fulfilled the three criteria for Gnosticism I indicated earlier—but on the basis not only of other lost sources but also most probably of a highly idiosyncratic reading of John's narrative. Those who wished to could easily take him as a paradigm of knowledge rather than simple faith: for instead of merely believing what the other disciples tell him, he declares that he will withhold his assent until he truly knows, until the precise epistemic conditions he has specified have been satisfied. What better example could be imagined of the preference for knowledge-based belief over groundless belief? The same readers could just as easily understand him to represent a tiniest and highest elite within the already very small elite of Jesus' closest disciples: for does not Jesus return a second time for him alone, and does Jesus not devote to him a final appearance and interchange?

But what of the third criterion, the disdain for all things bodily and the identification of the true person with his immaterial spirit? How could Thomas, who demanded to touch Jesus' body and to put his finger and hand into Jesus' wounds before he could believe in his resurrection, possibly be taken as the patron saint of an anticorporeal doctrine?

John does indeed tell first how Thomas asked to touch Jesus' body and then how Thomas acknowledged Jesus' divinity. But in between he nowhere explicitly asserts that Thomas actually touched Jesus' body; indeed, his text, read carefully, makes it clear that Thomas never did actually touch it. Those who wished to could see in this textual situation the proof that Thomas did not in fact touch that body, but came to recognize Jesus' divinity without making any material contact with it. For Gnostic readers of John's Gospel, the fact that Thomas did not touch Jesus' body but nonetheless acknowledged his divinity could be taken as evidence that Jesus' risen body was not material but purely spiritual, and hence as corroboration for the systematic privilege the Gnostics accorded to the spirit over the body. If Thomas did not touch Jesus' body, it must have been because he could not do so, because no one could do so—because in fact there was no material body to be touched.

This may be why no Gnostic apocryphal text makes the slightest explicit or implicit reference to Thomas's touching Jesus' body. Indeed, several of these texts provide narratives in which the act of touching a holy body, Jesus' or someone else's, is negatively valorized. Such scenes seem designed to be interpreted, in part at least, as implicit condemnations of any suggestion that someone as holy as Thomas might have wanted to thrust his hand into Jesus' wounds. For example, *Infancy* relates how the boy Jesus "went through the village, and a child ran and knocked against his shoulder. Jesus was angered and said to him, 'You shall not go further on your way,' and immediately he fell down and died" (§4.1). But the most striking example occurs near the beginning of *Acts of Thomas*, in the wedding at Andrapolis:

> And as the apostle looked to the ground, one of the cupbearers stretched forth his hand and struck him. And the apostle, having raised his eyes, looked at the man who had struck him, saying, 'My God will forgive you for this wrong in the world to come, but in this world he will show his wonders, and I shall soon see that hand that struck me dragged along by dogs.' (§6)

And sure enough, as soon as Thomas has finished singing an allegorical wedding song, this is just what happens (§8). If there were any hint in this text or any other Gnostic one that Thomas was thought to have actually touched Jesus' body or had even tried to do so, this scene might be interpreted as suggesting that Thomas had once erred but since then had learned from his mistake. But in the absence of any such hint it is more plausible to suppose that this scene in *Acts of Thomas* is implicitly suggesting that, whatever Thomas may have once said, he was not so sacrilegious as to have ever actually stuck his hand into Jesus' wounds.

❧

In this case, as in general among the New Testament Apocrypha, the mode of reading that lies behind the production of these writings appears to be enormously sensitive—indeed, hypersensitive—to the gaps within the narratives of the canonical Gospels, and it attempts to fill out these lacunae with additional information, seeking to provide a continuous narrative line for those who take both sets of texts together. As we saw earlier, such gaps are characteristic of both the Hebrew and the Christian Bibles; presumably a religious community that was centered upon such texts could scarcely ignore these breaks. More likely, such a community would have tended to develop speculative and competitive lines of argument to explain what was missing and why it had been left out, would have worked through the merits and demerits of such lines in controversial debate, and would eventually have crystallized the most successful ones into a new and more stable orthodoxy (or, as the case might be, heterodoxy).

The approach tried out in Part I used psychological material in order to fill out some of the evident gaps in the Gospels. Often the authors of the Apocrypha deploy the same strategy: where a lacuna seems to open up between two moments of the holy narrative, they ask what events, actions, and psychological dispositions must be assumed in order to bridge it. For example, the canonical Gospels tell of no event in Jesus' life between his birth and the scene at the Temple in Jerusalem when he was twelve years old. Readers who did not doubt Jesus' divinity must have wondered what powers he already possessed as a child—it is after all not self-evident why he only became a miracle-worker after the onset of puberty. In like manner, to take an example from pagan Roman culture, readers who were astonished by the technical sophistication of Virgil's first published work, the *Bucolics*, asked whether he had written other, earlier poems but withheld them from publication.

The Virgilian question was provided with an answer, apparently satisfactory to many, by such sophisticated forgeries as the *Culex*; the Christian one, by the apocryphal Birth and Infancy Gospels. Thus *Infancy* begins when Jesus was five years old (§2.1) and concludes with the scene at the Temple when he was twelve (§19.1–5), thereby ensuring a seamless connection with the Gospel of Luke (Luke 2:42–51)—indeed, the last lines of *Infancy* ("Jesus . . . was subject to his parents; but his mother stored up all that had taken place," *Infancy* §19.5) are virtually a citation of the last words of the story in Luke ("he . . . was obedient to them; and his mother kept all these things in her heart," Luke 2:51). Similarly, the various apocryphal Acts of the Apostles, including the *Acts of Thomas*, filled out what eventually came to be felt as the gap left at the end of the New Testament Gospels, which told the story of Jesus' life to the very end (and even beyond) but left open the question of what became of most of his disciples.

In the case of the secret doctrines imparted by Jesus to Thomas and transmitted in various Gnostic Apocrypha, matters are not very different. John himself had done what he could to exclude such unauthorized supplementations of his own Gospel by citing Jesus as explicitly declaring, "I have spoken openly to the world; I have always taught in synagogues and in the temple, where all Jews come together; I have said nothing secretly" (John 18:20). Yet the temptation to suppose that Jesus might have made additional pronouncements only to some hearers, and not to others, would have received strong support from various passages in the synoptic Gospels, in which Jesus has private discussions with the disciples (Mark 4:10) or says that for them he is reserving a secret knowledge, but to those outside the group he will speak only in parables (Mark 4:11, 34). Indeed even within the group of disciples there is what could be understood as at least one unambiguous reference to the existence of an inner circle, privileged with private instruction, consisting of Peter, James, John, and Andrew (Mark 13:3, and compare the related though different Transfiguration).

Such passages, (mis-)understood by an (overly) alert readership, seem to have suggested the kind of material that could be inserted into what may have seemed a crucial gap between one sentence in the Gospel of John, Jesus' offer to Thomas to touch his body (John 20:27), and the very next one, Thomas's pious exclamation acknowledging Jesus' divinity (John 20:28). For if it was not the act of touching Jesus' body that convinced Thomas (and no Gnostic could possibly have believed that the risen Jesus had possessed a material body that Thomas could have touched), then what could have persuaded him? For a religion that gave the highest priority to knowledge and hence to teaching a salvational doctrine, there could have been little doubt: it must have been a secret instruction that Jesus spoke to Thomas, but that John himself did not report in his Gospel, either because he was not deemed worthy of receiving this doctrine or because he chose to reserve it for himself and his closest associates. In either case, many readers may have felt an overwhelming desire to know these hidden words. For on this view it was precisely these unknown words that led Thomas to recognize Jesus' divinity. Must they not therefore have carried an enormous charge of mystic knowledge and redemptive power?

Such considerations may have helped generate Gnostic texts like *Gospel* and *Contender*, which consist almost entirely of brief utterances by Jesus to Thomas (or, very rarely, to one or more of the other disciples), sometimes in response to questions, sometimes not, or like *Apocalypse*, which takes the form of an extended monologue, once again spoken by Jesus to Thomas. The contents of the doctrines expounded tend to overlap with sayings and views attributed to Jesus in the New Testament, though much of the material cannot be paralleled from canonical sources and hence probably goes back to lost ones; and even when there are canonical parallels, these Gnostic writings place far more emphasis upon redemptive knowledge, upon a redeemed elite, and upon the unimportance of the material body—or the dangers posed by it. Just what the relations are between these apocryphal and canonical texts, and to what extent the versions of the apocryphal writings now extant have been modified to make them more orthodox, or less so, are questions about which scholars have not yet reached a consensus; though these issues are certainly important, they are not directly relevant to the themes of this book, and hence are omitted here.

❧

To be sure, describing texts like these as "narrative developments" from the Gospel of John and other sources might seem to require that we attribute to them literary qualities they do not possess. After all, those people (probably few in any case) who turn to them in search of the literary effects we associate with well-wrought fictional or historical narratives—tension, suspense, foreshadowing, character development, and so forth—will be disappointed. However, I am using the term "narrative development" here not as a vaguely commendatory label guaranteeing artistic excellence, but in a highly specific sense, to indicate, on the one hand, that all these later texts are inserted imaginatively by their authors and readers into a particular, identifiable moment of some other narrative, and, on the other, that they are all characterized at the very least by a minimal narrative structure, namely the succession of discrete events marking different conditions in the same state of affairs regarding various relatively stable characters.

But a Gnostic author, for whom no knowledge is important except what is necessary for salvation and for whom such knowledge is usually known by authoritative figures from the very beginning, is not inclined to create effects of suspense or character development. That is why the doctrinal exposition goes point for point in an order that may seem random to us: what matters is the individual insight, and the cumulative power of the whole structure, rather than an orderly argumentative sequence. It is also why Gnostic narratives like *Infancy* and *Acts of Thomas* are made up of a sequence of individual episodes in which only the specific circumstances change, not the characters' personalities: for a Gnostic, such circumstances belong only to this material world and are ultimately devoid of reality, while the spiritual essence that is expressed in and through these holy characters is beyond time and change. Thus in *Infancy* Jesus as a little child already possesses all the knowledge and all the power that he will go on to display as an adult; in *Acts of Thomas* the Apostle Thomas is almost from the beginning a paragon of all possible virtues, filled with the self-assurance of true faith and therefore capable of converting even the most recalcitrant unbelievers.

When these texts do present the kind of narrative features familiar from other literary works, it is usually only at or near their beginning sections, where their link to the texts from which they arise is strongest. Only in its opening paragraphs, for example, does *Contender* show Jesus justifying his discourse to Thomas in terms of the latter's character and the relation between the two of them, before he goes on to propound doctrines that he could just as well have presented without any interlocutor at all. *Gospel* reserves until paragraph 13 the depiction of the dramatic situation in which Jesus invites various disciples to say what he is like and then rewards Thomas for his profession of ignorance by taking him aside and revealing to him the secret words, but afterward the text continues, for the most part, with a bare series of "Jesus said"s.

It is the beginning of *Acts of Thomas*, however, that provides perhaps the most literarily sophisticated scene of any of these Gnostic writings:

> At that time we apostles were all in Jerusalem—Simon called Peter, and Andrew his brother, James the son of Zebedee, and John his brother, Philip and Bartholomew, Thomas and Matthew the taxgatherer, James the son of Alphaeus and Simon the Cananaean, and Judas the son of James—and we portioned out the regions of the world, in order that each one of us might go into the region that fell to him by lot, and to the nation to which the Lord had sent him. By lot India fell to Judas Thomas, also called Didymos. And he did not wish to go, saying that he was not able to travel on account of the weakness of his body. He said, "How can I, being a Hebrew, go among the Indians to proclaim the truth?" And while he was considering this and speaking, the Saviour appeared to him during the night and said to him, "Fear not, Thomas, go away to India and preach the word there, for my grace is with you." But he would not obey saying, "Wherever you wish to send me, send me, but elsewhere. For I am not going to the Indians." (§1)

The episode begins by justifying itself as the first-person statement of one of the twelve disciples and by attaching itself closely, even in the order of the names, to the various catalogues of Jesus' disciples in the canonical New Testament (especially Matt. 10:2–4; also Mark 3:16–19, Luke 6:14–16, Acts 1:13). The character of Thomas, at this earliest stage of the narrative, is the one we are familiar with from John: he doubts the decision of the lot, disobeys the express order of Jesus even when this latter comes to speak only to him, and remains attached to the debilities of the material body.

At this point Thomas still has a long way to go before he can become a Gnostic saint. But when, in the very next paragraph, Jesus decides to sell him as his slave into India, we find ourselves confronted with a further, even more creative adaptation of the story in John's

Gospel. For Jesus seems here to be taking the first two words of Thomas' pious exclamation in that Gospel, "My Lord and my God!" quite literally, as a declaration on Thomas's part that Jesus is his lord in the sense of being his master or owner. Hence Jesus can declare at the marketplace that he possesses a slave; and when the Indian merchant Abban asks Thomas, "Is this your master?" the latter has no other choice than to quote his very own words from the Gospel of John and to answer, "Yes, he is my Lord" (§2). From that moment on Thomas has rediscovered his true identity and lost all his doubts forever—"On the following morning the apostle prayed and entreated the Lord, saying, 'I go wherever you wish, O Lord Jesus, your will be done'" (§3).

※

So far, we have been considering in this chapter only the Gnostic Apocrypha, those noncanonical writings in which Doubting Thomas figures prominently as a Gnostic saint, Jesus' dark twin brother, who begins by doubting him but ends up believing in him precisely without touching him, and thereby confirms a firmly anticorporeal dogma. However, not all the New Testament Apocrypha are Gnostic, and Thomas appears in non-Gnostic and anti-Gnostic apocryphal writings as well as in Gnostic ones. But two crucial differences must be noted: first, in these latter texts he never plays a central role but is always integrated into the stories of figures who are evidently far more important than he is; and second, none of these non-Gnostic texts suggests that Thomas did not actually touch Jesus, and many of them emphatically indicate that he or others did.

We may distinguish two kinds of cases: first, texts in which the character of Thomas himself, as he is presented in the Gospel of John, is introduced into a new action, and second, those in which some motif connected importantly with his story in the Gospel of John is detached from his person and attached to someone else.

First, one of the New Testament Apocrypha, the *Book of the Resurrection* attributed to Bartholomew the Apostle, attempts to fill in one of the most striking lacunae in John's account by inventing a set of actions attributed to Thomas that can explain his mysterious absence from Jesus' first appearance before the disciples:

> Thomas was not with them, for he had departed to his city, hearing that his son Siophanes (Theophanes?) was dead. It was the seventh day since the death when he arrived. He went to the tomb and raised him in the name of Jesus . . . . Thomas and he went into the city to the consternation of all who saw them. He, Siophanes, addressed the people and told his story; and Thomas baptized twelve thousand of them, founded a church, and made Siophanes its bishop. Then Thomas mounted on a cloud, and it took him to the Mount of Olives and to the apostles, who told him of the visit of Jesus and he would not believe. Bartholomew admonished him. Then Jesus appeared, and made Thomas touch his wounds and departed into heaven. (E 671)

Thomas's unexplained absence from Jesus' first appearance to the disciples in John's Gospel is here provided a perfectly pious justification: Thomas's visit to his dead son is not only motivated by quite comprehensible paternal considerations but also permits him to perform a miracle that imitates Jesus' resurrection of Lazarus—the same episode in John's account in which Thomas made his first appearance (John 11:16). His own signal piety is further confirmed by his performance of a mass baptism and his foundation of a church; and if the son's transmitted name "Siophanes" is really to be understood as a corrupt form of "Theophanes," then Thomas will have named his own son in honor of "a God who has appeared" among men. Yet in trying to resolve one of the problems in John's account, this new version inevitably ends up creating new problems of its own: for how could so pious a follower of Jesus—and one, moreover, who has himself just seen the resurrection of his son from the dead—possibly doubt the resurrection of Jesus? Instead of venturing a second invention to solve this crux, the text concludes this episode by repeating from John's Gospel the scene of Jesus inviting Thomas to touch his wounds, thereby authorizing its own account by tying it back into the canonical text. Significantly, in doing so, it states explicitly that what convinced Thomas in the end was that he actually touched Jesus' wounds.

A similar textual strategy, combined with a marked tendency toward amplification, repetition, and multiplication (already characteristic of Luke, as we saw earlier), is found in the strongly anti-Gnostic *Epistle of the Apostles* (third quarter of the second century). Here the reappearance of Jesus after his death leads to a whole sequence of scenes of profound doubt and only gradually growing belief (E 561–63): first the three women weep at the tomb until Jesus appears, tells them who he is, and says that one of them should report the good news to the disciples (§10); Mary Magdalene does so, but the disciples refuse to believe her (§10); then Sarah (or, in another version, Mary again) goes to them, but this time they accuse her of lying (§10); then Jesus goes to them himself, together with the women, and even then he is not believed, for the disciples think that he must be a ghost (§11); whereupon Jesus attempts to prove his identity by telling them of Peter's betrayal, but even now he is still not believed (§11). Finally he invites a number of them to test his reality by a tactile inspection, and it is this alone that decisively convinces them:

> And he said to us, "Why do you doubt and do you not believe? I am he who spoke to you concerning my flesh, my death, and my resurrection. And that you may know that it is I, lay your hand, Peter, (and your finger) in the nail-print of my hands; and you, Thomas, in my side; and also you, Andrew, see whether my foot steps on the ground and leaves a footprint . . . ." But now we felt him, that he had truly risen in the flesh. And then we fell on our faces before him, asked him for pardon and entreated him because we had not believed him. (§§11–12)

Here the narrative pattern of disbelief and then faith that structures the conclusions of all four of the canonical Gospels is powerfully magnified and mechanically, indeed almost compulsively, repeated. It is only the actual act of touching Jesus' body that can provide the conclusive proof; hence this touching is so important that it cannot be reserved for Thomas alone but must also be accorded to Peter, a particularly authoritative (and notoriously disloyal) disciple.

Finally, Thomas plays an important role in the legend of the As-sumption of the Virgin. In the Latin account attributed to Joseph of Arimathaea (E 715–16), Mary summons all the disciples when she learns that she is about to die, and all of them come except Thomas (§7). It is only after they have buried Mary and, without their knowing it, angels have started to bear her to heaven, that Thomas shows up:

> Thomas was suddenly brought to the Mount of Olives and saw the holy body being taken up, and cried out to Mary, "Make your servant glad by your mercy, for now you go to heaven." And the girdle with which the apostles had girt the body was thrown down to him; he took it and went to the valley of Josaphat. When he had greeted the apostles, Peter said, "You were always unbelieving, and so the Lord has not suffered you to be at his mother's burial." He smote his breast and said, "I know it and I ask pardon of you all," and they all prayed for him. Then he said, "Where have you laid her body?", and they pointed to the sepulchre. But he said, "The holy body is not there." Peter said, "Formerly you would not believe in the resurrection of the Lord before you touched him: how should you believe us?" Thomas went on saying, "It is not here." Then in anger they went and took away the stone, and the body was not there; and they did not know what to say, being vanquished by Thomas' words. Then Thomas told them how he had been saying Mass in India (and he still had on his priestly vestments), and how he had been brought to the Mount of Olives and seen the ascension of Mary and she had given him her girdle; and he showed it. They all rejoiced and asked his pardon, and he blessed them and said, "Behold how good and pleasant a thing it is, brethren, to dwell together in unity." (§§17–21)

In the Gospel of John, Thomas had been separated out from the group of disciples after the death of Jesus, and was accorded the special privilege of a private appearance afterward. Here the same thing happens after the death, not of Jesus, but of Jesus' mother: Thomas is missing from the group that buries her, and is granted the unique honor of seeing her ascension to heaven. Of course he does not touch her body as he had touched Jesus'—to do so would be the deepest sacrilege, and anyway he is in no doubt this time—but he receives the next best thing: her girdle, which is now passed on to him as proof of her ascension. This text is marked not only by close parallels to the Gospel of John, but also by clever, indeed almost witty, reversals of John's narrative. This time, for example, it is the disciples who are disbelieving, not Thomas (he demonstrates his remorse for his earlier doubt and proves his piety by explaining that his absence was due to his officiating at a Mass in India, thereby presupposing and validating the stories of his eastern mission); it is they who become angry; and it is they who must become convinced and beg forgiveness. And finally, in a nice touch, it is, of all people, Thomas, the outsider, the loner, who concludes the story with an edifying moral drawn from the opening of Psalm 133, pointing out to them all how wonderful social cohesion is.

Second, transferences of motifs from Thomas to other characters appear with some frequency in literary texts, ancient and modern. One example from non-Christian late antiquity is provided by Philostratus' *Life of Apollonius*, from the early third century A.D., which seems to preserve a pagan version of a story much like that of the miracle of Jesus' resurrection (though by precisely what mediations and transmissions is far from clear). In this scene, the holy man Apollonius is being mourned by his followers Damis and Demetrius, who are unaware that he has been transported miraculously from the scene of his trial at the Emperor's palace to a temple of the nymphs at Dicaearchia, where he had sent Damis ahead:

> Damis broke into loud laments and said something like, "Oh gods, shall we ever see our fine and good companion?" Apollonius heard him—for in fact he already happened to be present in the temple of the nymphs—and said, "You will see him, or rather, you have seen him." "Alive?" asked Demetrius. "For if dead, we have never stopped mourning you." Then Apollonius stretched out his hand and said, "Take hold of me, and if I escape you, then I am indeed an image coming to you from Persephone, such as the gods of the underworld reveal to those who are depressed from mourning. But if I resist when I am grasped, then persuade Damis too that I am alive and have not cast away my body." They were no longer capable of disbelieving, but

jumping up they clung to the man and kissed him. (8.12 = 1.328.7–20 Kayser)

The holy man's miraculous apparition in the secluded chamber before the disciples who are lamenting his death, their mourning and doubt, his friendly offer to let himself be touched, their consequent joyous acceptance of the reality of his reappearance—all of these motifs are familiar to readers of the Gospel of John; and, though it cannot be entirely excluded that both Philostratus' account and John's go back to the same unknown source independently of one another, or that they were both composed without any awareness of each other, it seems much likelier that Philostratus' version is ultimately derived from John's account by lost intermediaries.

Transferences of this sort occur in the New Testament Apocrypha as well. For example, the *Acts of John* (second century) tells how John crept up behind Jesus to watch him while he was praying and was astonished to see him change shape and increase in size; whereupon Jesus turned back into a small person, tugged John's beard, and said to him, "John, be not unbelieving, but believing, and not inquisitive" (§90, E 317). Here the words Jesus addressed to Thomas (John 20:27) have been recycled and redirected to another disciple, John (after all, it was in the Gospel of John that these words had first stood). Again, an apocryphal letter of Jesus to Abgar Ouchama the Toparch begins by praising him in terms similar to those with which Jesus had reacted to Thomas's acknowledgment of his divinity in the Gospel of John: "You are blessed; you believe in me, and you have not seen me" (E 542, compare John 20:29).

But the most amusing example of such a transference is the obstetric variant that appears in the apocryphal reports concerning the birth of Jesus. The version of this story found in the *Gospel of Pseudo-Matthew* provides Mary with two midwives, Zelomi and Salome:

And when Zelomi had come in, she said to Mary, "Allow me to touch you." And when she had permitted her to make an examination the midwife cried out with a loud voice and said, "Lord, Lord Almighty, mercy on us! It has never been heard or thought of that any one should have her breasts full of milk and that the birth of a son should show his mother to be a virgin. But there has been no spilling of blood in his birth, no pain in bringing him forth. A virgin has conceived, a virgin has brought forth, and a virgin she remains." And hearing these words, the other midwife with the name Salome said, "I will not believe what I have heard unless I also examine her." And Salome entered and said to Mary, "Allow me to handle you, and prove whether Zelomi has spoken the truth." And Mary allowed her to handle her. And when she had withdrawn her hand from handling her it dried up, and through excess of pain she began to weep bitterly and to be in great distress, crying out and saying, ". . . behold, I am made wretched because of my unbelief, since without a cause I wished to test your virginity." (§13, E 93–94)

Things do not end badly after all: shortly after Salome's repentance she will go on to be miraculously healed. It seems that the Redeemer's birth is too joyous an event to allow such a punishment to be permanent.

The logic of this narrative transference is obvious. To events at the death of Jesus correspond events at his birth: to Jesus' miraculous ability, after his death, to pass unhindered through the physical boundary of the locked door behind which his disciples are hiding corresponds, at his birth, a no less miraculous ability to pass through the hymen, the physical boundary of Mary's womb, without leaving any trace of his passage. At least for some people, such a miracle must be verified if it is to be believed; and what other way is there to do so than to touch the sacred body? Here, of course, that sacred body is not Jesus', but Mary's, and in consequence Thomas himself can no longer play the role of the doubter—even aside from the question of Thomas's age at Jesus' birth, no ancient author could have tolerated the notion of his (or, for that matter, of any man's) inserting his dubious finger into the holy vagina. Hence this function must be transferred to the only figures who could have performed such an act in contemporary Palestinian culture, female midwives. The author of this story has not the slightest doubt that an act of physical touching does indeed take place: but he does not seem to have quite made up his mind whether touching this holy body is something extremely positive (because it alone can confirm the miracle) or extremely negative (because it is motivated by doubt, as though the miracle required confirmation). With tactful even-handedness, this particular version leaves both options open, assigning the purely positive aspect to one midwife, Zelomi, and the purely negative one to the other, the similarly but ominously named Salome (starting with Josephus, *Antiquities* 18.5.4, this is the name given to the dancing daughter of Herodias who demands and receives the head of John the Baptist on a platter). The same question is dealt with in different ways by the other versions of this legend extant in the Apocrypha. On the one hand, the *Protevangelium of James* tells only of the negatively valorized midwife, Salome (§§19.3–20.4, E 64–65); so too, the *Arabic Infancy Gospel* knows of only one midwife, an old Hebrew woman who doubts, is punished, and is finally healed (§§2–3, E 102–103). On the other hand, the medieval Latin infancy gospel referred to by scholars as Arundel 404 *(Book of the Savior's Infancy)* presents a narrative in the first person spoken by the positively valorized midwife herself (no other, negative midwife appears here): she describes the baby's miraculous birth and appearance, and in touching his body confirms his extraordinary nature (E 110).

❧

It would be both instructive and entertaining to trace the many versions of Doubting Thomas throughout the history of world literature. Even in those cases in which his metamorphoses might well have been predicted on principle, their specific details can still surprise us. For example, the transference of Jesus' wounds to Saint Francis of Assisi, in the form of the stigmata that famously marked his body, leads inevitably to numerous scenes in the early biographies of the saint in which various associates of his attempt to view and even to touch them, and sometimes actually manage to do so. But it is impossible within the boundaries of this survey to examine all such material systematically. Hence I will conclude this chapter by considering only one modern text that seems in some ways to recycle John's foundational narrative, not only because this one is intrinsically interesting but also because it raises important methodological issues.

"Marienkind" ("The Virgin Mary's Child"), the third story in the Grimm brothers' nineteenth-century collection of fairy tales, is, in spite of its attractive style and happy ending, in fact one of its very harshest. It tells of the daughter of a woodcutter who is so poor that he cannot afford to feed his family and hence finds himself obliged to accept the Virgin Mary's offer to adopt his child when she is three years old. The girl enjoys a jolly time in heaven until, on her fourteenth birthday, the Virgin summons her and announces that she is going away for a while. During her absence the girl is to take care of the keys to the thirteen doors of the kingdom of heaven—but she is only permitted to use twelve of them to open the doors and admire the wonderful things inside: the Virgin expressly forbids her to open the thirteenth door. Girls will be girls: naturally she promises obedience; naturally she opens, one after the other, the twelve licit doors, and marvels at the dazzling apostle behind each one; naturally she can hardly resist the growing temptation to open the only door that really matters, the thirteenth one. And naturally, one day when her guardian angels conveniently leave her alone, she gets her chance:

> She looked for the key, and when she held it in her hand she also put it into the lock, and when she had put it into the lock she also turned it. Then the door sprang open, and there she saw the Holy Trinity sitting in fire and glory. She stood still for a little while and looked at everything in astonishment. Then she touched the glory a little with her finger, and her finger became completely golden. She immediately felt a terrible fear, slammed the door shut and ran away. And the fear did not go away, whatever she did, and her heart pounded constantly and would not calm down: and the gold remained on her finger and did not go away, however much she washed and rubbed it.

Now that the girl has failed in her ordeal, the Virgin returns to ask her whether she has opened the thirteenth door. When the girl adds mendacity to disobedience, and obstinacy to mendacity, the Virgin looks at her golden finger, deems her unworthy of heaven, and sends her back to earth. Here she spends years suffering hunger and cold in the forest; having used her voice to tell Mary a lie, she even loses her faculty of speech; eventually she is covered by nothing except her long hair. But then a king discovers her by chance, takes her to his palace, and marries her. Every year, for three years, she gives birth to a child; every year the Virgin asks her whether she opened the thirteenth door, and, when she refuses to confess, takes the baby away from her and vanishes; every year the king's subjects become more convinced that the real reason for the disappearance of each of her children is that she has been eating them. The third time the people's patience is exhausted and she is put on the stake to be burned. Only when the flames rise around her does the "hard ice of her pride" finally melt, and she cries out, "Yes, Mary, I did it!" Immediately rain descends from the clouds, dousing the fire, and the Virgin herself appears together with all three children from the heavens, to announce the story's moral: "Whoever repents his sins and confesses is forgiven."

It is easy to recognize in this story a collage of motifs familiar from various sources, mostly religious or quasi-religious: the Virgin protectress; menarche as the beginning of moral responsibility; the unlucky number 13; Bluebeard's castle; Griselda; Mary Magdalene as a hermit; repentance and redemption; martyrdom and salvation. They have been organized along the temporal axis of a series of reversals in the girl's fortunes: a starting point of economic and psychological distress; a change for the better with the Virgin's first descent; one for the worse with the girl's expulsion from heaven; another for the better with the king's intervention; a series of steps down toward the worse with the three successive births and denials, culminating in the worst possible situation, the apparent loss of all three children and the threatened loss of her own life; and a final, decisive change for the better with her confession and rescue. Together the themes and the plot conspire to transmit a severe, indeed almost intimidating message about the importance of obedience, submission, honesty, and contrition.

In the present connection, it is the girl's golden finger that attracts attention, for it seems not unlikely that this motif in the Grimms' fairy tale ultimately goes back to the story of Doubting Thomas in the Gospel of John (just as the many triplets in the story and the girl's repeated denial of Mary seem to go back to Peter's triple denial of Jesus). The deeply Christian character of all aspects of the story; the basic theme of defiance and distrust; the prolonged refusal of acknowledgment of divine superiority despite divine benefaction; the final, liberating expression of contrition and subordination—all these features of "Marienkind" make it hard not to think of Thomas's skeptical demand that he touch Jesus' risen body when the girl disobediently reaches out to touch the Holy Trinity. Remarkably, the earliest extant version of the story, published in the seventeenth century in Italy, lacks the motif of the girl's finger altogether: this has been added at some later point during its evolution, presumably in the course of its transmission through a culture deeply familiar with the New Testament, as early modern Germany certainly was. Perhaps, within a northern European Christian context, such a story of disobedience and contrition reminded storytellers and their listeners so strongly of Doubting Thomas that they inserted into it this specific feature, so closely identified with him.

Viewed in this light, the fairy tale may even provide a coherent, if very lopsided, implicit interpretation of John's narrative. Certainly it transforms numerous features of the Gospel account. Not only are the characters and the plot different in many obvious ways; more important, the fundamental theological issue here is not doubt but rather disobedience. This theme is not altogether without precedent: for Jesus' words to Thomas, that he should be not unbelieving (ἄπιστος) but believing (πιστός, John 20:27) can mean in Greek not only "not unbelieving but believing," but also "not disobedient but obedient." Thus the fundamental point of the story is no longer the importance of faith even without visual evidence but rather the importance of repentance and confession. The culture of early-nineteenth-century Germany, embodied in the person of the Grimms' informant, Gretchen Wild, seems to have put a much higher premium upon obedience and submission to authority than did that of first-century Palestine.

Applying the German fable to John's narrative suggests that its authors and audiences may have believed that Thomas not only demanded to touch Jesus' body but also actually did touch it, that his doubt about the resurrection of Jesus was in fact a manifestation of his insubordination with regard to authority, that this was a terrible sin to commit, and finally that his climactic outburst, "My Lord and my God!" was an expression not so much of pious acknowledgment overcoming skepticism but rather of contrite submission overcoming arrogance. The German text seems far more preoccupied with sinners than the Greek text is, and indeed it is also far sterner with them: for the communities in which this fairy tale flourished, the final divine absolution cannot be granted unless the sinner has been made to endure enormous suffering. As it were, the momentary gap in John's account between Jesus' invitation that Thomas touch him (20:27) and Thomas's acknowledgment of Jesus' divinity (20:28) has been expanded here into many years of terrible physical distress and psychological anguish.

Thus the fairy tale, in comparison with the Gospel, is marked not only by striking similarities but also by no less evident differences. This is hardly surprising, given that we are dealing with two texts belonging to two very different genres deriving from two widely separated times and cultures; but it does raise the methodological question of how we as interpreters can tell that, despite the observed differences, the observed similarities are significant enough to justify correlating the two texts involved not just in a loose association of analogy, but in a far stronger intertextual relation. After all, not every parallel is meaningful: not every textual finger is Thomas's (the Gospel of John is not a pertinent precursor for Arthur Conan Doyle's "Adventure of the Engineer's Thumb" or for Ian Fleming's *Goldfinger*), and not every literary Thomas is a descendant of the Doubter (neither Tom Sawyer nor Tom Thumb is a Doubting Thomas, despite the former's curiosity and the latter's nickname). How, if at all, can we persuade doubters that it is useful to think of the Gospel of John when reading "Marienkind"?

In fact there is no algorithm for determining when two texts are related intertextually and when their similarities are merely accidental or due to wider generic or cultural factors. Nonetheless, two general rules can be suggested: first, that individual elements of content in themselves tend not to be significant markers of intertextuality unless they function in some clearly marked way toward the communication of central themes of the text as a whole; and second, that the more elements of different kinds, each separately linked with parallel phenomena in the precursor text, are involved in mutually supporting and systematically cohesive correlations, the likelier is their meaningful relation as a whole with that precursor. In the present case, the first rule suggests that what matters is not so much the girl's finger, but rather her touching the radiance with that finger as the incontrovertible act of disobedience; and the second rule focuses the reader's attention upon the links within the story between such elements as touching, disobedience, submission, the Virgin, the apostles, and the Holy Trinity.

"Marienkind" can be understood without the slightest acquaintance with the Gospel in a way that provides considerable satisfaction—obviously, for otherwise generations of children would not have enjoyed it—and in this regard it presents a very different case from the exegetical texts examined earlier in this chapter. But by the same token, knowing the Gospel does enrich our understanding of the fairy tale, with respect not only to its genesis (surely whoever introduced the motif of the finger into this fairy tale had heard of Doubting Thomas) but also to its intrinsic meaning (precisely its divergences from the Gospel are the clearest indicators of its own deepest ideological commitments). Comparing the fairy tale with the Gospel can throw light upon John's narrative as well, for the later text can be read as a creative response to the earlier one, implying an interpretation of it that is probably unconscious and certainly erroneous (as nearly as we can judge) but may nonetheless claim our attention both as an expression of implicit hermeneutic possibilities contained within the earlier text and as a manifestation of one way in which a later culture adopted, appropriated, and distorted the creative impulses transmitted to it by an earlier, authoritative one.

❧

The Grimms' fairy tale is like the non-Gnostic texts discussed earlier in this chapter in one crucial regard: however the tale and the texts valorize touching the holy body, none of them seems to have any doubt at all that that body not only could be touched but indeed actually was touched. Applied to the story of Doubting Thomas in the Gospel of John, this can only mean that many readers have presupposed as evident that Thomas not only demanded that he touch Jesus' body and that Jesus not only invited him to do so, but that Thomas also in fact did so. As we have seen, however, this interpretation of the Gospel account is devoid of support from the words of John's text. Gnostics, in contrast, however else they may have misunderstood or distorted the Gospel of John, seem to have recognized correctly in it the message that Thomas, despite his doubt, did not touch Jesus' risen body, but became convinced of Jesus' divinity by some other, nontactile means.

In short, Gnostics and non-Gnostics seem to have read the same text, the Gospel of John, in two remarkably different ways. To explain how this could happen, we must look at the tradition of orthodox Christian exegesis of the Gospel of John.

Exegetical Reactions: From the Church Fathers to the Counter-Reformation

We have considered a number of reactions to John's account of Thomas in which interpretation assumed the form of narrative. For these writers, John's Gospel seems to have been sanctioned not only by his own authority or by intrinsic qualities of the text, but also by the momentous nature of the characters, actions, discourses, and situations that it recounted. In their fascination with the events John narrated, such writers tried their best to penetrate through his text with an urgent and pious gaze. They sought the realities that lay beyond it and that they believed alone could save them—not words alone, not even his words, but that Word "which became flesh and dwelt among us, full of grace and truth" (John 1:14). The fewer the obstacles the text posed to their devotion, the more undistractedly they could address themselves to the Redeemer: at best, the text became a window, transparent to the very events that promised salvation—or, even better, the window suddenly, miraculously, opened, so that a holy spirit could breathe through it unimpeded onto the anxious countenances of those who were waiting to be inspired by it.

For such readers, to understand the text with due piety meant to interpret not its mere linguistic density but the authentically real events to which it gave access; and to venerate this story meant to retell it, to narrate it anew, filling the gaps, supplying the motivations, clarifying the message. John's text is lacunary; the Apocrypha supply what seems to be missing, but create new gaps in the very act of filling old ones. John's text shows a Thomas whose character and actions hover ambiguously between positive and negative values: the Apocrypha decide firmly for one or the other—thereby suppressing the problem of his evaluation rather than resolving it once and for all. John's text introduces characters whose motivations, actions, and even ontological status oscillate between contradictory possibilities: the Apocrypha choose one alternative alone—thereby violating the apparent intention of John's rich and problematic text.

Interpreting by narrating tends inevitably to devalue the source text, for the original text ends up as just one version of the events among others, while some new narrative is presented as more complete and hence as no less authoritative. However pious the authors of the New Testament Apocrypha may have been and however much they believed their narrative elaborations to remain safely within the narrow confines of a faith sanctioned by the founding text and guarded by the institutions of their religious community, nonetheless their imaginative efforts inevitably had the effect of making John's voice seem but one more in an increasingly loud and discordant chorus.

The counter-tendency to such narrative interpretations, then as always, was textual exegesis, which restored the founding text to its position of unchallenged centrality by generating a second, non-narrative, argumentative text, one that followed the first one from beginning to end of whatever section was of interest (from the individual word to the whole document) and sought to elucidate it. Against the unruly wanderings of the narrative imagination, the exegetical imperative trained the spirit in self-discipline and an ascetic concentration upon what was given and could not be freely chosen; against the typically pagan freedom to tell the holy stories in whatever way each new audience could find most plausible, exegesis restored a characteristically Jewish veneration for the inalterability of the single holy text as the hallowed word of God himself. Above all, against the potentially unchecked proliferation of stories, versions, communities, and patterns of belief, it imposed the singleness of a limited canon of authorized texts, each one in a putatively stable and unchanging form. If ordinary readers in informal circumstances tend to generate further narratives out of the narratives they experience, it usually requires strong institutional constraints to induce them to limit their discursive freedom and to focus their attention instead upon the consideration of textual exegesis. Freedom was of course not banished but was redirected, from the generation of stories rivaling the foundational texts to the elaboration of interpretations subordinated to them. And in the course of time that elaboration itself came to stand under more or less well defined and controlled systems of rules, inherited and adapted partly from Jewish tradition, partly from the great Hellenistic exegetical schools of Alexandria and Pergamon. On the textual level, the canonization and codification of the New Testament permitted, and was further reinforced by, a millennial tradition of textual exegesis; on the institutional level, this normalization was permitted, and further reinforced, by the cultural domination of an established church that could define itself as apostolic (and hence as possessing unquestionable legitimacy) and universal (and hence as possessing a monopoly on legitimacy). In the lengthy process of demarcation, stabilization, and centralization of a determinate body of holy scripture we can trace the textual outlines of that much larger process whereby the institutions of the Catholic and Orthodox churches gradually became consolidated and strengthened.

But the focus upon a small body of writings to be interpreted did not at all mean that the activity of interpretation could itself be brought to a swift conclusion. Texts change every time they are copied; even if the texts stay the same, the meanings of many of the words they contain inevitably develop over time; even if the meanings sometimes remain fairly stable, ever new audiences approach the same texts with ever new experiences and questions; even if in the short term the audiences remain fairly constant, new interpreters constantly arise for whom the earlier interpretations seem not fully satisfactory. Ordinary experience teaches that the more one tries to explain what one really means, the more one finds oneself having to

explain the explanation—how much more so when what one is trying to explain is not what one meant oneself, but what John or Mark
or Paul (or their texts) meant. The exegetical imperative has no
difficulty in establishing a single, clear starting point for the activity of interpretation, but it cannot define with equal clarity a final
ending point at which a complete and definitive interpretation has
ultimately been reached. On the island Glubbdubdrib, granted one
wish, Gulliver asks to see the ghosts of Homer and Aristotle together
with those of all their commentators. As he observes his two heroes
and the rest of the huge crowd that results, Gulliver discovers that,
contrary to what was reported through the ages, Homer was not
blind and Aristotle, so far from being a Peripatetic, could scarcely
walk. Nor did these two bear any relationship to their commentators:
"I soon discovered that both of them were perfect strangers to the
rest of the company, and had never seen or heard of them before."

With nothing to stop it and a strong internal dynamic propelling it
onward, interpretation is quite capable of going on until the end of
time—or until it is interrupted, because the institutions supporting it
have fallen into crisis and people have become reluctant to continue the effort to derive from the ancient founding texts truths
that by then seem to have only limited utility for their own very
modern lives.

❧

Various intrinsic difficulties in John's account of Doubting Thomas
might well have attracted exegetic attention in any case; but these
certainly did so all the more once his text had become established as
one of the four canonical Gospels of the New Testament. The seeming contradictions between neighboring parts of the narrative are too
blatant to be ignored—for example, Jesus can pass through locked
doors (20:19, 26) but can offer his body to be touched (20:27); Jesus
refuses Mary's attempt to touch him (20:17) but invites Thomas to
do just this (20:27); Thomas angrily demands an aggressive bodily
examination before he will consent to believe (20:25) but cries out
a hyperbolic declaration of belief, apparently without ever having

fulfilled the conditions he himself had postulated (20:28). Moreover, the statements attributed to the risen Jesus himself—his refusal to let Mary touch him because he has not yet gone up to the father (20:17), his gift to the disciples of the holy spirit and the office of forgiveness of sins (20:22–23), and his praise of those who believe although they have not seen (20:29)—are portentous in their implications yet enigmatic in their meaning.

But John 20 is of capital importance for another reason as well, for it raises, in acute form, the question of what Jesus' doctrine of resurrection from the dead really means. This doctrine is at the very center of Jesus' teaching; yet for those who could not bring themselves to believe it without receiving some sort of corroborative proof, there were only two instances of resurrection that could be cited in its support, those of Lazarus and of Jesus himself. Attention naturally focused on the latter, if only because Lazarus presumably went on to die a natural death sometime later, whereas the risen Jesus could be supposed to have lived on forever, and it was this kind of resurrection that most people were interested in. On the one hand, it is obvious that the resurrection of the son of God could not be thought to be identical in all regards with the resurrection of all humans. On the other hand, it is no less obvious that just as the fact of Jesus' attested resurrection could be considered as good evidence for a promised future general resurrection of all men, so too the nature of Jesus' resurrection might indicate the kind of resurrection those who believed in him could look forward to.

In particular, was Jesus' resurrection, and by implication that of all men, a resurrection of the body or of the spirit, and if of the body then of what kind of body? John had furnished details suggesting varying degrees of corporeality in the risen Jesus: he passes through locked doors (20:19, 26); he shows the disciples his hands and side, which must be presumed to bear the marks of all the wounds he suffered at his death (20:20); he invites Thomas to touch his wounds, and surely the invitation is seriously meant (20:27). Of these passages the first one suggests the immateriality of Jesus' resurrected body, but the second and third ones seem to imply not only its physical reality but also its continuing to bear the same signs of terrible suffering that disfigured it at the moment of its death. How were these various indications to be reconciled with one another?

※

Paul's First Letter to the Corinthians indicates that by the decade of the 50s the question of the precise physical nature of Jesus' resurrected body provoked acute anxiety and confusion, at least among the Christians of this one Greek city. Although it would be inexact to claim that what was bothering the Corinthians were questions of textual exegesis in the strict sense, there can be little doubt that they were responding to, and trying to understand, oral (and perhaps also written) reports of Jesus' resurrection that must have run more or less along the lines of John's later account. Their worries were symptomatic of deeper concerns that for many centuries would go on to shape Christian exegesis of John's narrative.

After Paul's departure from Corinth, the Christian community there, which he had been instrumental in founding, had fallen into internal strife and doctrinal disarray. Christians were suing one another in Roman courts (1 Cor. 6:1–8); against both Roman and Jewish law, one Christian man had reportedly married his stepmother (5:1–2); there was growing resentment against Paul's prescriptions regarding matters, crucial to everyday life, such as sexual license (6:9–20), marriage (7:1–16), and the eating of sacrificial meats (8:1–13). All of these difficult issues Paul deals with rapidly, effectively, and unambiguously; it is questions concerning the resurrection that he postpones climactically to the end of his letter, as the most important and difficult ones.

Here too he begins with the easier, though more fundamental issue: he reminds his readers of the *fact* of the resurrection of the dead (15:1–34). Evidently at least some of the Corinthian Christians had begun to doubt this; just what their grounds were, is far from clear. Perhaps they believed that they themselves had already been resurrected spiritually in this life by reason of their initiatory baptism into Christianity; or they thought that Jesus' resurrection was a unique exception and that only those who happened to be alive at Jesus' second coming would form part of his kingdom; or they supposed, like many Greek pagans, that only the soul was immortal; or they could not conceive that a life worth living could follow death. At any rate, they were probably not emphatically denying Jesus' resurrection, but at the very least they must have been attaching far less weight to it than Paul thought appropriate; perhaps they were suggesting that what had been raised from the dead had been a mere spirit rather than Jesus' physical body. Against such views, Paul argues for the centrality of Jesus' resurrection after death as a warrant for the central Christian belief in the resurrection after death for all mankind: "But if there is no resurrection of the dead, then Christ has not been raised; if Christ has not been raised, then our preaching is in vain and your faith is in vain" (15:13–14).

But it is here that the real difficulties arise. Up to this point, Paul has tacitly but systematically been assuming that resurrection, be it Jesus' or ours, must be bodily resurrection if it is to be any resurrection at all; but it is not at all clear what that could possibly mean. Paul can dismiss as foolish the questions posed by an anonymous worrier, "How are the dead raised? With what kind of body do they come?" (15:35), but in fact the difficulties these queries raise are far too acute for him not to take them seriously. So the last section of the letter must be directed to the *manner* of bodily resurrection. Using the quotidian (but also philosophically prestigious) analogy of the sown seed, Paul argues, passionately yet obscurely, that what dies is reborn with a new body given by God, and he goes to considerable trouble to illustrate his claim that the number and variety of possible God-given bodies are very great indeed, certainly far greater than his readers might have imagined. He makes it clear that the new body with which men will be resurrected will be entirely different from the kind of body they had in life: it will be "imperishable" (15:42, 50, 52, 53, 54), will put on "immortality" (15:53, 54), will be "raised in glory" (15:43), will be "raised in power" (15:43), will be "from heaven" (15:47, 48)—as he puts it, mysteriously, "It is sown a physical [ψυχικόν: literally, an 'ensouled' or 'living' or 'psychic'] body, it is raised a spiritual [πνευματικόν] body. If there is a physical body, there is also a spiritual body" (15:44). And yet he insists that what Christians will be reborn with will be a body—a spiritual body, to be sure, but nevertheless their very own one.

Paul is treading a very thin line here. On the one hand, he cannot ascribe to the risen body precisely the same material corporeality that had characterized it in life: for to do so would undermine all hope of a final escape from the transience and suffering of life as we know it in this world. If materially embodied life is ineluctably and radically defective, then what is the point of hoping for a reincarnation in the form of that same kind of body, for yet one more time? A defect doubled is not a benefit; pain repeated is not joy. But on the other hand, Paul does not want to deny that what is resurrected is a body, our body, of some kind: for to do so not only would imply the ultimate worthlessness of the whole material creation, but would also create enormous difficulties for understanding what kind of personal identity would be involved in the resurrection. For however we try to imagine ourselves in our deepest identity, it seems to be extremely difficult or indeed quite impossible for most people to envision themselves in total isolation from any bodily dimension whatsoever. If we are who we are at least in part because we are embodied, then what good would it do us to be resurrected without a body that demonstrates an essential continuity with the one we have known, loved, and suffered with? Without some sort of body, we could not recognize ourselves in the resurrected person. The only resurrection worth having, for many people, is one in which we are raised again in our own bodies: a resurrection not involving our body would not, in a crucial sense, involve us.

Caught between these twin impossibilities, Paul invents the paradoxical notion of a "spiritual body"—something that he can certainly name and analogize, but that neither he nor anyone else seems capable of clarifying. And in the closing lines of this section he recurs, twice, to a no less paradoxical formulation in order to designate the combination of personal continuity and radical transformation which he proposes to the Corinthians as their sole hope and their greatest belief: "we shall all be changed" (πάντες δὲ ἀλλαγησόμεθα, 15:51), "we shall be changed" (ἡμεῖς ἀλλαγησόμεθα, 15:52)—indeed, the second time he even adds the grammatically unnecessary first person nominative plural pronoun in order to emphasize that it is *we ourselves* who shall be changed. Caroline Walker Bynum puts the paradox nicely: "when Paul says 'the trumpet shall sound . . . and we shall be changed,' he means with all the force of our everyday assumptions, both 'we' and 'changed.'" We shall no longer be the same persons we were; and yet at the same time we shall be we ourselves, as changed; and moreover we shall know it.

What can this possibly mean?

❧

It is precisely this question which underlies the earliest references to Doubting Thomas among the church fathers. The first explicit discussions of Thomas in patristic texts are found in the first decades of the third century, probably a little more than a century after the composition of the Gospel of John. They occur in Tertullian and Hippolytus, in the context of their impassioned polemics against all forms of thought tending to deny the materiality of the resurrected body, be it Jesus' or ours. In his letter to the Corinthians, Paul would seem on any interpretation to have been emphasizing the radical difference between the kind of physical corporeality familiar to us in our unresurrected body and the kind of spiritual nature we can hope for in our resurrected one. But he could thereby be thought to have opened the door to Docetists, Gnostics, and others who wished to claim that Jesus' resurrected body, and our future ones, were in some way or another not fully material.

Hence Paul must be rescued by John; and Thomas would seem to be a helpful ally. After all, for any reader of John's account who understood him to mean that Thomas had not only demanded to touch Jesus' body but had also succeeded in doing so, the episode provided incontrovertible proof that Jesus' risen body really was material and was identical with the body that had hung upon the cross. It must have been tempting to interpret John's difficult and lacunary text in just this way: to deny that Thomas had actually touched Jesus would have meant depriving Christian theology of an apparently irrefutable piece of evidence in its struggle against heretical views. So it will not surprise us to find that Tertullian uses the Thomas episode against Marcion as the last and most conclusive stage in a series of proofs for the materiality of Jesus' risen body:

> For so too Marcion preferred to believe that he [Jesus] was a phantasm, and disdained the truth of the whole body in him. And yet not even in the case of the apostles was his nature seen to be a mockery, but it was trustworthy when he was seen and heard on the mountain, and trustworthy when he tasted the wine (and so too before, at the wedding in Galilee), and then it was trustworthy when he was touched by believing Thomas. (*On the Soul* 17.14 = *CChr SL* 2.806)

Tertullian's other references to Thomas are similar in content, but somewhat more disparaging in evaluation: Thomas is an example of someone who can only believe if he hears and touches (*On the Soul* 50.5 = *CChr SL* 2.856), and he is contrasted with Mary Magdalene, a believer who wished to touch Jesus out of love, not out of curiosity and incredulity (*Against Praxeas* 25.2 = *CChr SL* 2.1195–96). So too, Hippolytus' *On the Resurrection* tells how Jesus invites Thomas to touch him in order to convince the doubting disciples that he was the same resurrected as he had been when he died (Greek Fragments 7 = *GrChrSchr* 9.1.253); although this fragment of Hippolytus, transmitted by Theodoretus, does not include a specific statement that Thomas did indeed touch Jesus, we are surely intended to think he actually did. Noteworthy here is that it is not Thomas's doubts that are to be laid to rest by a tactile demonstration, but all the other disciples', so that Jesus' invitation seems to be designed to invalidate any eventual Gnostic heresies long before they could possibly be invented.

Yet given the stakes at issue, what is surprising is not that Tertullian and Hippolytus make use of Thomas for their polemical purposes, but that they make so little use of him. For aside from these passages, Thomas does not make a single additional appearance in any of Tertullian's or Hippolytus' texts—indeed, not even in those anti-Gnostic writings in which he might above all have been expected to appear, such as Tertullian's *Against Marcion* or *On the Resurrection of the Dead*. Tertullian's *On Christ's Flesh* is a case in point: not only is there no mention of the episode of Doubting Thomas anywhere in this treatise, which is devoted to determining the exact nature of Jesus' risen flesh (a question for which the story of Thomas might be thought to provide good evidence). What is more, when Tertullian, in order to prove that the risen Jesus was not a phantom, lists the bodily actions he performed, he does not include Jesus' invitation to Thomas to touch him (9.7 = *CChr SL* 2.892), and when he wishes to prove Jesus' material resurrection he does so by citing not John's resurrection account but Luke's (24:39) (5.9 = *CChr SL* 2.882). In fact, Tertullian's text does not quote a single passage from the Gospel of John later than 19:37 (at 24.4 = *CChr SL* 2.916). The same applies to another author writing anti-Gnostic polemics shortly after 200 A.D., Irenaeus, who on several occasions in his *Against Heresies* refers to the fact that the risen Jesus showed the disciples the wounds of the nails in his flesh, but never indicates either that Thomas was among them or that he or anyone else actually touched him (5.7.1 = *SC* 153.84–88, 5.31.2 = *SC* 153.392–96). Ignatius of Antioch's *Epistle to the Smyrnaeans*, written about a century earlier (if it is genuine, as is likely), already proves that Jesus was resurrected in the flesh by citing his offer to the disciples to touch him as proof that he was not a bodiless demon (3.1–3 = *SC* 10.156); but even though Ignatius claims that these followers touched him and therefore believed, his textual reference is probably to apocryphal gospels (or just possibly to Luke 24:39) and certainly not to John 20, and he makes no mention at all of Thomas.

Why the anti-Gnostic polemicists did not make more use of the evidence Doubting Thomas could be thought to afford them so splendidly is an interesting question. Perhaps the accidents of transmission play some role in reducing Thomas's presence in such texts, though this seems unlikely to be a decisive factor. Was there a preference among these authors for the other Gospel accounts of the Resurrection over John's? If so, why? Might John have been considered suspect in some way? Was Thomas perhaps too compromised by his status as a Gnostic saint to be readily used as a weapon against the Gnostics? Might some lingering hermeneutic scruple have suggested that it was not correct after all to interpret John's narrative as indicating that Thomas had really touched Jesus?

❧

In any case, the fact that Thomas entered into Christian theology within the context of anti-Gnostic polemics that emphasized the question of the materiality of Christ's body played a decisive role in the subsequent interpretation of his story in both Catholic and Orthodox Christian exegesis of the New Testament throughout late antiquity and the Middle Ages. But why should the context of origin have continued to weigh with its heavy hand upon the choices of exegetes writing many centuries later? Gnosticism was no longer a vital heresy posing an urgent danger to orthodox belief a thousand years after the heyday of Marcion and Valentinus. Yet Christian commentators continue to attack Gnostics and Manichaeans, Nestorians and Arians, Docetists and Antinomians, throughout the Middle Ages. But the polemics rapidly become ritualized, and their targets increasingly abstract. The persistence of the commentators' emphasis upon the materiality of the risen body cannot be explained in terms of the persistence of the Gnostic danger; to do so would be not only historically improbable (for the Gnostics did not in fact persist) but also methodologically circular (for it does not explain why the Gnostic heresy should have provoked so insistent a reaction in the first place). Bynum has argued that the sufferings of the martyrs were important in focusing continuing theological attention upon the problematic relation between the mutilated, very material dead body and the glorious, but no less material risen one; but martyrdom too was no less ephemeral a fashion than Gnosticism was, and so cannot explain the abiding urgency of this concern.

Part of the explanation must lie in the very traditionality of the interpretive process: despite their occasional declarations to the contrary, commentators are always engaged not only with the canonical text on which they are commenting but also, and sometimes even more intensely, with the exegetical tradition of which they are part. Indeed, the dialogue with hermeneutic precursors often seems to take precedence, at least psychologically, over the engagement with the text itself. This general tendency was greatly exacerbated by central characteristics of the late ancient and medieval Christian exegetical traditions: the stakes involved in theological questions involving an omniscient and omnipotent, monotheistically conceived and redemptively intentioned divinity were very high, so that any disagreement, even on a matter of detail, tended to be pursued to its most far-reaching and fundamental consequences. Compromise came only with difficulty, if at all; and the monopoly on scriptural interpretation often claimed by the Catholic and Orthodox churches provide only favored interpretations with the massive sanction of the church's authority and power. Symptoms of this conservatism can be found throughout this tradition: most concretely in the practice whereby whole blocks of exegetical material are repeated from author to author, anonymously or by ascription, in the form of excerpts, commentaries, translations, and so on; most frequently in the deferential citation of the unquestionable authority of the great predecessors, like Augustine and Gregory the Great. Even in the period of Scholasticism in the High Middle Ages, the rational exertions of the exegetes are directed far more toward unraveling the philosophical puzzles generated by Thomas's allegedly touching the risen body than toward reexamining the fundamental premises of the traditional interpretation that he did indeed touch it. Thus in Thomas Aquinas's magisterial commentary on John the possibility that Thomas might not really have touched Jesus is momentarily raised—but then is immediately suppressed, by means of a mere reference to Gregory the Great's authoritative claim that Thomas did touch Jesus after all (*The Gospel according to John,* chap. 20, lectio 6.4 = Ed. IV Taurinensis, vol. 2, p. 502).

But such an explanatory hypothesis in terms of institutional constraints remains one-sidedly formal, and cannot tell us why the particular problem of whether Thomas touched Jesus should have focused so many interpretative issues for so long. To understand this, we must also invoke other, more enduring factors, ones of content; and here the crucial issues were the very ones of personal identity and individual embodiedness that had already so perplexed Paul's factious Corinthians. In purely philosophical terms, the temptation presented to them and later commentators by the Gnostics is easy to understand: at least within the Platonic tradition, divinity and immortality were strictly associated with immateriality, and it was this tradition (and not that of the Epicurean or Stoic thinkers, for whom it was not difficult to conceive of material gods) that most decisively influenced both the early and the later stages of Christian theology. For philosophers trained within this tradition, the very idea of a material god must have seemed a self-contradiction: a truly material god could not truly be a god. The notion of bodily resurrection could not help but raise all kinds of insoluble difficulties. To name only a few: What would become of the reproductive and the excretory organs? Which stage in the development of the dead person's body would be resurrected? What about bodies that had been mutilated or otherwise defective at death? Or bodies that had been devoured by animals? Or ones that had been eaten by animals that had then gone on to be consumed by other people? For logically trained minds, the paradoxes that result from the very idea of the risen flesh quickly become vertiginous.

For centuries, various kinds of institutional and psychological pressures helped persuade most philosophers not to insist too much upon logical consistency. At the same time, most other people found it quite impossible not to insist upon their bodies. To conceive of any kind of a resurrected self quite devoid of the corporeal dimension intimately and necessarily associated with the unresurrected self during all its lifetime requires an enormous effort that exceeds most imaginative capacities. What use to anyone was a resurrection that would not be individual? But what kind of individuality could be imagined independent of space, time, matter, and the body? The only life we know is our embodied one in this world; our only reason to hope for resurrection is to enjoy forever an improved version of that life, not some completely different one. What good is resurrection if I cannot embrace my Aunt Betty once again? And how can I recognize her if she does not have that mole on her right cheek?

Jesus knew that if he wanted the disciples to recognize him after his resurrection he had to bear all the terrible wounds of his Passion visible upon his glorious body. If medieval artists always depicted resurrected souls as improved bodies, this was due not only to the constraints of the visual medium but also to their obligation to make themselves understandable to viewers who could not conceive of such souls in any other way than as perfected versions of real bodies with their contingent specific features. Iconoclasm, as in eighth-century Byzantium, could censor paintings; but no Iconoclasm, however rigorous, could possibly alter that.

❧

In Origen, who belongs to the generation immediately following that of Hippolytus and Tertullian, we can already see at work the strict constraints under which New Testament criticism was obliged to operate.

Despite the fragmentary nature of the evidence, two different interpretative positions emerge from Origen's repeated discussions of the Thomas episode. On the one hand, Origen shows himself keenly aware of the contradiction between those interpreters who point to Jesus' demonstration to Thomas of the wounds of the nails in his hand and those who emphasize his ability to pass through locked doors (*On Saint Luke, Homily* 17.5 = *GrChrSchr* 49².104f. = *SC* 87.257); and from the apparent contradiction between these two passages he himself derives the conclusion that after the Resurrection Jesus was "as it were in a certain intermediate state (ὡσπερεὶ ἐν μεθορίῳ τινὶ) between the density of his body before the Passion and the manifestation of a soul deprived of this sort of body" (*Against Celsus* 2.62). In such texts Origen is evidently attempting to resolve the discrepancies in John's account, but he can do so only at the cost of having to deny the full material continuity between Jesus' body before and after the Resurrection. On the other hand, in other passages Origen views Thomas as an accurate and cautious judge who is not distrustful of the reports of his fellow disciples, but instead is careful to make sure that what is involved is not just some phantasm (Fragments from Catenae 106 = *GrChrSchr* 11.4.561) and to prove that Jesus has really been resurrected in a body that offers resistance to the touch (ἀντιτύπῳ: alternatively, "one that is a copy of his real body" or "one that is identical to the body he possessed before," *Against Celsus* 2.61). If, Origen maintained, the pagan anti-Christian philosopher Celsus supposed that after Jesus' death he no longer truly existed with his wounds but instead emitted a mere image of those wounds (*Against Celsus* 2.61), the episode of Thomas proved on the contrary that Celsus was mistaken to assimilate the risen Jesus to all other phantoms and visions (*Against Celsus* 2.62). The section in Origen's *Commentary on John* which discussed the episode with Thomas is not extant; but in an earlier passage of that commentary Origen explicitly contrasts Mary Magdalene, who was not entrusted with the honor of being the first person allowed to touch the risen Jesus, with Thomas, whom Jesus invited to do just this (*Commentary on John* 13.30.180 = *SC* 222.132).

It is certainly not impossible to reconcile these two positions: Origen seems to believe that the continuity of Jesus' body before and after the Resurrection was guaranteed not by its materiality but by a kind of somatic form (εἶδος σωματικόν) sufficient to resist Thomas's touch but still capable of passing through locked doors. But by the same token he could all too easily be taken to be pointing in two quite different directions, toward a radical difference between Jesus' pre- and post-Resurrection bodies (and hence toward the less than full materiality of the latter) but also toward the full materiality of Jesus' post-Resurrection body (and hence toward the complete identity of this with his pre-Resurrection body). The same oscillation between what could seem to be incompatible positions marks Origen's view of the value to be attached to the Gnostic legends regarding Thomas found in the apocryphal New Testament writings: in one passage Origen seems to accept their validity, since he etymologizes Thomas's name "Twin" by explaining that, like Jesus, Thomas had written down secret doctrines for his disciples while speaking to outsiders in parables (Fragments from Catenae 106 = *GrChrSchr* 11.4.562); but in another, though admitting that he knows of a Gospel of Thomas, he explicitly condemns all such apocryphal texts, declaring that faith must remain content with the four canonical Gospels accepted by the church (*On Saint Luke*, Homily 1.2 = *GrChrSchr* 49^2.32 = *SC* 87.100).

Whether such apparent inconsistencies are to be explained in terms of the development of Origen's thought, either in response to adversaries or as a consequence of his own reflection, or whether they are rooted more deeply in permanent tensions within his conception of human and divine identity, his subtle attempt to combine doubts about the materiality of Jesus' resurrected body with certainty about Thomas's touching it was ultimately untenable, since it was exposed to attack on the grounds that he was attempting to mediate between one position close to those of certain Gnostics and another one that had already been established as Christian orthodoxy—and that in doing so he was stepping outside the confines of that orthodoxy. Origen's staunch defender Pamphilus of Caesarea could insist with all his force (and against all evidence) that Origen had always maintained that Jesus' body was material and remained entirely identical both before and after the Resurrection (*In Defense of Origen*, PG 17.585B, 587B, 595B, C)—but in vain. For Origen's ardent opponent Methodius of Olympus maintained no less vehemently that only a complete material continuity could guarantee the persistence of personal identity, that Origen had failed to recognize this and had thereby opened himself up to the charge of Gnosticism, and that it was above all the episode of Thomas that proved the materiality of Jesus' risen body (*On the Resurrection* 1.26.1 = *GrChrSchr* 27.253; 3.12.5–7 = *GrChrSchr* 27.408–9). The anti-Origenist dialogue *Adamantius* also cites this episode in order to prove that Jesus was composed of flesh (De la Rue 4.851d, Caspari 5.3 = *GrChrSchr* 4.178–79).

In the end, it was Methodius and his allies who carried the day.

Origen was attacked for centuries and was finally condemned for heresy at the Council of Constantinople under Justinian in 533. After Origen, the notion that Thomas had actually touched Jesus' wounds was never seriously contested throughout the Middle Ages. Origen's condemnation may have helped ensure that for many centuries Christian orthodoxy would be defined in part by its insistence that Thomas did in fact touch Jesus.

❧

In the whole of late ancient and medieval Christian exegesis, there seem to be only four moments when the possibility that Thomas might not have touched Jesus after all emerges briefly, only to be suppressed at once.

First, Augustine discusses this episode in many of his writings, including numerous exegetical, polemical, and dogmatic texts, sermons, and letters. In only one passage does he ever cast doubt upon Thomas's having touched Jesus, in his *Treatise on John* (121.5), where he notes that Jesus does not say "Have you believed because you have touched me?" (John 20:29) but rather "Have you believed because you have seen me?" Augustine's explanation for this apparent difficulty is that sight is being used here as a general term for any kind of sensory perception whatsoever; but then he adds, "And yet it might be said that the disciple did not dare to touch when the other [Jesus] offered himself to be touched; for it is not written, 'And Thomas touched.' But whether it was only by seeing, or also by touching, that he saw and believed . . ." (*CChr SL* 36.667–68); Augustine's formulation recurs, slightly varied, in the *Glossa ordinaria* once ascribed to Walahfrid Strabo (*PL* 114.424). Augustine mentions the eventuality that Thomas might not have actually touched Jesus as a mere possibility, registers it without elaborating or refuting it, and attaches so little weight to it that in the very same sentence he already moves on to the next problem.

Second, the early-twelfth-century theologian Euthymius Zigabenus, in his commentary on the Gospel of John, explains John 20:28 with the words, "When he [Thomas] saw in his [Jesus'] hands the sign of the nails, and his pierced side, then at once he believed, and did not wait to touch him." But then he immediately goes on to correct himself by adding, "But others say that after he had touched him he cried out, 'My Lord and my God!' " (*PG* 129.1489A). And a few lines later he asks how it was possible for Jesus' risen body to be touched, and answers that this happened supernaturally and by divine dispensation (ὑπερφυῶς τε καὶ οἰκονομικῶς, 1489C). Zigabenus says that the interpreters are divided; but he does not indicate just who it was who thought Thomas did not touch Jesus, and the further course of his own interpretation strongly suggests that he himself was convinced that Thomas really did touch Jesus.

Third, in his commentary on John 20:27–31, the thirteenth-century German theologian and philosopher Albertus Magnus devotes considerable attention to the problem of precisely what kind of palpability and incorruptibility are to be assigned to Jesus' risen body, given that it passed through locked doors, displayed wounds, and was touched by Thomas. At the very end he turns to the same problem which Augustine mentioned, the reference to sight alone at John 20:29: "But pay attention to what he says: 'Because you have seen me.' And he does not say: 'Because you have touched me?' Because of this, some people say that although the Lord offered his hands and side to be touched, nonetheless out of reverence the apostle did not dare to touch him. Augustine says this too, though doubtfully. But it is not known what the truth is about this, except that one can believe piously that he did touch the Lord, as a greater proof of the Resurrection" (*On the Gospel of John*, chap. 20.28–31 = vol. 24, p. 695 Borgnet). Here too the possibility that Thomas did not touch Jesus is attributed to anonymous interpreters, but is ultimately rejected as being less pious than the alternative, that Thomas did touch him.

Fourth, in his own commentary on the Gospel of John, Thomas Aquinas deals with most of the same issues as his many predecessors. Here too, as in Albertus Magnus, the Augustinian problem is taken up again together with the Augustinian solution, and a slightly novel twist is added: "But there is a second cause for doubt, since when Thomas asks, 'Unless I see and touch,' God offers him both, i.e.

touch and sight; and so he ought to say, 'Because you have seen and touched, you have believed.' I answer that we should say, according to Augustine, that we make use of the sense of sight for any sense organ whatever . . . Or we should say that Thomas became confused within himself when he saw the wounds and the scars, and before he inserted his finger he believed, and said, 'My Lord and my God'; but nonetheless Gregory [the Great] says that he did touch, and that he professed his faith at the sight" (*The Gospel according to John*, chap. 20, lectio 6.4 = Ed. IV Taurinensis, vol. 2, p. 502). Thomas is inclined to accept Augustine's solution of the difficulty; as we saw earlier, he is capable of recognizing for a moment an alternative, that Thomas did not touch Jesus—but only for a moment: then the authority of Gregory the Great intervenes to bring him back into the traditional course of the standard exegesis.

That is all. In over a thousand years of detailed, intense, devout exegesis of John 20, only two interpreters seem to have recognized on their own, and each one only for a moment, that Thomas might not have actually touched Jesus: one Latin scholar, Augustine (and a couple of authors who derive from him); and one Greek one, Zigabenus (and no author seems to derive from him).

Tradition is powerful.

❈

Minor differences of emphasis are apparent between the interpretations of John 20 prevalent in the Western medieval church and those to be found in Eastern Orthodoxy. Nonetheless, as a whole the late ancient and medieval tradition of Christian exegesis of the story of Thomas is structured by five basic hermeneutic strategies.

1. *Detextualization.* John's narrative is read not as a text composed by a human author in order to achieve certain effects upon its readers, but as a transparent window onto a set of events arranged by God in order to achieve certain effects upon the world. What passes for exegesis of the text is usually in fact analysis of the events to which the text refers. What we would recognize as the marks of John's authorial intention in so structuring his textual account as to produce particu-

lar rhetorical effects upon his readers are instead viewed as the signs of God's economy in so organizing the sequence of real events as to produce the right effect upon Christians. Thus the question why Thomas was absent from Jesus' first appearance to the other disciples is often answered by the claim that this happened by divine dispensation: God was making sure that Thomas would not be there the first time precisely so that Jesus could return a second time in order to assuage his doubt and thereby provide an important lesson for all of us (so, for example, John Chrysostom, *PG* 59.681–62 and Gregory the Great, *Homily* 26 [= *PL* 76.1201C]). God is the author of the book of the world, and the Gospel is true because it mirrors that first book faithfully.

2. *Retrojection*. The contemporary concerns of the interpreter are projected back into the events of the text as prophetic intentions on the part of the ultimate, omniscient divine author, which were expressed back then and are still fully relevant, now and always. Thomas can be said to doubt not the Resurrection itself, but the precise nature of the Resurrection, which he wants to clarify in the same way that Christian theology does (so, for example, Ambrose, *CSEL* 32[IV].519–20 and Paulinus of Nola, *Epistle* 31.6 [= *CSEL* 29.275.3–6]). So too, divine economy has ensured that Thomas would doubt, so that from the beginning any would-be future doubters would already be persuaded to believe, and any heresies would be deprived of their foundation: among the numerous examples of this interpretative claim that might be cited, see especially Gregory of Nyssa (*PG* 46.633), Cyril of Alexandria (*PG* 74.724A), Ammonius of Alexandria (*PG* 85.1520B), Paulinus of Nola (*Poem* 27 [= *CSEL* 30.262–91, esp. lines 416–24]), Petrus Chrysologus of Ravenna (*Sermon* 84 [= *PL* 52. 439A–B]), and Bruno of Asti (*PL* 165.596A–B). In general, Thomas, the Gnostic saint, is reread within the church as the fiercest champion of orthodoxy against every heresy, and all heresies are reread as versions of Gnosticism, denying the materiality of Jesus' body and the possibility of redemption for the material universe. Thomas is not only rescued from the clutches of the Gnostics: he becomes a fully convinced champion in the struggle against them.

3. *Displacement.* The focus is shifted from what appear to be the fundamental concerns of the text to secondary issues generated by larger commitments independent of it. The interpreters' certainty that Jesus' risen body was identical with his crucified one leads them to focus not upon the question of whether Thomas touched his body, which they take for granted, but upon that of how Jesus was able to enter miraculously through the locked doors of the room despite the materiality of his body: the story becomes a classic locked-room mystery. Thereby it is the quality and nature of Jesus' body that becomes the central issue in interpreters as diverse as Origen (*GrChrSchr* 49.104), Epiphanius (*GrChrSchr* 25.111–12), John Chrysostom (*Homily* 87 = *PG* 59.474), Proclus of Constantinople (*PG* 65.684A), Cyril of Alexandria (*PG* 74.725A), John of Damascus (*PG* 94.1189C and 1220–28), Hilary of Poitiers (*PL* 10.87B–88A), and Augustine (*Sermon* 247 = *PL* 38.1157). Why does Jesus' perfect, risen body retain wounds received during the course of his life? Does the risen Jesus bear wounds or scars, or images of wounds or scars, or nothing of the sort? In their focus upon such questions, the interpreters repeat Thomas's fascinated obsession with Jesus' body—something of which John himself had implicitly but strongly disapproved.

4. *Disambiguation.* The polyvalence of Thomas's attitude and character, as presented by John, is clearly felt to be intolerable by much of the tradition. So it tends to be simplified, in one direction or the other. Either Thomas is very good indeed, and is a model for what we must do and be in our lives (so, for example, Origen, *GrChrSchr* 10.561–62; Ambrose, *PL* 15.1593C–94A; Pseudo-Augustine, *Sermon* 161 = *PL* 39.2063; and John Cassian, *CSEL* 17.280–81), or, or he is very bad indeed, and is a negative example teaching us what we must at all costs avoid (so, for example, John Chrysostom, *Homily* 87 = *PG* 59.473–74). As for his disbelief, most interpreters refuse to believe the text's evidence that he is simply disbelieving (the rare exceptions include Augustine in many passages of his works, and Asterius, *Homily* 20 [= *Homily* 1 on Psalm 11]). They think otherwise, presumably in part because Thomas does end up professing belief, but also because they are uncomfortable with the notion that one of Jesus' disci-

ples might actually not have believed in him; instead, they substitute some closely related but less ambiguous concept for the one found in John's text. Thus Thomas is said to be merely slow to believe, or inclined to believe little, or curious, or a seeker, or mournful, or full of desire for Jesus, or stupid (*slow to believe:* Leo the Great, *Sermon* 73.1 = *PL* 54.394C–D, the Venerable Bede *CChr SL* 120.67, and Albertus Magnus, *On the Gospel of John,* chap. 20 [= vol. 24, p. 689 Borgnet]; *believe little:* Cyril of Alexandria *PG* 75.564A–B; *curious:* Ammonius of Alexandria *PG* 85.1520B; *seeker:* Pseudo-Augustine, *Sermon* 161.4 = *PL* 39.2063 and Petrus Chrysologus of Ravenna, *Sermon* 84 = *PL* 52.439A; *mournful:* Ammonius of Alexandria *PG* 85.1520B and Cyril of Alexandria *PG* 74.721D; *desire for Jesus:* Basil of Seleucia *PG* 28.1084C, John Chrysostom, *Homily* 87 = *PG* 59.473, and Gaudentius of Brescia, *Sermon* 18 = *PL* 20.961B; *stupid:* John Chrysostom, *Homily* 87 = *PG* 59.473, Theophylactus *PG* 124.300C, John Cassian *CSEL* 17.280, and Haimo of Halberstadt *PL* 118.494D).

But for the most part, the tradition does its best to redeem Thomas—after all, was not he too a disciple, chosen by Jesus himself? The differences between Thomas and the other disciples, upon which John insists, tend to be reduced or canceled out altogether: Thomas reverts to the condition of most or all of the others; he acts for them or with them (so, for example, Theodotus of Ancyra, *Homily* 4 = *PG* 77.1411A; Ammonius of Alexandria, *PG* 85.1520B; and Paulinus of Nola, *Epistle* 31.6 = *CSEL* 29.274–75). The very emphasis upon divine economy also tends to palliate the offense of Thomas's doubt; for if from the beginning God had been planning the whole episode for the sake of our edification, then what blame can possibly attach to Thomas?

5. *Mystification.* Although the interpreters make extraordinary efforts to render the text intelligible to their readers, their ultimate goal is to emphasize the limits of intelligibility and the inferiority of human reason before the wonders of God. The miracle of the locked door, like the miracle of Jesus' risen body, surpasses the capabilities of human understanding—which is seen to be precisely the point of the story of Doubting Thomas. Instead of a Gnostic embodiment of the

importance of knowledge and the transmission of a secret doctrine of salvation, the orthodox exegesis sees in Thomas the proof that we should not try too hard to understand and should be prepared to believe even without understanding (so, for example, Pseudo-John Chrysostom, *PG* 59.684; Hilary of Poitiers, *PL* 10.88B; and Werner of St. Blasius, *PL* 157.936C–D). Tertullian's celebrated dictum, "It is certain because it is impossible," is, in this abbreviated, decontextualized, and thereby more drastic form, only the most lapidary expression of an attitude that the church found convenient. Even Augustine, for all his strenuous and unremitting intellectual effort, could declare in this context, "Where reason fails, that is where faith is constructed" ("Ubi defecerit ratio, ibi est fidei aedificatio," *Sermon* 247 = *PL* 38.1157). For centuries, Christian intellectuals were willing, and indeed often quite happy, to apply their individual capabilities of rational criticism only up to a certain point—and then, rather than pursuing them to their ultimate logical conclusion, to sacrifice them upon the altar of institutionalized communal belief.

After all, had not Thomas himself once done the very same thing?

❧

It is only with the Protestant Reformation that for the first time a new and quite different interpretation of the story of Doubting Thomas becomes possible. German followers of Luther, like Johann Bugenhagen (*Ungedruckte Predigten*, p. 324), tend either to deny altogether that Thomas actually touched Jesus, or, if they do retain this tradition, they reduce his act of touching to the status of a mere allegory or metaphor; Calvin (*Commentaries on the Gospel of John*, pp. 370–71), followed among others by Erasmus Sarcerius (*Holiday Postilla on the Gospels*, pp. 20–24), argues that Thomas's requirement that he touch Jesus before he could believe proves that he failed to understand the difference between empirical belief based upon knowledge and true religious faith; indeed, one mid-sixteenth-century Protestant interpreter, Wolfgang Musculus, even condemns Thomas's preference of the evidence of his senses over the holy word of God, paralleling it with the preference for Satan over God, and in the end accuses Thomas of popery (*Commentaries*, pp. 957–58, observation 3). In all these regards, the encrusted and familiar habits of thirteen centuries of traditional exegesis seem suddenly to be called into question—as though the Reformers had decided to read directly the text of John itself, and not just to approach it through the mediation of the many volumes of learned exegesis that linked it with them and separated them from it.

To be sure, one must treat this impression with caution. For one thing, the collective term "Reformers" can be misleading in its suggestion of a greater degree of doctrinal harmony than in fact existed among these disparate and often highly polemical figures; and many of the seeds first planted by the Reformers did not flower until a century or more later, for example in Pietism. And yet the Protestant Reformers did tend to be more innovative in their interpretations of the story of Doubting Thomas than their contemporaries—by contrast, the Catholic humanist Erasmus, for one, was notably traditional in his account of the episode, insisting in his *Paraphrase of the Gospel of John* (ad xx.28 = *Opera Omnia* 7.645B,D) and in his reply to Stunica's criticisms of his first edition of the New Testament (*Opera Omnia* IX.2, p. 126 ed. de Jonge) that Thomas did indeed touch Jesus and interpreting Jesus' words, "Have you believed because you have seen me?" along the lines established by Augustine more than a thousand years earlier.

Second, and more important, this North European Protestant tendency does not come out of nowhere, but has its own lengthy prehistory: just as the Reformers took over their principle of "sola Scriptura" ("the Bible alone") from certain minor tendencies in late medieval theology, so too their interpretations of Doubting Thomas were not completely novel but were anticipated to a certain degree by a very few late ancient and medieval metaphorical understandings of Thomas's act of touching. In the fourth century, Ambrose allegorizes Thomas's touching of Jesus' body with his finger as the act that opens the door of resurrection for us (*PL* 15.1593C–D, 1594A). And in the twelfth century, Gottfried of Admont provides an elaborate allegorical exegesis interpreting Thomas's demand to touch Jesus' hand as the desire to understand his commandments correctly, his demand to put his hand into Jesus' side as the desire to be active and useful in the church, and his demand to put his finger in the wound left by the nails as the desire to distinguish correctly between Jesus' works and his own (*PL* 174.314B–D). But even here the difference between the pre-Reformation and Reformation allegorizations is evident: for the former accept the reality of Thomas's touching Jesus as a historical fact and then invoke the doctrine of divine economy so as to attach to this real event further symbolic significations intended by God when he devised it; the latter question the historical accuracy of the report and attribute to it, if anything, a merely spiritual significance. In this case, metaphor, for the Reformers, does not so much support literal reference as substitute for it.

The tendency of the Reformers to reduce or even to question the concreteness of Thomas's act is a direct result of some of their fundamental tendencies.

First, the Reformers' renewed focus upon the text of the Scriptures as the sole source for legitimate faith leads them to distinguish sharply between the New Testament, to which they attribute sole authority, and all noncanonical writings. Thus Luther begins one of his discussions of Thomas by peremptorily dismissing all the accounts of his activities except those in the New Testament as "stinking lies" ("erstuncken und erlogen": *The Gospel on Saint Thomas's Day* = *Werke* 17.II, p. 289); Melanchthon goes so far as to say that we "must rely upon the promises [contained in the Scriptures], even if new voices should sound out from the heavens among thunder and lightning, as on Mount Sinai" (*Interpretation of the Gospel of John*, chap. 20 = *Corpus Reformatorum* 15.433). The result is that, stripped of the various kinds of apocrypha in which Thomas had played such diverse and important roles and which continued to some degree to haunt Christian interpretation throughout the Middle Ages, John's account remained as the sole source of information for readers who wished to know more about the disciple.

Second, the Reformers' disdain for any texts outside the Gospel was extended to apply not only to the ancient apocrypha but also to the whole vast body of interpretative commentary that had gradually been built up around the slender founding texts. One senses everywhere in the Reformers a new willingness, indeed an eagerness, to break with the Catholic interpretative tradition and the hermeneutic monopoly of the church; thus Melanchthon can mention contemptuously the age-old question of the nature of Jesus' risen body and its scars, only to reject it immediately as an uninteresting Scholastic quibble (*Interpretation of the Gospel of John,* chap. 20 = *Corpus Reformatorum* 15.431). If God does indeed speak to men through the Bible, the Reformers seem to believe, then surely he ought to be able to do so directly, without needing the mediation of a human institution in order to make himself understood to mankind.

Third, this strong inclination toward the acceptance of texts as the only appropriate basis for faith leads to an emphasis upon Jesus' spoken words as they are quoted in the New Testament as the sole reliable manifestation of his divine intention rather than upon the miracles that he is also reported to have performed there. To understand what Jesus wanted us to comprehend, the Reformers take his speeches to be a far more reliable guide than his actions, to say nothing of the actions of others. Thus Luther interprets Jesus' words, "Blessed are those who have not seen and yet believe" (20:29), to mean, "The disciples do not believe in public signs, but blessed are those who have not seen and believe the Word alone" (*The Gospel on Saint Thomas's Day* = *Werke* 17.II, p. 289). So the Protestant interpreters concentrated far more upon Jesus' speeches in analyzing this episode, and far less upon Thomas's actions; whether or not Thomas actually touched Jesus becomes quite unimportant in the end.

And fourth, the Reformers' emphasis upon faith alone, rather than human works, as the sole source of redemption leads them to focus in interpreting the story of Thomas not upon what Thomas did or did not do, but upon what Jesus did or did not do. In their eyes, to presume that Thomas could actually achieve faith by touching Jesus would accord to this merely human disciple far too much autonomy and power: if he can indeed be saved, this must be due not to any action of his own but to his faith, and that faith can come only from Jesus, not from him. According to Luther, Jesus shows his hands and feet to the disciples "and especially to dear Thomas" in order to indicate to them that it is his works alone that can procure salvation and not anyone else's (*The Gospel on Saint Thomas's Day* = *Werke* 17.II, p. 294, cf. 291); and Melanchthon says that it was already Jesus' action in offering himself to Thomas that saved the latter, not anything that Thomas might have done himself (*Interpretation of the Gospel of John*, chap. 20 = *Corpus Reformatorum* 15.432). It is the deeds of Jesus that fascinate the Protestant interpreters, not those of Thomas.

We must of course not exaggerate the caesura produced by the Reformation within the history of the Christian interpretation of the story of Doubting Thomas. Even Luther accepts in one or two passages an actual physical contact between Thomas and Jesus (*Sermon on 12 April 1523* = *Werke* 10.I.2, p. 229; *Sermons of the Year 1540*, Nr. 26 [4 April]* = *Werke* 49, p. 159), as do some of his followers, like Musculus (*Commentaries*, p. 957) and Spangenberg (*German Postilla*, p. 10r). Given the power of tradition, such traces are not surprising; what is surprising is the Reformers' marked tendency to put into question the millennial view that Thomas touched Jesus. In doing so, they contribute the first genuine novelty to this exegetical tradition since Tertullian.

❧

Unsurprisingly, the Catholic Counter-Reformation responded vigorously and polemically to the Protestant challenge within the tiny field of the exegesis of John 20 just as it did in so many other larger and more important areas of contention. The Counter-Reformers of the latter sixteenth and early seventeenth centuries are no less convinced than their pre-Reformation predecessors were that Thomas did indeed touch Jesus—indeed, they seem to be far more stridently so. But for the first time they must acknowledge conspicuously that there are some who think that Thomas did not touch him, and so they now find themselves obliged, as their predecessors were not, to try to find good evidence to prove that he did. The wave of innovation started by Luther inevitably invests his opponents too; it is no longer enough for the interpreter, whatever his faith, simply to repeat traditional views: now these must be defended, if possible with new arguments, if not then at least with louder ones. The result is partly that some new arguments are indeed adduced that had not previously been invoked and partly that the traditional arguments, and the argument of traditionality itself, are now brought forward with a greater methodological awareness and polemical clarity than ever before.

A good example is provided by Alfonso Salmerón, a Spanish exegete from Toledo, who wrote a commentary on the New Testament published in 1604 (about three years after Caravaggio painted his celebrated version of Doubting Thomas). Salmerón begins by quoting Thomas's words, "My Lord and my God," and then explains them:

> These words seem to have been said by Thomas after he touched. And although some people wonder whether he did touch or did not—since the text says nothing explicitly about this matter, and Euthymius asserts that he did not touch out of reverence but remained content with the sight of Christ's presence and wounds—nevertheless it seems to be more probable, and more consonant with the truth, that he did touch. First, because Christ said to him: "Because you have seen me, Thomas, you have believed": but sight is customarily understood for every sense because of its perfection and evidence, so that everything which we perceive with the other senses, or indeed which we apprehend with our intellect, we are said metaphorically to see . . . Then [second] the very word of the beloved disciple [1 John 1] proves it . . . Third, that Thomas's finger has been preserved with veneration and is displayed in the church of the Holy Cross in Jerusalem: therefore he touched, as is reported, otherwise there was no reason why his finger should be preserved more than other people's . . . Fourth, the Fathers themselves testify to this explicitly. [There follows a long list of authorities, including Athanasius, Epiphanius, Theophylactus, Ambrose, Augustine, Leo the Great, Thomas Aquinas, and Albertus Magnus.] Fifth, reason itself proves this: first because Thomas would have obeyed the Lord when he ordered him, "Put your finger here, etc."; then because Christ

showed himself to all the senses to be recognized; then again, lest Thomas might perhaps have regretted that he did not touch, and said, "If only I had touched, then maybe I would have found something different"; and then finally for our sake, for whom this touching, and so great a slowness, were intended to be useful. (*Commentaries*, vol. 11, treatise 27, p. 216)

Salmerón is here applying the most up-to-date exegetical method available to him, the sixteenth-century Spanish Dominican theologian Melchor Cano's *loci theologici* (theological modes of argument), and is taking pains to demonstrate the harmony between his own interpretation and all the conventional sources of authority, including scripture, the church fathers, recent theologians, and the light of reason. Nonetheless, exegetically speaking, what he offers is very heterogeneous indeed. The very accumulation of arguments, which are heaped up in an order that seems quite random despite their numeration, is clearly designed to have a rhetorical effect, to silence doubters by burying them under a huge mass of incontrovertible proofs. Yet this very feature allows his profusion of demonstrations also to be read just as easily in the opposite way, as a symptom of an anxiety that no single truly decisive argument is available to prove the case once and for all: better, then, perhaps, to offer twenty bad arguments than to have to admit that there is not one good one. Salmerón's first argument is derived ultimately from Augustine's explanation of why Jesus referred only to sight; his second one misunderstands the first lines of the First Epistle of John to refer not to his having heard and seen and touched Jesus during his life but to his having done so after the Resurrection; his third one is an appeal to the sacred relic of Thomas's finger (to which we shall return later), which of course proves at most only that some people once believed that that finger might have touched Jesus, not that they were right to do so; his fourth one sets the most celebrated exponents of the tradition into battle array without demonstrating that they were fighting on the right side; and the fifth brings a list of suggestions that may indeed be new but by and large are captious and trivial.

Other sixteenth- and seventeenth-century Catholic exegetes fare no better, whether they try to bring new arguments or remain content with recycling old ones. Some, like Francisco de Toledo (*Commentaries*, vol. 2, chap. 20, annotation 27, p. 363D–E) and Juan Maldonado (*Commentaries*, vol. 2, p. 1120), are satisfied with simply listing the church fathers who thought Thomas touched Jesus. Others try to be more original. One scholar, Francisco de Ribera, suggests, ingenuously, that when Jesus told Thomas to put his finger into the wounds, John would certainly have mentioned it if Thomas had not done what Jesus told him to do (*Commentaries*, p. 504). Another, Cajetanus Potesta, reports that some people first adopt the idea, suggested by Thomas Aquinas, that Thomas became confused by Jesus' words and did not dare to touch him—but then go on to add, as a bizarre compromise solution, that Christ himself at that point grabbed the disciple's hand, brought it near the wound in his side, and made him touch it (*Gospel History*, vol. 2, chap. 91, verse 28, 3912, p. 597).

In the same years, Catholic sermons sometimes seem to take pleasure in summoning up painful images of Jesus' wounds, and in doing so the preachers often remind their audiences that Thomas proved their reality. These speakers seek to mobilize their listeners' whole sensory apparatus in order to make them empathize with Jesus' sufferings as deeply as possible, so that they will break through the barrier of self-satisfied habit, recognize their sinfulness, and change their ways.

Thus in a homily on the Passion of Jesus delivered by San Carlo Borromeo in the cathedral of Milan on March 23, 1584 (when Carravagio was about eleven years old), this leading figure of the north Italian Counter-Reformation used all the considerable rhetorical force at his disposal to make his audience read attentively, and not just in any text, but in

> this swollen and distended body of Christ, these holy wounds, the lacerations of his flesh! . . . Do you know how it should be read? This reading must move us to the point that we feel in our own flesh all the tortures which the Lord felt in his; that these nails pierce our hands and our feet, that these wounds and these injuries be renewed within

us; that we too be struck by scourges and disfigured by spittle. Listen to the Apostle who teaches us how what is written on the outside of this book must be read: 'Have this mind among yourselves, which is yours in Jesus Christ' [Phil. 2:5]; feel it, Oh children, I say, not with only one or two senses, but with all of them, apply your eyes and contemplate with care this livid flesh and these wounds; lend your ears to this mockery, these insults, finally to these blasphemies, supreme outrages to the divine glory and majesty, which inflicted deeper wounds upon Christ than the lance; smell this cadaverous stench which emanated from Calvary where our Lord was crucified, a seasoning of torture added to the numberless pains which he endured: taste this very bitter gall, this sour beverage in which wine and vinegar were mixed with myrrh; arouse the sense of feeling of which every one of your limbs is susceptible so that you think you feel all the torments of which the body of the Son of God was tortured. Oh happy he who knows how to read this book in this way! (*Homélies et discours* 350–51)

With a combination of sophisticated psychological manipulation and passionate visualization, San Carlo works on every sense organ of his audience to make them feel Jesus' sufferings as intensely and as viscerally as possible. Visualization is only one element, albeit a crucial one, in the panoply of all the sense organs, which culminates in the most basic and unsettling one of all, touch, deployed here in an insistent rhetoric that suggests not only contact with the sacred flesh, but redemptive penetration into it:

All these wounds are in effect just as many openings: it is by means of them that the Lord wants us to enter, if we wish to read. Do you not recall that after his Resurrection, still bearing upon his body the traces of his wounds, the Lord appeared to the apostles and that he said to Thomas in particular, "Put your finger here, and see my hands; and put out your hand, and place it in my side" [John 20:27]. This is the invitation which the Lord is still addressing to us today, for his desire is that we enter into his wounds and that we read in them what is written inside them. Oh, what teachings you would discover in them, Christian, if you would put out your hand!

Put your hand into these wounds and you will understand all the value of your soul . . . *Put*, Christian, your hand *into this side*, and you will understand how much God is horrified by the excesses of the flesh, by cupidity, vanity, pride, impurities . . . *Put your hand into this side* and you will recognize how beautiful virtue is. (*Homélies et discours* 352–53)

This extraordinary passage can only attain its shattering climax if the materiality, sensuality, and passion that run through it can be focused onto the envisioned image of Jesus' wounds and Thomas's act of touching them. These sacred realities demand the listeners' unquestioning belief. Nothing would have been more detrimental to the whole rhetorical impact of this saintly homily than the slightest hint of doubt concerning whether Thomas really did touch Jesus' body.

Thus by the beginning of the seventeenth century the frontier dividing the world of Christianity into two hostile camps passed not only through the map of Europe: it also divided the interpretative field surrounding John 20, opposing to each other those who doubted that Thomas had ever touched Jesus and those who were more convinced than ever that he must have done so. Upon the exiguous trace of this one exegetical difficulty, we can see the heavy shadow of momentous historic transformations.

Pictorial Versions:
Thomas in Sacred Images

We have examined Doubting Thomas in two complementary varieties of text: first, ones in which the specificity of John's account faded
away and ultimately yielded to a fascination with the events he narrated, so that these could be further elaborated in ever new narratives
devised by later storytellers hoping to get the story finally right; and
second, ones in which the linguistic materiality of John's story thick-
ened, condensed, became an object of intense attraction and systematic attention in its own right, generating ever more refined exegetic
strategies devised to demonstrate that it was not only faultless, but
infallible. In both cases, words were the indispensable medium for
the definition and propagation of traditions that demonstrated both
a rich creativity and an obstinate continuity through the succession
of many generations.

Hence my logocentric focus up to this point has not been inappropriate. Part of what makes language so fitting a medium for the transmission of the Doubting Thomas story is that the content of this
story is itself highly verbal. From Mary's opening outcry of disconsolate dismay to Jesus' climactic judgment on Thomas and on later believers, this chapter in John is articulated as a dramatic sequence of
strikingly individual verbal utterances—the thirty-one verses of John
20 contain no fewer than eighteen quotations of direct speech (20:2
Mary; 13 the angels; 13 Mary; 15 Jesus; 15 Mary; 16 Jesus; 16 Mary;

17 Jesus; 18 Mary; 19 Jesus; 21 Jesus; 22–23 Jesus; 25 the disciples; 25 Thomas; 26 Jesus; 27 Jesus; 28 Thomas; 29 Jesus). Verses 30–31 then close the story (and probably also concluded John's original Gospel) with a double reference to the written form of his account: "many other signs . . . which are not written in this book; but these are written that you may believe." For that matter, is not the first sentence of this same Gospel, "In the beginning was the Word" (1:1)?

But then again, just what sort of "Word" are we meant to think of when we read that opening sentence? The final verses specify the language of John's Gospel as written down in the form of a book, but it is only an extremely strained metaphor that could let us imagine the word announced at its opening as being in any kind of written form. Certainly, Christianity inherited from Judaism the focus upon a sacred scripture as the stable core around which the institutions of belief were to be organized, and it is an essential aspect of the self-presentation of the Gospels that they are written texts (though of course they go back to oral accounts). Yet it was not until after the Protestant Reformation that the capacity of all believers to read that scripture themselves and to found their belief upon their experience of reading it came to assume anything like the same degree of centrality in some versions of Christianity that it had long held in most varieties of Judaism. Yet even in the sixteenth century, and for that matter well into the nineteenth, most Christians were in fact illiterate—and even now, many continue to be. Any attempt to exclude the uneducated from participation in the practices of Christian belief would have contradicted Jesus' universalist message—to say nothing of being tactically not very shrewd. Thus the history of Christianity is also a history of strategies devised to mediate between a written message of salvation, on the one hand, and communities of partially or fully illiterate believers, on the other.

If we bear in mind that these Christians have been unable to read, it becomes clear that the exegetical tradition provides only a necessary, but not a sufficient explanation for the fact that many people continue to believe that Thomas really did put his finger into Jesus' wounds despite the evidence of the Gospel of John. For until the last several centuries literacy was not widespread enough in Europe to allow large segments of the population to confront even the text of John directly themselves, to say nothing of learned commentaries upon it. Instead, the Bible was mediated to them as a linguistic document by the sermons of their priests, who accompanied the text with an authorized interpretation that had been elaborated and sanctioned within the exegetical traditions of the church. Most of the small minority of believers who could study the New Testament text themselves would no doubt have found John's narrative difficult and confusing, and we may well imagine that many of them were relieved to take refuge in the church's authoritative interpretation. If the church fathers, and their local priest, concurred in telling them that Thomas had touched Jesus, and if the text of John did not blatantly contradict this claim, then who were they to question it?

Thus the single written text could only become socially intelligible by finding a place within a much wider context of oral utterances: discussed, explained, expounded, elaborated, the scriptural source provided an ultimate reference point for the more variegated oral discourse within which Christian belief flourished.

❧

But to approach such issues involving the reception of John's account solely in terms of orality and literacy is to neglect a cultural fact of critical importance: for most of the history of Christianity, the access that the vast majority of Christians have had to the Bible text, be it written or oral, has been mediated by visual representations. The mosaics and frescos on the walls of churches, like the miniatures in sacred manuscripts, never fulfill a merely decorative function but are, above all, directed toward a vital communicative purpose: they present the holy text to believers, transmitting the basic outlines of the fundamental episodes to those who do not know them, recalling to those who do the plots of the sacred stories, and illustrating for those who are more expert the specific doctrines and meanings implied by the iconography. The priest who illustrates his Sunday sermon not only by citing passages from the episodes in the Scriptures but also by pointing them out to his congregation in the mosaics or painted images arranged along the walls of his church may be taken as one paradigmatic instance of this vital interaction between verbal and visual media. But there are others as well: the individual worshipper who identifies the names of the figures represented and together with their names calls to mind the stories attached to them; the partially literate viewer who helps his less well educated fellow to decipher the explanatory inscriptions that often accompany the images; the parents who ask their children, the children who interpret for their parents. The medieval church is not only an architectonic expansion of a fully illustrated manuscript of the Holy Scripture: it is also the concrete manifestation of a fully semioticized universe, in which there is almost no detail that does not reveal itself to the pious gaze to be the bearer of a message of salvation perfectly understandable to every Christian, even the least literate.

Can it be doubted that, for most viewers, the lucid power of the visual image tended to prevail over the ambiguities of the spoken word, to say nothing of the obscurities of the written one? We tend to emphasize the importance of icons especially in considering the Orthodox traditions; but there are few varieties of Christianity in which such aids to visualization have not played a significant role. Indeed, even Luther—despite his stubborn insistence in according the sole theological privilege to the Word of God—was sensitive to the power that visual images could exert in shaping believers' moral intelligence. For the text can be animated only by the exercise of the listener's or reader's own visual power, which may remain uncultivated or relatively limited. But the pictorial or sculptural image, thanks to the artist's fertile imagination and refined technical skill, can be immediately intelligible, presenting itself as a second reality sometimes no less vivid than the viewer's own.

In Byzantium, the Iconoclastic controversy temporarily interrupted the long-lasting tradition of the propagandistic use of visual representations of sacred scenes—but only temporarily. In the West, where it was not until the Reformation that the display of religious images in churches was widely assailed, this tradition was never seriously questioned for well over a thousand years. In the early fifth century, Paulinus of Nola gives an entertaining account of his application of sacred paintings to the wall of his church in order to strengthen the Christian faith of the illiterate local peasants ("peasantry of unbroken faith but unlearned in reading," *PL* 61.660, Poema XXVII, line 548)— or at the very least to distract them temporarily from their festive appetites for food and wine. Two centuries later, Gregory the Great wrote two letters to Serenus, Bishop of Marseille, in which he provided a classic formulation of the doctrine that religious paintings were for the illiterate what religious texts were for the educated:

> That is why an image is displayed in churches, so that, at least by looking on the walls, those who are ignorant of letters can "read" what they are incapable of reading in manuscripts. (*Epistle* 9.105, *PL* 77.1027–28)

> For what scripture provides to those who read it is provided by an image to the laymen who view it, since even those who are ignorant see in it what they should comply with, those who are ignorant of letters "read" in it. Whence an image has the value of reading, above all for laymen. (*Epistle* 11.13, *PL* 77.1128)

Throughout the Middle Ages Gregory's formulations were cited repeatedly in the context of what came to be known as the doctrine of *muta praedicatio* ("preaching without words"). Sacred images were not to be venerated as religiously efficacious in their own right—unlike the statues of the gods in pagan temples for their heathen worshippers, and despite the frequency with which various forms of Christian superstition too have yielded to the temptation of idolatry. Instead, these pictures and sculptures were to act as mere signifiers, pointing to something that was higher than they and genuinely sacred, the truer world of religious episodes and figures for which they were to serve as the community's instructors and admonishers.

Thus the history of visual representations of the story of Doubting Thomas is not of merely ancillary or antiquarian interest, but is rather an inherent, indeed an essential component of any full account of the reception of John's narrative. For images of Thomas have had at least as important a role in determining the understanding of his story

among Christians and non-Christians alike as any written texts—
perhaps even including the Gospel of John itself—could possibly
have had.

❦

The iconographic tradition of Doubting Thomas is long and complex. We may enter into its riches through the portal of a particularly impressive and significant version, painted by Michelangelo
da Merisi, better known as Caravaggio (Ill. 1). The painting probably dates from around 1601, and may have been commissioned by
Marchese Vincenzo Giustiniani for his private collection and painted
while Carravagio was living in Rome in the house of Cardinal
Ciriaco Mattei (but the early reports are contradictory and incomplete, and there is much uncertainty regarding all these indications).
In any case, by 1606 the painting was included in the Giustiniani collection, and with the acquisition of this collection by the royal family
of Prussia in 1816 it moved to Berlin. Today it is displayed in the picture gallery at the Neues Palais of Sanssouci in Potsdam.

Caravaggio's *Doubting Thomas* serves well as a focus around which
to organize the complex iconographical traditions of this story, not
only because of its intrinsic high quality but also because of its considerable historical significance. For Caravaggio's painting has a rich
and sophisticated relation to earlier treatments of Thomas's doubt; at
the same time, from the very beginning it seems to have had a profound impact on many viewers. We can best judge this by its considerable influence on other painters, who in their own paintings display their interpretative responses to the paintings that have most
moved them. No other painting of Caravaggio's was copied as frequently during his lifetime as this one was. Four copies are known to
have been made and shown within a few years after the original was
first displayed, including one in Cardinal Mattei's own collection.
And for decades thereafter, painters like Rubens and Strozzi (see Ills.
24 and 25, below) demonstrated that the best, and perhaps the only,
way for many other artists to treat the theme of Doubting Thomas
satisfactorily was to think their way critically through Caravaggio's

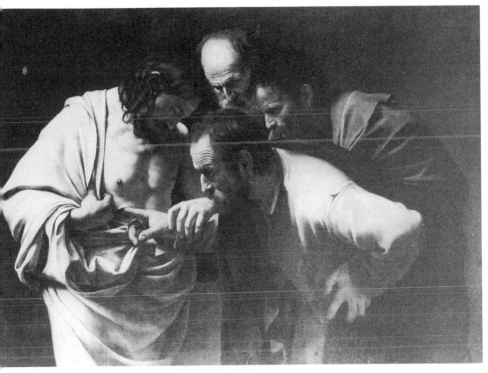

1. Caravaggio, *Doubting Thomas*, ca. 1601.
Gemäldegalerie, Neues Palais, Sanssouci, Potsdam.

compositional choices. We shall turn later to interpretations of Caravaggio's painting versions like these seem to imply; but for the moment it is enough to hazard the generalization that, for many artists since Caravaggio's time, to see Doubting Thomas is to see him as Caravaggio did.

❧

What do we see when we look at Caravaggio's *Doubting Thomas?*

We see three men, and an other. Their four heads form a perfect cross, only slightly off-center to the left in the upper half of the painting. In their outlines, the four of them compose various diagonals, triangles, and other geometric figures of mathematical precision. But the diversity of their color, attitude, age, and other characteristics divides them sharply into various contrasting groups.

They stand in an abstract, unidentifiable space before an obscure, indistinguishable background. Cut off from any identifiable setting, they seem to bear their meanings entirely within themselves, in their own attributes, postures, and gestures—that is to say, in an entirely implicit and unstated relation to earlier iconographic traditions—and are presented to us as curious specimens for our inspection, or as venerable icons for our worship. The light falls upon them from our space, high up on our left, and picks out various areas and details—Jesus' body, wound, and hands, the disciples' foreheads and shoulders—while leaving others—above all, irritatingly, provocatively, Jesus' face—in dark shadow.

On the left stands Jesus. His skin is pale—sepulchrally so—and he is clothed in a light-colored winding sheet that is draped around him like a classical philosopher's robe. His body is posed statuesquely, but its build is slight, delicate, almost feminine—a subtle nuance of effeminacy is conveyed by the long, lank hair partly gathered behind his ear, and by the prominent nipple and curve of his right breast, accentuated by a cross-shaped shadow along his chest. His neck is sharply bent and his face is directed downward. The deep shadow on his countenance allows us only to recognize its features but not to determine any emotion that might be animating them; aside from the fact that his gaze seems to be fixed upon his left hand and his mouth seems to be slightly open, we can tell nothing. With his right hand he is pulling back his mantle like a theatrical curtain, baring his breast and wound for a dramatic visual and tactile inspection. But it is in his left hand that much of the energy of this painting is concentrated. For Jesus' left hand has seized Thomas's right wrist with a virile, indeed superhuman power which contrasts sharply with the delicacy of his body. But just what is the precise intention expressed by this gesture? Is he guiding Thomas's hand? Is he forcing Thomas's finger farther into the wound? Is he stopping it from penetrating any farther? We cannot tell. Jesus' gesture expresses an absolute force and control, but its purpose remains entirely hidden from us. Perhaps, if Jesus' face were illumined, his expression would reveal the answer to these questions—then again, perhaps not.

The three disciples are painted in the deep red and brown colors of blood and earth; they embody a forceful vitality, betokening not only life in general (as opposed to death), but also terrestrial, common, vulgar life in particular (as opposed to ideality and abstraction). Their clothes are rude, peasant cloaks; their bodies seem burly, stocky, muscular; their hair is carelessly shorn, their beards untrimmed; they are all at least one generation older than Jesus. All three express varieties of extreme tension. Thomas's gaze, like that of the disciple on the right, seems to be directed at the exact point where his finger vanishes into Jesus' wound; the older disciple in the background seems, like Jesus, to be staring at Jesus' left hand gripping Thomas's wrist. But while of the other two disciples we can see very little besides their concentrated stares, Thomas's whole body expresses a remarkably dynamic tension. He stands coiled like a spring: his left hand propped on his hip for support, his left elbow thrusting out disturbingly into our own space, his whole body is focused upon the movement of his finger and upon his gaze which follows it. At the point where his left upper arm joins his shoulder, the tension of his stance has burst open a seam in his jacket: this vertical tear in the fabric of his garment is symmetrical with the horizontal gash in the skin of Jesus' body. We see both holes; Thomas sees one of them, and touches it.

But what Thomas does is not merely to touch Jesus' wound; rather, Caravaggio has used all the artistic resources at his disposal to lend Thomas's gesture an active, dynamic quality, so that we seem to see his finger gradually penetrating deeper and deeper into the wound. The viewer's gaze is directed in a forceful downward spiral that begins at the brightly lit bald forehead of the older disciple who is standing in the background staring downward, then moves forward and down toward the right to the spot of light on the forehead of the other disciple standing on the right staring down and to the left, and finally moves along the line of his gaze through Thomas's own fixed stare across the temporary visual obstacle of Jesus' fingers to reach climactically Thomas's own finger, whose tip we can surmise but not see, since it is hidden in the wound. Reinforcing this vertical spiral is another, horizontal one which draws us irresistibly into the painting by beginning at the point of Thomas's uncannily projecting left elbow closest to us and moves back into the picture plane along his left upper arm through the bunched muscular expanse of his shoulder, then extends along his right arm through Jesus' hand to the same truncated fingertip. The impression of movement is further reinforced by the small fold of brightly lit skin above Jesus' wound, which seems to be yielding to the pressure with which Thomas's finger is pressing against it.

The result is that Thomas's inquisitive gesture takes on a drastic, energetic, almost brutal quality. The contrast between the elegance and delicacy of Jesus' wounded body and Thomas's crude violation of it is concentrated in the vulva-like form of Jesus' wound, the stiffly erect shape of Thomas's probing finger, and, in what is perhaps the single most disagreeable detail of all, his dirty, blackened thumbnail. We need not search for hidden psychoanalytic meanings for these unequivocally sexual overtones: it is enough to recognize them as part of the rhetorical strategy of this painting, designed to evoke the reader's emotions of compassion, horror, outrage, and disgust. We seem to be viewing not an inspection, but a rape. But if so, can we be quite sure that we can tell who is raping whom here? Thomas's finger is indeed penetrating Jesus' wound. But what is the meaning of the gesture with which Jesus has seized Thomas's hand, and what is the emotion we seem to be able to read expressed upon Thomas's countenance?

More generally, how are we to characterize the general import of this painting of Caravaggio's as a whole? Will we understand it better if we take it as expressing religious faith or skeptical doubt? Do we see in this painting more a miracle of faith that is embodied in the risen though mortally wounded Jesus and seems to be recognized by the disciples, or more an obstinate disbelief that demands the graphic materiality of a probatory test before it will accept the reality of Jesus' wound? In his 1990 book on Caravaggio, Maurizio Calvesi reprinted an earlier essay entitled "Caravaggio or the Search for Salvation," in which he argued that this painting "testifies not so much to doubt (one might say) as rather to a certitude which has been firmly acquired"; but two years later, Ferdinando Bologna took this same painting as emblematic for what he called "the incredulity of Caravaggio" in his own book-length study of the painter which bore this title and in which he maintained that a rigorous demand for evidence and verification, as was typical of contemporary natural science, was one of the painter's salient characteristics. Which Caravaggio, and which *Doubting Thomas*, if either, shall we prefer?

❧

At first glance, the iconography of Doubting Thomas might be thought of simply as a minor variation upon a traditional image in which Jesus shows us his wounds so that we can believe in his resurrection. In countless pictorial images (Ill. 2) and a few sculptural ones, Jesus presents himself to our view and draws our attention to his graphically depicted wounds. The ultimate textual sources for such a scene are the Gospel episodes in which the risen Jesus shows his wounds to his disciples (Luke 24:39–40, John 20:20), but this iconographic tradition is not to be understood primarily as a historical illustration of an episode in the Gospel narrative. The viewers to whom Jesus is addressing himself in these images are not so much the disciples in a particular moment of the past, as rather ourselves in our fallen present time and in Jesus' redemptive timelessness. Seeing those wounds, we are meant to recall our own state of sin and the sacrifice God has made for us; the image functions persuasively to steel our resolve and help secure our salvation. If the image in question is painted and not sculpted, the impression of three-dimensionality necessary to convey to the viewer a representation of Jesus' wounds can only be the result of an optical illusion created by the painter's technical skill upon the two-dimensional surface of the canvas: an artistic illusion must convince us of a redemptive truth.

2. Petrus Christus, *Christ as Savior and Judge,* ca. 1450.
Birmingham Museum and Art Gallery.

No doubt the message of the images of Doubting Thomas is at least in part likewise directed toward us as viewers, with the very same function and paradox. But this time we ourselves, as viewers, have entered into the picture and appear in the guise of Thomas, who is always represented inspecting Jesus' wound. To transpose a figure for the viewer into the visual plane of the image and to place him there together with the Redeemer upon whose wounds that figure gazes is to invent no innocent variation: it sets up powerful new complexities and tensions. For now the relation between Savior and viewer not only is enacted by the picture but is also represented by it, so that we find ourselves introjected into it. We discover an image of our own viewing that cannot help but deeply influence the nature of our own response to what we see.

But what is more, the identification of this figure for the viewer as Doubting Thomas and not as just any worshipper whatsoever immediately links the image we see to a specific moment in a familiar story, so that the picture comes to function both as a reminder of a distant past and as an indicator of an anguished present. Thomas both does and does not represent us: we must strive to be as like him as possible in certain regards and as unlike him as possible in others. Moreover, the fact that Doubting Thomas asked not only to see Jesus' wounds but above all to insert his fingers and hand into them raises a further paradox: for a painting can only be appreciated by being seen, not by actually being touched. Thus a pictorial image of Doubting Thomas must try to persuade us to believe in Jesus' resurrection by permitting us only to see, and not to touch, an image of someone who achieved notoriety for claiming that seeing is not enough and that only touching provides real proof.

It is along the fault lines of this field of paradoxes, involving visuality and evidence, proof and belief, truth and illusion, sight and touch, recognition and self-recognition, that the artistic traditions of Doubting Thomas take shape and develop through the centuries.

❦

Images of Doubting Thomas do not begin to appear until the late fourth century, rather later than visual representations of other

3. Scenes from the New Testament: sarcophagus relief, ca. 400.
S. Celso, Milan. Doubting Thomas is at the far right.

scenes from the story of Jesus' resurrection. Probably the earliest still
extant is found on a sarcophagus relief in the church of San Celso in
Milan dating from about 400 (Ill. 3). Did patrons hesitate to concentrate artists' attention upon someone whose fame derived from
the fact that he had doubted the divinity of Jesus? Be that as it may,
once these images begin to be produced they become very popular
throughout the Middle Ages, in both the West and the East—indeed, perhaps somewhat more so in the latter, where icons showing
the so-called *psilaphisi* ("touching") continue to play a prominent role
in Resurrection cycles to this day.

Two basic trends in medieval representations of the saint can be
identified.

First, the image of Doubting Thomas always forms part of a cycle
of holy images, and never stands alone. Three such cycles are of particular importance in medieval depictions of the saint: the Passion
and Resurrection of Jesus; the missionary activity and martyrdom of
Thomas in India; and, to a much lesser extent, the death and As-
sumption of the Virgin and her gift of the holy girdle to Thomas. Although a full account of the iconography of Thomas would have to
consider all three of these traditions, I will limit my discussion to the
first one. For this is the only one that derives solely from the account

in the Gospel of John (whatever visual or verbal mediations it may have passed through along the way), whereas the other two refer back to later legends of the saint.

Second, Doubting Thomas, like all other characters represented in medieval sacred depictions, is always portrayed in full figure. Whether the image is as tiny as an elegantly worked tenth-century Byzantine ivory tablet in London which measures a mere 4.2 × 5 cm (Ill. 4) or as vast as the late-twelfth-century mosaic in San Marco in Venice (Ill. 5), it invariably shows the figure in its full vertical extension from head to foot. Therefore emotion can be conveyed not by facial expressions, which are scarcely distinguishable, but only by more conspicuous means: the posture and gesture of the body, limbs, and head as a whole; the coloring and lighting; the attitudes of the other figures.

These two features conspire together to make identifiability the primary goal of these images, not the transmission of a specific interpretation of the action represented in them. Of course some view of the nature and value of Thomas's character and actions is always implied by the specific manner in which these are depicted. Yet the location of this image within a narrative sequence, combined with the restriction of the representations to full figures, sets narrow limits to the kinds of detailed interpretations that can be suggested. Instead, the viewer usually seems to be supposed to be satisfied with simply succeeding in identifying the figures and actions represented.

The very possibility of this identification is based in part upon the strictly maintained iconography of the details within the image itself—Jesus, bearded and fully clothed, is most often standing centrally with his (usually right) arm raised while he pulls aside a fold of his garment with his (usually left) hand in order to expose no more (or very little more) than the wound on his (usually right) side; Thomas, usually beardless until the thirteenth century, usually bearded thereafter, is almost always crouching or approaching on Jesus' (usually right) side and is touching Jesus' wound with an extended finger of his outstretched (usually right) hand; the other disciples, usually ten of them, surround the scene, usually on both sides;

4. Scenes from the New Testament: ivory tablet, tenth century. Victoria and Albert Museum, London. Doubting Thomas is in the far right corner of the facing page.

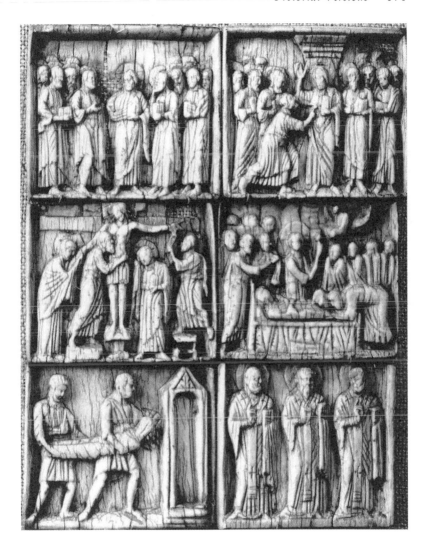

5. The women in the garden, and Doubting Thomas: mosaic, ca. 1190.
San Marco, Venice.

the action most often takes place within a room or house and in front of a closed door.

However, it is only in part that this internal logic establishes the identifiability of the scene. Instead, it is above all the relation between this scene and other ones depicted together with it or implied by it that makes it possible to tell just which one this is. For one thing, this scene is placed syntagmatically (to adopt Roman Jakobson's linguistic terminology) within a sequence of identifiable episodes from Jesus' Passion and Resurrection, such as the Crucifixion, the women at the tomb, the appearance at Emmaus, and so forth; and it is rendered distinguishable from each of these by a series of evident similarities and differences.

Above all, it is the paradigmatic parallels and contrasts with the scene in which Mary Magdalene mistakes Jesus for the gardener that help most significantly to establish the meaning of the scenes of

Doubting Thomas. Just as in the text of the Gospel of John the two episodes of "Do not touch me" (or *"noli me tangere"*) and of Thomas's doubt symmetrically structure chapter 20 as a whole, so too within the pictorial traditions derived from that text the images of Mary and of Doubting Thomas form a structural pair in which the meaning of each image derives from the binary opposition of highly determinate similarities and differences established between them.

Consider, for the sake of convenience, an attractive example from the German Renaissance, the two images painted by the workshop of Martin Schongauer in the fourth quarter of the fifteenth century on two adjacent panels in the Altar of the Dominicans at Colmar (Ill. 6). What links the two images is that these are the only two scenes, both in this Altar and in other depictions of the events after the Passion, in which the resurrected Christ stands erect (often in the center) and is approached on the side by a single other person. This fundamental similarity is what gives to all the many differences between the two images their full significance: in the one case Jesus' interlocutor is always a woman, in the other always a man; in the one she almost always kneels, in the other he usually crouches; in the one Jesus always refuses her, in the other he always accepts him; in the one Jesus almost always turns away from her, in the other he always turns toward him; in the one Jesus almost always stretches his arm downward toward her, in the other usually upward away from him; in the one there are never any witnesses, in the other there usually are, the disciples; the one always takes place outdoors in a garden, the other almost always indoors within a house.

And above all, there is virtually never any direct physical contact whatsoever between the two figures in scenes of *"noli me tangere,"* while there almost always is in ones of Doubting Thomas. The empty central space that separates the bodies of Mary and Jesus in the *"noli me tangere"* of Schongauer's workshop, defined by the dynamic tension with which Mary reaches for Jesus and Jesus moves away from her and delimited by the minimal space between her outstretched fingers and his, is an emotionally charged locus of intense longing and keen disappointment. In contrast, the central image of contact with which

6. Workshop of Martin Schongauer: left (Ill. 6a) *"noli me tangere"* and right (Ill. 6b) Doubting Thomas, from the Altar of the Dominicans, last quarter of the fifteenth century. Musée d'Unterlinden, Colmar.

7. Wounded Amazon: left (Ill. 7a)
Sosicles from Phidias?; right (Ill. 7b)
Mattei from Cresilas? Museo
Capitolino, Rome.

Jesus' hand holds Thomas's wrist and Thomas's finger touches Jesus' side recompenses for the melancholy of Jesus' refusal of Mary's desire and provides a consoling image of communication between man and god (purchased, to be sure, at the cost of Jesus' wound, to which Thomas's finger and our eyes are drawn). Thus one reason why Thomas is almost always shown touching Jesus in pictorial representations is that this element forms an indispensable part of the basic semiotic system which differentiates him structurally from Mary Magdalene; we shall see shortly that there is another important reason as well.

Within the Doubting Thomas tradition in the Middle Ages, Jesus is normally shown with one arm raised. Why? Nothing in the text of John or in the logic of the image itself seems to require such a gesture, yet it forms an intrinsic part of this tradition for a thousand years. It seems most likely that it has been inherited by Christian iconography from a "pathos formula" (to adopt Aby Warburg's term) in ancient Greek and Roman art whereby a wounded or exhausted figure—most notably an Amazon (Ill. 7), but also, for example, Adonis or Aeneas—raises his arm to support him- or herself upon a spear. Emotionally, the gesture denotes weariness or languor; at the same time the raised hand draws our eyes to the sculpted figure, soliciting our attention and compassion. Moreover, if the figure is wounded in the side, the gesture frees that part of the body for our gaze; and if it is a woman, it lifts her breasts up and outward, suggestively, provocatively.

It remains uncertain whether or not a direct causal link can be established between Jesus' raised arm and that of these pagan sculptures. It is worth noting in any case that Adonis is frequently found on late ancient sarcophagi, and that the combination of eroticism and suffering embodied by the wounded Amazon seems to have made this one of the most popular sculpture types in antiquity—twenty-eight statuary copies have been found, distributed throughout the whole Roman Empire, to say nothing of the countless gems and miniatures that popularized this image at a more affordable price.

In any case, the very uselessness of the gesture in the case of Jesus, the fact that it was not constrained by a determinate situational logic, gave medieval artists considerable leeway in interpreting it as they chose—but always within the limits of the canon of identifiability. In the sarcophagus of San Celso (Ill. 3), Jesus seems to be doing nothing more than exposing his side; perhaps he is covering his head, though why he should do so is unclear. In the tenth-century ivory tablet in the Victoria and Albert Museum (Ill. 4), it seems that he is saluting

Thomas, and may also be blessing him. In the mosaic of San Marco (Ill. 5), he is exposing the wound of the nail on his hand, and may also be bestowing a blessing upon the viewers. In other cases he appears to be performing a typical declamatory gesture of the classical orator (in which case we are no doubt intended to recall his utterances to Thomas during this episode in John's narrative), or pointing up to the heavens to indicate that it is divine salvation which is the ultimate goal of the believer's faith. Rarely, he does not raise his arm but uses it for some other purpose: to point to the wound, lending it even greater emphasis; to invite Thomas to place his finger in the wound; exceptionally, to grasp or even seize Thomas's arm, perhaps to indicate that it is his wish that Thomas touch him or even that this is happening against Thomas's will.

As for Thomas, he is almost always shown actually touching Jesus' wound—the medieval exceptions in which he does not actually touch the Savior's body can probably be counted on the fingers of one hand. One reason for this has already been indicated: the systematic contrast with Mary in *"noli me tangere."* But there is another reason, one dependent upon the constraints of the visual medium. In a picture (especially in one that does not show facial expression but only bodily posture), one cannot easily represent a modal verb: one can show "he touches," but hardly "he should touch" or "he may touch" or "he must touch" or "he wants to touch." How, then, can a painter show Thomas's desire to touch Jesus' wounds? If he merely shows Thomas pointing with his finger toward them, he will be taken to be representing someone who is signaling Jesus' wounds, demonstrating their reality and significance; and then there will be no reason to identify this figure as Thomas (for there were others too for whom this would be no less appropriate a representation). The only thing that distinguishes Thomas from all other characters in the New Testament narratives is his expressed desire to put his finger and hand into Jesus' wounds. So there is no other way for the artist to represent Thomas in an unmistakably identifiable manner than by showing him actually touching the wound.

In most representations, Thomas is shown in an oddly crouching or stooping posture beside Jesus (Ills. 3, 4, 5). This tradition has evident pictorial advantages: visually, it places Thomas in an inferior position next to Jesus and helps viewers to focus their attention upon the true protagonist of the episode, Jesus with his wounds. Moreover, in dramatic terms, this posture brings Thomas's head down closer to the height of Jesus' side wound and to his own probing hand, indicating thereby more clearly that Thomas's desire is both to touch Jesus' wound and to see himself doing so. But the structural contrast with Mary Magdalene, who in the *"noli me tangere"* tradition is always shown kneeling before Jesus, suggests another significance for this motif. For crouching is an uncomfortable, usually temporary posture halfway between standing and kneeling. A standing Thomas would be defiantly unbelieving; a kneeling Thomas would already be fully believing. The Thomas of John's narrative is both: and so must the Thomas of medieval iconography be if he is to be identifiable. If we wish, we can interpret the very instability of his crouching posture as an expression of a dynamic process: Thomas is shown in the process of falling gradually to his knees; he began by standing up, expressing doubt, but has already started to fall to a position expressing adoration; once he reaches a completely kneeling position he will have fully acknowledged Jesus' divinity and can be thought to be crying out, "My Lord and my God!" and thereby fulfilling Jesus' command, "Do not be faithless, but believing'" (John 20:27–28).

As for the other disciples, most medieval depictions show all ten of them, present as witnesses, just as in the Gospel narrative (Ills. 4, 5). In comparison, the representations that include only one other disciple or a few other ones are far less numerous and can be explained as the result of spatial or compositional constraints (Ill. 3). Almost always, the ten witnesses are gathered together into the same visual plane, in one or two compact groups: they represent a coherent community of largely undifferentiated, fully convinced believers. Thomas, by contrast, is revealed by his placement, posture, and action to be (still) fundamentally different from them: an individual, who transgresses not only the visual symmetries and boundaries of the chorus of believers but also the unquestioning solidity of their

faith. In some depictions, this contrast between the group and the individual can come to assume an accusatory dimension, indeed, in a
few cases, almost a menacing one.

Finally, the location in which this episode takes place is usually
identified as being inside or in front of a house or a room; often
the indication consists of nothing more than a prominent doorway
placed centrally behind the figure of Jesus (Ills. 4, 5). In literal terms
this locale recalls John's narrative, in which Jesus came to the disciples through the locked doors behind which they had sought protection, and thereby helps further both to anchor these images in the
Gospel story and to recall to the viewer further details of it. But it can
hardly be doubted that this represented doorway has a metaphorical
sense as well: it is also the gate to heaven, to eternal life, which will
remain closed forever to the unbeliever but is open for those who believe, on condition and by means of their faith and Jesus' mediation.
Theologically, this figural meaning must be taken to be at least part,
perhaps even an essential part, of the message that such medieval
representations of Thomas intended to convey to the communities of
their viewers.

❧

In certain regards, the images of Doubting Thomas produced during
the Renaissance display a high degree of continuity with the medieval ones. All representations are still full figure, the iconographic elements typical of the medieval representations tend to be maintained, cycles of images of which the scene of Doubting Thomas is
an integral part are still occasionally found. But in the Renaissance,
for the first time, we also find solitary representations of this episode
that are not integrated into any larger narrative cycle. In such cases,
the identifiability of the image can no longer be entrusted to its specific syntagmatic location within a visible narrative sequence. Rather,
identification must depend partly upon the competent viewers' recognition of the traditional iconographic elements within the picture
itself, and partly upon their memory of other images to which this
one is related paradigmatically, such as *"noli me tangere."* These repre-

8. Cima da Conegliano, *Doubting Thomas*, 1504. National Gallery, London.

9. Girolamo da Treviso, *Doubting Thomas*, 1505–1506. San Niccolò, Treviso.

sentations of other scenes, even if not physically co-present, continue to contribute latently to the meaning of this image by their structural relation to it.

In northern Italy, especially in the Veneto, the basic medieval traditions are maintained with considerable continuity, but there are significant innovations in detail. In Cima da Conegliano's painting of 1504 in the National Gallery in London (Ill. 8), as in Girolamo da Treviso's painting of 1505/6 in S. Niccolò in Treviso (Ill. 9), we see two large altar paintings evidently commissioned and intended for public worship. As in the medieval images, Jesus is the central figure around whom all the others are arranged, Doubting Thomas is represented as bearded and stooping or moving in an unstable, dynamic posture, the episode is located in what is easily recognizable as a room, and the other disciples are depicted as a compact community of witnesses (with the addition, in the bottom register of Girolamo's painting, of contemporary witnesses, apparently including the patron). In Cima's painting, Jesus extends his right hand downward toward Thomas in a gesture of invitation; in Girolamo's, he grasps Thomas's hand and pulls it to the wound—both motifs have medieval precedents. New in both, as we might expect, is the greater degree of individuation of the characters, the concentration upon the expression of emotion through facial as well as bodily gestures, the perspectival interior space of the room, and, in Cima's painting, the relatively realistic depiction of landscape through the two apertures set into the wall.

But the most important novelty in both paintings is the representation of Jesus in heroic half-nudity, garbed only in a light-colored winding-cloth which he wears like a philosopher's mantle. Revealed by his partial nudity, Jesus' statuary elegance in the paintings of this tradition and his evident health and vigor in spite of the visible wounds provide a compelling image of the miraculous perfection of the body of the resurrected Jesus, especially in contrast to the old age, full and heavy clothing, and cramped attitudes of most of the disciples. Furthermore, the philosophical implications of his garb identify him as someone who possesses and communicates a timeless

10. Marco Pino, *Doubting Thomas*, 1573. Cappella Teodoro, Duomo, Naples.

11. Mariotto di Nardo, *Doubting Thomas*, after 1395.
Former Monastery of Santa Brigida al Paradiso, Florence.

12. Bicci di Lorenzo, *Doubting Thomas*, ca. 1439. Santa Maria del Fiore, Florence.

13. Andrea del Verrocchio, *Doubting Thomas*, 1463–1483. Orsanmichele, Florence.

and redeeming wisdom, just as the classicizing elements of his posture and depiction set him outside the historical moment inhabited by the disciples and temporarily visited by himself, and identify him as someone who dwells most properly in a transcendent, timeless dimension.

This North Italian tradition exerts considerable influence upon generations of painters throughout Italy (and elsewhere in Europe), as can be seen for example in the Sienese painter Marco Pino's 1573 altar painting in the Cappella Teodoro of the Duomo at Naples (Ill. 10). But at the same time, beginning as early as the end of the fourteenth century, a specifically Florentine tradition develops which presents a number of singular, indeed anomalous features. One early predecessor of this local tradition is to be found in a little-known fresco by Mariotto di Nardo painted after 1395 in the former Monastery of Santa Brigida al Paradiso in Florence (Ill. 11). But the earliest surviving representative of it in its full form is a fresco by Bicci di Lorenzo from around 1439 in S. Maria del Fiore (Ill. 12), followed for example by Andrea del Verrocchio's celebrated bronze statue of 1463–1483 in the church of Orsanmichele, both in the same city (Ill. 13).

In these representations, and in the others which belong to this same narrow tradition, Jesus has lost his unchallenged and unique centrality: now it is the pair of Jesus and Thomas together around whom the space in the image is arranged. And the focus upon this pair is so exclusive that other participants, such as the witnessing disciples, are almost always absent. In these Tuscan images, Thomas is always young and beardless; he could be Jesus' son; he is uncertain and tentative in his gesture and posture. Jesus is usually fully clothed except for a narrow slit in his cloak which reveals his wound; he is always bearded, and he lays his arm protectively around Thomas's shoulders, not only authorizing him to test his wound, but going further, encouraging and emboldening him to do so. Jesus' whole attitude is tender and affectionate, full of love and understanding for this adolescent whose desire he justifies and even approves.

In the peculiarities of this local tradition we can easily detect the pictorial repercussions of conditions specific to the political and religious culture of Renaissance Tuscany, where Thomas was a favorite saint of the Medici family, who devoted various churches to him; where he functioned as the patron saint of the mercantile courts, justifying the importance of the principle that one must test carefully before pronouncing judgment (it was the Mercanzia which commissioned Verrocchio's sculpture for an external niche at Orsanmichele); and where the holy girdle of Mary, given to Thomas, was preserved in Prato as a religious relic, the "sacra cintola," of central importance to the city's cultural identity.

❧

If we consider Caravaggio's painting within the context of earlier trends, it is obvious that, just as we would expect, he has almost nothing in common with the Tuscan tradition. In Caravaggio's version, Jesus and Thomas are not alone, Thomas is no hesitant adolescent son, Jesus is no lovingly understanding father, and the emotional tone is anything but tender and compassionate. More seems to link Caravaggio with the Venetian tradition: in both cases we find a half-naked Jesus cloaked in the philosopher's mantle, a bearded Thomas, and witnessing disciples. Nonetheless, the differences that separate Caravaggio from the Venetians are unmistakable: the body of Caravaggio's Jesus is suffering and effeminate, not majestic and virile, and his hand has forcefully seized Thomas's wrist, and is not just holding it or inviting his investigation. Above all, in Caravaggio's painting Thomas's fingers do not merely touch Jesus' wound but penetrate disturbingly into it.

How can we explain the origin of these striking characteristics of Caravaggio's painting? Of course he might simply have invented them on his own; but religious painting tends to be conservative, and in other cases Caravaggio demonstrates a considerable awareness of earlier artistic traditions and a sophisticated relation to them. If so, just which earlier traditions might have supplied him useful suggestions in the present case?

Since the pioneering works of Roberto Longhi, we have learned to

14. Bernardino Butinone, *Doubting Thomas*, ca. 1475. Pinacoteca Malaspina, Pavia.

think of the northern Italian region of Lombardy, where Caravaggio began his career, as a creative matrix in which to look for the sources of many elements of his pictorial compositions. But in the present case this approach does not get us very far. For Doubting Thomas was apparently not a popular subject in fifteenth- and sixteenth-century Lombard art; and of the few examples I have been able to discover, such as the small panel painted by Bernardino Butinone around

1475, in Pavia (Ill. 14), and the altarpiece painted by Bernardino Campi in 1568, in the Brera in Milan, none shares any important features with Caravaggio's painting, and most, like these, are far closer in spirit and composition to the prevalent Italian conventions than to his remarkable creation.

Indeed, the most striking features of Caravaggio's painting seem to be quite unparalleled in earlier Italian art. But if so, then to find comparable elements in the medieval and Renaissance artistic traditions preceding Caravaggio we must move north of the Alps, to a German iconographical tradition which can be detected at least since the thirteenth-century pediment of the Church of Saint-Thomas in Strasbourg (Ill. 15) and which goes on to flourish throughout the North, especially in Germany, starting in the fifteenth century. In images like the Altar of the Dominicans of Schongauer's workshop (Ill. 6b), the right wing of the Ehninger Altar that was painted by a follower of Dieric Bouts around 1479 (Ill. 16), or a painting by Bartholomäus Bruyn the Elder, composed around 1520 (Ill. 17) and derived from the celebrated Thomas Altar painted by the Master of the Bartholomäus Altar two decades earlier, as well as in a number of wooden sculptures of the same period, we find close parallels to certain aspects of Caravaggio's painting. Here too Jesus' body is shown half-naked, not as a manifestation of power and glory, but instead in order to demonstrate the horrible traces of all he has suffered: he is the "Schmerzensmann," the "Man of Sorrows," and we are meant not to admire his majesty but to pity his torments. Here too Jesus seizes Thomas's hand forcefully, drawing it ever farther into the wound. And here too Thomas's finger or fingers penetrate deep into it. What is more, in a number of these German images, just as in Caravaggio's painting, Thomas is shown approaching Jesus not from Jesus' right side (as in most medieval and Renaissance Italian versions) but from his left side, so that Thomas's own hand does not obstruct the viewer's gaze and thereby make it sometimes difficult to tell whether he is touching Jesus or not: in this position the gesture of physical contact is free of any ambiguity. The general atmosphere of transfigured violence, of heightened suffering, is typical of much of medieval

15. Jesus and Doubting Thomas between Saints Peter and John; ca. 1230. Tympanum of the Church of Saint-Thomas, Strasbourg.

and Renaissance German religious art as well as of contemporary mystical writings.

To explain the origin of these elements of Caravaggio's painting of Doubting Thomas, we seem to have no alternative other than to postulate some form of northern influence upon him. But it remains uncertain by exactly what means this influence might have reached him, and of exactly what image or images it may have consisted. Walter Friedländer suggested that Caravaggio's version might have been influenced by the woodcut of this theme in Albrecht Dürer's *Small Passion*, printed in Nuremberg in 1511 and circulated throughout Europe (Ill. 18); and indeed in the depictions of Jesus, Judas, and an armored soldier in another woodcut in the same series, showing Jesus taken captive in the garden (Ill. 19), and Caravaggio's recently rediscovered painting on the same theme (Ill. 28, below), there are evident close similarities. Yet what is most distinctive about Dürer's woodcut of Doubting Thomas—its placement of a majestic, hero-

16. Follower of Dieric Bouts, *Doubting Thomas*, right wing of the Ehninger Altar,
ca. 1479. Staatsgalerie, Stuttgart.

17. Bartholomäus Bruyn the Elder, *Doubting Thomas*, ca. 1520.
Gemäldegalerie, Berlin.

ically nude Jesus, his head enhanced by a nimbus, in the very center
of the composition—is in fact not at all similar to Caravaggio's picto-
rial arrangement and emotional tone and far more reminiscent of the
Venetian tendency (unsurprisingly, given Dürer's close contacts with
Venice). What it does have in common with Caravaggio's painting—
Jesus' nudity, his violent grasping of Thomas's wrist, Thomas's finger

18. Albrecht Dürer, Doubting Thomas, *Die kleine Passion* (Nürnberg, 1511).

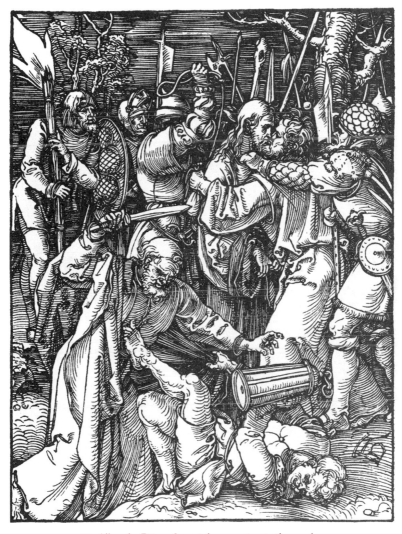

19. Albrecht Dürer, Jesus taken captive in the garden,
Die kleine Passion (Nürnberg, 1511).

20. Hans Schäufelein, Doubting Thomas, in Wolfgan von Män, *Das Leiden Jesu Christi vnnsers Erlösers* (Augsburg, 1525).

21. Hans Schäufelein, The Disrobing of Christ, in Wolfgan von Män,
Das Leiden Jesu Christi vnnsers Erlösers (Augsburg, 1525).

which penetrates deep into Jesus' wound—it also shares with many other North European examples of this theme.

Thus it does not seem likely that Dürer's book was Caravaggio's prime or sole means of access to the northern iconographic tradition for this particular image. So too, the seventeenth-century German artist and art historian Joachim von Sandrart reported that Caravaggio was especially fond of the pictures of Hans Holbein the Younger and strongly influenced by them. Yet Holbein never depicted the theme of Doubting Thomas in any medium, and none of his other paintings, drawings, or printed illustrations displays a strong similarity to Caravaggio's composition.

However, it seems most unlikely that, if Caravaggio really did study the works of Holbein in the form of printed illustrations, he would have only been interested in this one North European artist. Is it not likelier that he would have drawn ideas from other printed images as well? Alas, the modern repertories of North European printed illustrations of the fifteenth and sixteenth centuries are still woefully incomplete. Yet, even so, they contain a number of images that present striking affinities with Caravaggio's painting. For example, the sixteenth-century German artist Hans Schäufelein published a Passion series in which a Doubting Thomas (Ill. 20) has a compositional arrangement that, despite some obvious differences, is in certain regards quite close to Caravaggio's—a rustic, heavily cloaked Thomas has been put in the center and is inserting two fingers into the wound in Jesus' naked side while Jesus firmly holds on to his wrist. In the same series, a Disrobing of Christ (Ill. 21) displays other similarities— Jesus' delicate and suffering nudity, and the intense observation by an only partially visible man in the background.

It is not possible, at least in the current state of the evidence, to prove definitively that Schäufelein was in fact the key mediator between the Germanic tradition and Caravaggio. But illustrations by other artists to be found in the repertories point in the same direction; and given the incompleteness of the published collections, and the enormous diffusion of such northern printed reproductions throughout Europe in the fifteenth and sixteenth centuries, we may suspect that Caravaggio encountered the proximate source of his inspiration in a printed book, where it may still be awaiting scholarly rediscovery. If so, then a written text, and indeed a printed one, will have been an important link in the production of an image of Doubting Thomas which was commissioned by a highly erudite patron—but which ended up achieving a form in which it can be appreciated even by the illiterate.

❧

Set against the context of these various iconographical traditions, Caravaggio can be seen to have innovated in two crucial regards in his own version of the Doubting Thomas tableau.

1. Caravaggio's is the first major version of the scene in which the persons depicted are shown not in their full vertical extension but rather in half-figure. Indeed, Friedländer suggests that Caravaggio's painting might have been the very first such half-figure version at all, but this is not strictly true; however, the only earlier example that I have been able to discover, the early-sixteenth-century Stein triptych by Simon Bening, in the Walters Art Gallery in Baltimore, is very small (6.8 × 5.2 cm) and hence quite schematic, and Doubting Thomas is only one element in a set of sixty-four miniatures that does not seem to have become widely known or influential.

2. Caravaggio's is the first major version of the theme in which Thomas is set in the very center and foreground of the composition, displacing Jesus to one side and the other disciples to the back and other side. The only earlier examples I have found for this compositional arrangement are in printed German illustrations such as Schäufelein's.

The former innovation means that we spectators must approach quite close to the picture in order to have a good view of it. As a private commission for display in an aristocratic collection—the painting measures only 107 by 146 cm—it is not an object for public and institutional cult from a distance but rather for private and individual appreciation close up. We are obliged to come nearer to the painting, and thereby cannot avoid participating more fully in the pathos it depicts and transmits: as its smallness draws us in toward it, the repulsiveness of some details which we gradually begin to notice drive us away again, and we find ourselves in an emotionally fraught oscillation.

The latter innovation means that the story that this picture tells us is not so much one about Jesus, about something that happens to him involving Thomas, as rather, in its essence, one about Thomas, about something that has happened to him involving Jesus. This is why Jesus' face can be obscured by shadow, for ultimately the question of his own expression and motivation, interesting and perplexing as it may be, is merely secondary. Instead, it is Thomas's emotional state that Caravaggio has depicted for us with ineluctable clarity.

Just what then is the emotion expressed by Thomas's facial aspect, and indeed by his whole bodily posture? Given the possibilities suggested by John's highly complex narrative, one can think of a number of subjective states, any one of which might be depicted—doubt, belief, anger, aggressiveness, contrition, shame, terror, curiosity, incredulity, persuasion, concentration. All of these emotions or attitudes find some precedent and justification in the various traditions of Doubting Thomas we have considered.

But the body language that Caravaggio has provided for Thomas points unequivocally in a different direction. The upwardly directed furrows in Thomas's forehead—they are incised so severely and emphasized so forcefully by the contrast of light and shadow that, after Jesus' wound, they are the single most notable skin feature in the entire painting—indicate that his eyes are opened as wide, and the eyebrows pushed up as far, as they can possibly go. By contrast, the other two disciples' brows are furrowed downward and their eyebrows are pulled together and down toward the bridge of their noses. In the semiotics of the expression of human emotion, the meaning of both aspects is unmistakable: the other two disciples are shown under the pressure of intense visual and mental concentration; but Thomas is shown in the grip of an overwhelming astonishment (Ill. 22). The two other disciples, like doctors in the audience at a public anatomy lesson (Ill. 23), are concentrated, observing, serious: they

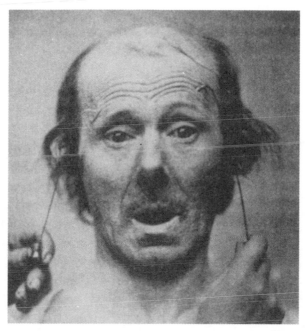

22. The facial expression of astonishment (from G.-B. Duchenne de Boulogne, *Mécanisme de la physionomie humaine,* 1862, pl. 56).

are careful and conscientious empirical investigators who are encountering an unusual phenomenon and want to be sure that no detail of it escapes their meticulous gaze. Thomas's situation is different: his eyes are open so wide that we might even say that he is no longer seeing in the conventional sense of the term. Instead, he has become the locus of a religious miracle.

In short, Caravaggio's painting is organized in terms of an action and a reaction. The action of Thomas's touching Jesus is concentrated into a pair of significantly opposed hands: Thomas's hand—human, penetrating, forceful—is set into evident contrast with Jesus'—divine, gripping, even more powerful. The reactions to these gestures are assigned to the foreheads of the three disciples: Thomas's upward-directed furrows of astonishment are opposed to

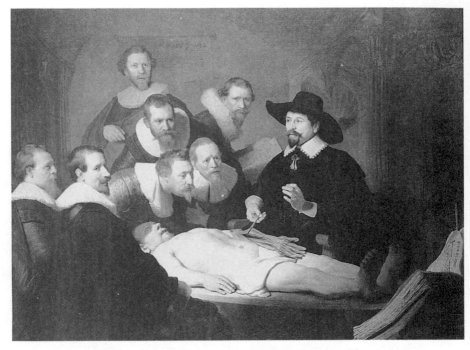

23. The facial expression of concentration (Rembrandt van Rijn, *The Anatomy Lesson of Dr. Nicolaes Tulp*, 1632, Mauritshuis, The Hague).

the other two disciples' downward-directed furrows of concentrated attention.

Traditionally, the other disciples were often set off against Thomas as the community of believers against the lone skeptic. Here too a gulf divides Thomas from the other two disciples, however closely they may press against him from behind—but this time the values are reversed. Here the other disciples are not linked with Jesus against Thomas. Instead, Thomas and Jesus determine one plane of the picture, while the other two disciples form another one. Despite the evident cross composed by the four characters' heads, it is in fact not really the case that Thomas is in front, Jesus and the disciple on the right just behind Thomas at the same level, and the oldest disciple

further back behind the other three. Instead, Caravaggio has somewhat distorted the perspective so as to bring Jesus slightly forward
together with Thomas into a diagonal plane almost aligned with the
picture plane itself. This diagonal plane begins at the right front with
Thomas's projecting elbow and ends at the left back in Jesus' shoulder. Together, Jesus and Thomas define the plane of the painting as
the domain of a religious miracle, embodied by the former and experienced by the latter. Thomas's penetration of Jesus' wound is coun-
terbalanced by Jesus' grip upon Thomas's wrist: between the two
characters who participate directly in this miracle, strength and
weakness, mastery and subjection, control and constraint are distributed—but unequally, for there can be no doubt that Jesus is fully the
master of this wonder.

But if the plane of the picture represents in Jesus and Thomas a
scene of religious sublimity, the two disciples placed behind them in
a neutral, uncharacterized space, peering intently at this scene and
crowding in to get a better view, correspond by an almost perfect
horizontal symmetry through the plane of the image to the real
viewers of Caravaggio's painting who stand before it and move closer
and closer to it in order to see its details more clearly. It is with good
reason that Caravaggio has obscured every single aspect of their
bodies that is not directly related to their activity of viewing: for it is
in this activity alone that their essence lies. They observe and witness, they guarantee the veracity of a miracle by sight, while Thomas
himself participates in that miracle by touch.

As it were, Caravaggio has displaced the subjective disposition of
doubt, which John attributed to Thomas alone, from Thomas himself
(whose astonishment here leaves no space for doubt) to the other
two disciples (who in John felt no doubt at all). The two disciples examine closely what they observe, but Caravaggio does not tell us
what judgment they will eventually come to on the basis of their
careful investigation. Will they remain skeptical? Will they be convinced? Even in the latter case, their ultimate conviction will be
based not upon a leap of faith but upon their cautiously pondered
and scrupulously punctilious inquiry. The world inhabited by the dis-

ciples—and by us with them—is the everyday one of ordinary doubt and commonplace inspection. Into that world has erupted for them Jesus' encounter with Doubting Thomas—and for us Caravaggio's painting of that encounter. Thomas's elbow juts out disturbingly into our space: we cannot remain indifferent.

Thus Caravaggio's painting is a representation neither of faith nor of doubt, neither of religious belief nor of scientific skepticism, but rather of the irreconcilable conflict and the indispensable interdependence between them. Caravaggio displays both attitudes accurately and fairly, but only in their profound tension with one another. In a letter of 2 August 1603, Cardinal Ottavio Paravicino wrote of Caravaggio that he had painted "some paintings which were in that middle between piety and profanity, such that I would not have wished to see them from afar" ("qualche quadro, che fusse in quel mezzo tra il devoto, et profano, che non l'haveria voluto vedere da lontano"). The *Doubting Thomas* may well have been one of the paintings the cardinal had in mind, for it certainly assumes a paradoxical middle position between piety and profanity. No doubt, when the cardinal wrote that he would not have wanted to see such paintings from afar, he meant that he would not have wanted to see them at all; but other viewers must have reacted by wanting to see them not from afar, but instead from very close up.

Caravaggio's painting may therefore be interpreted as a dramatization of the conflict between faith and skepticism. The ambiguity with which both attitudes are brought to convincing expression must have made it a highly suitable picture for both ecclesiastical and secular viewers and collectors, and no doubt helps to explain its extraordinary success in the first decades of the seventeenth century. At the same time, it resolutely maintains the reality and physicality of the miracle of Doubting Thomas against any who might have tended to doubt or discount it—such as, for example, the German reformers, who pursued this tendency, though no extant documentation proves such a conscious intention or actual use of the painting. As such, it is certainly a characteristic document of the Italian Counter-Reformation. It may be interpreted as a drastic visual equivalent of the effort to imagine Thomas's probing of Jesus' wounds that San Carlo Borromeo had called for so passionately in his Milan sermon seventeen years earlier. The fact that Caravaggio's painting makes strategic use of a specifically German Renaissance iconographic tradition in a way that decisively opposes a German Protestant exegetical tradition is a piquant irony of history—just as is the fact that this painting, in which a German theme is seen afresh with Italian eyes, left Italy for Germany in 1816 and has been there almost without interruption ever since.

¥

Caravaggio's dramatization of the problem of faith and doubt can have deeply disturbing effects upon the viewer, not only because it shows Thomas touching Jesus' wound with such graphic physicality, but also because it ambiguously juxtaposes Thomas's attitude with that of his two fellow disciples as equally plausible alternatives without deciding clearly for or against either one. Mockers of Jesus had always been an acceptable theme in Christian iconography, for example in scenes of the flagellation or the crowning with thorns, but they had almost always been disqualified by being shown as repugnant, hideous, subhuman. The two witnessing disciples in Caravaggio's painting are no less attractive figures than Thomas is, however, and indeed, as figures for the viewer who is deeply engaged in the study of this scene, perhaps even more so. This openendedness evidently did not disturb Caravaggio's first viewers enough to prevent the immediate and considerable popularity of the painting—on the contrary, it was probably an important contributory factor, since it permitted widely different ideas about faith and miracles to seek and find justification in the very same image.

Yet we can see in the versions of the theme painted by Caravaggio's followers how much easier it must have been for less courageous painters to simplify, sweeten, and above all disambiguate the most disturbing aspects of the original. Both of the versions by Rubens (Ill. 24) and Strozzi (Ill. 25) maintain certain key elements of

24. Peter Paul Rubens, *Doubting Thomas*, 1612–1615 (central panel). Koninklijk Museum voor Schone Kunsten, Antwerp.

25. Bernardo Strozzi, *Doubting Thomas*, about 1620. Compton Verney House Trust.

Caravaggio's painting: the half-figure composition; the reduction of the number of characters to Jesus, Thomas, and two other disciples; the contrast between Jesus' nudity and the clothed disciples. Yet at the same time they both transform Caravaggio's original in a way that renders it less disquieting, above all by clearly illuminating Jesus' face and removing any doubt about his emotional expression.

Rubens has maintained most closely the original compositional arrangement of Caravaggio's painting, but perhaps only in order to make his thematic transformation of it all the more striking. Jesus' body is now muscular and heroic; all four characters are far better groomed, particularly in their hair; the expression of Jesus' face and hands is one of calm, dispassionate invitation; his left and right hands open his body to a purely visual inspection; the disciple on the far right, who seems to represent Thomas, is dulcified by a return to the Florentine tradition of the tentative adolescent; he and the other two disciples gaze at Jesus and his wounds with seriousness and attention but with neither transcendent wonder nor rapt concentration. Above all, there is no wound visible at all in Jesus' side—it may have been painted out, and if so an original intention to follow the model of Caravaggio's painting more closely was later rejected, presumably because it was too disturbing. In consequence, Thomas does not put his finger into a wound in Jesus' side but is satisfied by seeing the wound in his extended hand—the gesture of Thomas's own hands, especially of the right one, seems to express not only surprise but also a recoiling at the very notion of touching his Lord. If Caravaggio shows us a scene that is in fact missing from the Gospel of John, Rubens has corrected him by conflating the two moments that would have taken place just before and just after it: Jesus' invitation to Thomas to touch him (John 20:27) and Thomas's pious outcry (20:28). What is most disturbing in Caravaggio's painting—Jesus' gaping wound and Thomas' brutal penetration of it—has been entirely suppressed.

Strozzi (Ill. 25), on the other hand, has maintained Jesus' weak and delicate body (though without any hint of effeminacy), the scruffiness and lankness of the hair and beards, and even, with considerable exaggeration, the tear at the seam of Thomas's jacket. But he has completely shifted the arrangement of the figures so as to provide a different interpretation for them. Now Jesus has returned to his traditional position in the center of the composition, and it is his face which is by far the most brightly and completely illuminated; Thomas's, by contrast, is turned almost entirely away from us. Although here too Jesus grasps Thomas's wrist and Thomas's finger penetrates into Jesus' wound, the emotional tonality of the gestures is quite different from that in Caravaggio: here Jesus has not seized

Thomas's hand with overmastering force but is gently and firmly guiding it; and despite the frontality with which Jesus' wound is displayed, it is shown here as less gaping, raw, painful; likewise, it is only the very tip of Thomas's finger which touches the wound, not a whole section of the finger which disappears into it. If Caravaggio showed us something about Thomas, Strozzi shows us something about Jesus, whose head is surrounded by a nimbus and who expresses his loving concern for mankind in his compassionate gesture to Thomas. Thomas himself, approaching Jesus from the front, like us, is an evident figure for the viewer—so much so that the other two disciples can be banished to the very edges of the painting. We can be sure that Thomas reacts to his experience with pious faith, as we ourselves should to this painting of it. But anything beyond this rather facile point is irrelevant to the painter's purposes, at least theologically. If Caravaggio's painting is upsetting and ambiguous, Strozzi's is reassuring in its naïveté.

※

It is precisely the most disturbing aspects of Caravaggio's *Doubting Thomas*—those which are systematically suppressed in these two paintings—that make it so characteristic of his work. This image brings together into a single, particularly concentrated and complex form a number of basic themes and motifs that recur throughout his oeuvre. The frequency with which such motifs are found in Caravaggio's works has often been interpreted psychologically, as a symptom of his own obsessions, desires, and fears, and this has given birth to an extensive literature devoted to attempts to use this evidence in order to analyze his personality. But painting, through most of history and certainly during the lifetime of Caravaggio, was not thought of as an exercise in private self-expression, but rather as part of a social system involving secular and ecclesiastical authorities, the art market of wealthy collectors and patrons, and the rivalry among competing painters for the highly limited resources of prestige and commissions. All in all, it seems better to interpret such thematic recurrences rather in terms of the tastes and interests of the society for which and within which Caravaggio worked so successfully, and in particular with reference to the patrons who gave him his commissions and whose expectations he tried to satisfy. It is their tastes, shaped no doubt in part, but only in part, by Caravaggio himself, that we see reflected in these paintings, and not Caravaggio's alone.

The consistency and coherence of these tastes make it easy to recognize in Caravaggio's *Doubting Thomas* thematic choices familiar from many of his other paintings: the problematic of belief and the danger of credulity (at least since *La Buona Ventura*, ca. 1594, at the Louvre, and *The Cardplayers*, ca. 1594/5, at the Kimball Art Museum in Fort Worth); paradoxes of sight and the visual medium (especially *Narcissus*, ca. 1597, at the Galleria Nazionale d'Arte Antica in Rome); drastic wounds, the signs of painful and violent damage to human flesh (for example, *Judith and Holofernes*, 1598, at the Galleria Nazionale in Rome; *Medusa*, 1600/1, at the Uffizi in Florence; *David with Goliath*, 1607 or 1609/10, at the Galleria Borghese in Rome); Jesus' suffering body (especially *The Crowning with Thorns*, ca. 1602/4, at the Kunsthistorisches Museum in Vienna; and *The Flagellation of Jesus*, 1607, at the Museo di Capodimonte in Naples); hands seizing wrists (for example, the executioner grasping St. Matthew's right wrist in *The Martyrdom of St. Matthew*, 1599/1600, at S. Luigi dei Francesi in Rome; or the angel grabbing Abraham's right wrist in *The Sacrifice of Isaac*, 1603, at the Uffizi in Florence; and cf. already *La Buona Ventura*); an extended finger unexpectedly caught and trapped (*Boy Bitten by a Lizard*, in the Collection Longhi in Florence).

But it is in particular with three other paintings of his that Caravaggio's depiction of Doubting Thomas invites comparison. Two of these represent Jesus' supper at Emmaus, one dating from around 1600/1 and now in the National Gallery in London (Ill. 26) and the other from about six years later and now at the Pinacoteca di Brera in Milan (Ill. 27). In both of these latter paintings as in the *Doubting Thomas*, Caravaggio has chosen to show us a scene of a religious wonder in which certain figures participate directly while others gaze on with apparent dispassion. In the London version (Ill. 26), the two disciples, seated, express the same overpowering astonishment in the

26. Caravaggio, *Supper at Emmaus*, ca. 1600–1601. National Gallery, London.

gestures of their hands, arms, and faces as Thomas does—note especially their wide-open eyes, raised eyebrows, and deeply furrowed foreheads. Here too, our space as spectators is invaded by elements of the painting—the disciple's outstretched left hand, a basket of fruit about to fall from the table—which jut out menacingly toward us and prevent us from regarding the miraculous events with indifference, as though they had nothing to do with us. And yet behind Jesus stands the innkeeper, unmoved, curious, watching: like the two other disciples in the *Doubting Thomas*, he is indeed involved, but only as an interested spectator like us, rather than as a deeply moved participant. So too in the Milan version (Ill. 27), in which the prosaic witnesses are doubled by the addition of the innkeeper's wife and the

27. Caravaggio, *Supper at Emmaus*, 1606. Pinacoteca di Brera, Milan.

contrast between the innkeeper's downward drawn, concentrated eyebrows and the disciple's upward drawn, astonished ones is even more forceful.

The last painting of Caravaggio's that invites particular attention in this connection has only recently been rediscovered, though it has been known from various copies for many years: the *Arrest in the Garden* in Dublin (Ill. 28). Here too we seem to find a violation, indeed something approaching a rape, committed upon the aristocratic, delicate, suffering Jesus, by a burly, rustic Judas; and here too

28. Caravaggio, *Arrest in the Garden*, 1602. National Gallery of Ireland, Dublin.

the weakness of Jesus' body is balanced by the extraordinary strength of his hands, which in the present case grasp not someone else's hand but instead each other, in an eloquent gesture of prayer, sorrow, and self-control; here too the aggressive proximity of Jesus and one of his disciples (Thomas too, it will be remembered, was later sometimes called Judas) is observed with varying degrees of dispassion but with strenuous attention by a series of other figures (including, at the right edge, what seems to be a self-portrait of the artist); and finally, here too Jesus is displaced toward the left side while the center is occupied by a massive, powerful body stretching its arm forward in a (vain) attempt to take control of Jesus' own body. The homoerotic and sadomasochistic implications that we may sense as a nuance of the *Doubting Thomas* seem here to achieve a particularly drastic expression.

❦

If it is still possible without embarrassment to apply the trite term "genius" to any artist, then we may say that Caravaggio was a genius. But his brilliance consisted not in an eruptive and merely self-directed urge to self-expression, but rather in his highly talented, trained, and circumspect understanding of how best to manipulate the possibilities inherent in the pictorial medium so as to establish the richest channels of communication with diverse communities of viewers. In this way, he can be taken as a paradigm—despite his uniqueness, in some ways an entirely typical paradigm—for all the artistic traditions that worked for many centuries to find ever more persuasive means with which to convince viewers of the reality, importance, and meaning of the story of Doubting Thomas. The success of these many, mostly anonymous artists can be measured in the very pervasiveness of the belief that Thomas did indeed put his finger into Jesus' wound, for it is to the effectiveness of the pictorial tradition that the prevalence of this belief can at least partly be attributed.

Thomas demanded not only to see Jesus, but also to touch him, if he was to believe. Viewers of these sacred images have only been able to see, and not touch, Thomas touching Jesus; yet many of them have believed because of these images that he really did.

※

The Holy Finger

Among the sacred relics of the Passion of the Lord preserved at Rome in the Basilica of Santa Croce in Gerusalemme, a short and squalid walk from the main train station, the astonished visitor can admire—next to one of the Holy Nails, two of the Holy Thorns, three small fragments of the Holy Cross, the whole crossbeam of the Good Thief's cross, part of the plaque nailed to Jesus' cross and naming him King of the Jews in three languages, and various smaller fragments of the Holy Sepulchre and of the Column of the Flagellation (and also of the Holy Crib as well)—the finger of St. Thomas, Apostle (frontispiece). Two phalanges of what seems, at least to this untrained observer, to be a human finger are clearly if only partly visible through the two lateral perforations along a silver repository, shaped like a pointing finger, within an oval monstrance with two crystal windows. The monstrance itself is surrounded by two palm leaves symbolizing Thomas's martyrdom, crossing at the top and bottom; the whole is surmounted by a small cross, while at the bottom a wax seal certifies the relic's authenticity against any possible doubters.

What is the nature of the fascination exerted by this peculiar object?

As we saw earlier, John implicitly but unmistakably criticizes Thomas's obsession with Jesus' material body as being misguided: according to Jesus' last speech to Thomas, the truly blessed are not those who need to see the Savior's body, let alone touch it, if they are to attain belief in his bodily resurrection, but instead are those who are capable of attaining such belief even in the absence of Jesus' body, those for whom it is enough merely to hear or read about Jesus' resurrection. Yet so compelling is John's narrative that it has ended up focusing the attention of many readers upon that very body, in a way and to a degree apparently not quite compatible with his intention, as far as we can identify it. Implicitly, John may well condemn Thomas's desire to touch Jesus' body: but explicitly John has allowed Thomas to formulate that desire so strikingly that it can scarcely be forgotten, and the very fact that John never explicitly condemns it nor explicitly states that it was not fulfilled permits it to linger in the reader's mind as a latent possibility.

With the doubtful exception of the Holy Prepuce, no trace of Jesus' body has remained in this world in all the historical time that has passed since the events of his Passion. None of us is likely, at least not before the Last Judgment, to see any part of that beloved and tormented body ever again, no matter how strongly we might wish to. But artistic representations of the holy body surround us on all sides throughout our lives, and surely they must tend to stimulate, without ever being able to fulfill, a desire to perceive that body itself, in its authentic reality, rather than just some portrayal or imitation of it. So strong can the desire to look upon the true holy body become that, frustrated as it will inevitably be, it must seek other, neighboring outlets. Various perplexing questions are thereby raised: If we ourselves cannot touch or even see Jesus' body, then what about the various objects that touched it themselves in one way or another? Can we touch them, or at least see them? Would not our doing so make the sacred accounts seem even more compelling? What of the nails and thorns that tore Jesus' flesh? And above all, what of Thomas's finger? After all, at least on some accounts, that finger was the only part of a human body to touch Jesus' risen body after the crucifixion. Mary Magdalene had been prohibited from touching Jesus, but Thomas had not: whatever became of his impious but venerable finger? Although the Gospel of John itself does not seem to attribute any importance to Thomas's own body, for many Christians that body has acquired a peculiar interest of its own, by default, as a proxy for another body, the one it is not, the one it alone could touch, lovingly and violently—the body of Jesus.

Just how strong this interest could become is suggested by the earliest source for the legend of Thomas's body, the account of his martyrdom in the apocryphal *Acts of Thomas*. As we saw earlier, this text is strongly Gnostic in character, and hence we would not expect it to devote much attention to matters of the body. Nonetheless, the *Acts of Thomas* recounts in detail the apostle's death: four soldiers pierce him with their spears (§168), multiplying and deepening in Thomas the wounds that Jesus experienced. Thomas himself explains why he must be pierced by four spears while one was enough for Jesus: Thomas is a mortal man and therefore is composed of four elements, but Jesus is a god and so is entirely unified (§165). And the text concludes by appending to the end of its account of Thomas's life a final scene indicating climactically the power of his body even after his death:

Now it came to pass after a long time that one of the children of Misdaeus the king was a demoniac and no one could cure him, for the devil was extremely fierce. And Misdaeus the king took thought and said, "I will go and open the sepulchre, and take a bone of the apostle of God and hang it upon my son, and he shall be healed." But while Misdaeus thought about this, the apostle Thomas appeared to him and said to him, "You did not believe in a living man, and will you believe in the dead? Yet fear not, for my Lord Jesus Christ has compassion on you and pities you of his goodness."

And he went and opened the sepulchre, but did not find the apostle there, for one of the brethren had stolen him away and taken him to Mesopotamia; but from that place where the bones of the apostle had lain Misdaeus took dust and put it about his son's neck, saying, "I believe in you, Jesus Christ, now that he has left me who troubles men and opposes them lest they should see you." And when he had hung it upon his son, the boy became whole. (§170)

As we might expect from a Gnostic text, this account betrays a certain discomfort with the power that it attributes to Thomas's body: the king's desire to use that body as a magic relic is rebuffed by Thomas himself, yet it is granted all the same; and the holy body turns out to be missing from the tomb (not because it was resurrected, as in the authorized Christian account of Jesus' body, but because the other disciples stole it and carried it away, as in the competing version which is cited and dismissed at Matt. 28:11–15), yet the dust in which it lay reveals itself to be not less potent (just as the body of Jesus is missing, but the mortal dust of Thomas's finger, which touched it, will retain a supernatural potency). It makes most sense to understand the text as a witness to a contemporary veneration of the relic of Thomas's body (localized perhaps in Mesopotamia, perhaps in Edessa in eastern Syria, at any rate probably not in India) that it reports, confirms, but does not wholeheartedly approve. Even in death, Thomas's bones know no peace.

The legends concerning the details of the death and afterlife of Thomas's body vary widely. Some authorities report that he died at Edessa and was buried there; indeed, Clement of Alexandria quotes the Gnostic Heracleon to the effect that Thomas himself died a natural death, unlike most of Jesus' other disciples (*Stromata* 4.9.71.3). Those authors who report that he died in India either suggest or assert that his body was left there, or else, much more often, find themselves obliged to explain how it came to be transported from India to Syria. Since the end of the Middle Ages, July 3, the traditional date for the translation of Thomas's relics to Edessa, has become the saint's day in the Western church. Is it coincidental that this date, unlike December 21, the saint's day in the Middle Ages, is as far from Jesus' birthday as the calendar permits? In any case, an active cult of Saint Thomas, centered on his grave at Edessa, is apparent in a number of texts dating from the end of the fourth or the beginning of the fifth century, such as the pilgrim Egeria's *Pilgrimage to Holy Places* (*CSEL* 61.23ff.), Rufinus' translation of Eusebius' *Ecclesiastical History* (11.5), and various sermons of John Chrysostom—one spurious sermon attributed to him even concludes by reporting how his listeners throw themselves down in front of the saint's grave and embrace his body (*Sermon on St. Thomas Apostle* = PG 59.500).

Thomas's bones, reportedly once buried in a vast church in Edessa and venerated in an impressive shrine there, are said to have been brought by Captain Leone degli Acciaiuoli on September 6, 1258, from the Greek island of Chios to the small port town of Ortona in Abruzzi along the southern Adriatic coast of Italy. To this very day they are still venerated there in the Concattedrale di San Tommaso Apostolo, which was restored after German troops blew it up on December 21, 1943, doubtless unaware that this was the medieval saint's day; a gilt urn under the altar of the crypt is said to contain the saint's mortal remains, while nearby stands a tombstone that bears a portrait and the inscription "Saint Thomas" in Greek and is reported to have come to Chios from Edessa.

The inhabitants of Ortona revere Thomas as the town's patron saint and derive no small measure of local pride from his presence among them. But for most other people the only part of Thomas's body that really matters is his finger, that sacred and sacrilegious digit which he demanded to insert into Jesus' wounds and which so many people believe he really did insert into them. In the monstrance of the Basilica of Santa Croce in Gerusalemme, Thomas's finger finds itself in holy, but also in rather ambiguous, company. All the other objects displayed are intimately associated with Jesus' body and partake of its sacred quality. Yet in most cases their association is not a matter of their having simply touched his body, to say nothing of lovingly caressing it, but instead is due to their having violently perforated it. Thomas's finger shares the same aggressively penetrating shape as the nails that drove holes into Jesus' hands and feet, and as the thorns that cut into his head: its very shape cannot help but remind us of the thrusting violence of Thomas's expression of doubt and of the means he demanded for resolving that doubt.

The monstrance is carefully designed to attract our gaze: like an ostensorium displaying the Host to the congregation at a Roman Catholic mass, its combination of a heavily wrought and elaborate frame surrounding an empty oval space in its center directs our attention to that center and above all to what is in the middle of that space, the repository; and the repository itself provides a further frame for the two bits of bone that are only partly visible through the two long slits of the lateral perforations. The repository, shaped like the finger that is implicitly assumed to have penetrated Jesus' wounds, itself seems wounded, as though it were a miniature body with a long lateral cut through which we can just see its bones, which we are being invited to inspect and confirm.

Thus Thomas's finger, in its display case in Rome, seems to put us too into Thomas's position and to involve us in complicated procedures of doubt and verification: for in this whole world it is the only surviving evidence for the resurrection of Jesus' body—if, that is, he did indeed touch it. The result is that we inevitably end up focusing our attention upon that finger, and may even forget what it touched. And yet, in this display, Thomas's finger points not sideways or downward but upward, beyond the cross whose truth it confirms to a heavenly domain to which Thomas himself only indirectly bore witness. The direction in which the finger is pointing invites us by implication not to waste our time in philological anxieties about whether Thomas really did touch Jesus' wounds, or in historical ones about whether what is being displayed here really are the mortal remains of his finger, but instead to think of heaven, and of how best to prepare ourselves for it.

For all of the other, perhaps even more sacred relics in the basilica, an inexpensive explanatory brochure for sale in the church provides a miraculous but highly circumstantial provenance, going all the way back to St. Helena's voyage to the Holy Land in the time of Constantine. But about the chain of intermediate sources that link the finger of Doubting Thomas presented in this display case back to its ultimate origin on one of his hands, this pamphlet prefers circumspectly to say nothing at all. How Thomas's finger got from Edessa to Rome—if in fact it really did—we shall doubtless never learn, at least not in this world. But we owe thanks anyway to whoever it was who gave us the finger, for in so doing he has made it possible for all those who believe to have their belief strengthened, and for all those who doubt to find their doubts confirmed.

But whether we believe or not, in any case we should recall what is alleged to be a Chinese proverb (but may after all, like so much else we believe, simply be apocryphal): "When the wise man points at the heavens, the fool looks at his finger."

Afterword

Doubting Thomas seems to have been devised by John largely in order to invoke, exaggerate, and then resolve doubt, and thereby to lay doubt to rest once and for all. Yet once Thomas has been invented, he is not so easy to get rid of: he lingers on, like the shadow of a guilty memory. Had John not introduced Thomas into his Gospel at all, he might well have worried that he had not done all he could in order to trace his readers' possible doubts to their most secret sources and to extirpate them right there; and had John not attributed to Thomas so hyperbolic an expression of doubt, he might well have felt that he had not revealed doubt to be so unmistakably godless and senseless an attitude that no reader of his would ever dare yield to it. If no one ever doubted, Thomas would not have been needed. Yet precisely by introducing this moment of negativity across the textual border from the outside world of faithlessness into the discursive realm of his holy Gospel, John has lent doubt an existence and even a kind of justification within that positive domain. And his decision to assign it so drastic a form has ended up making Thomas's skeptical outburst unforgettable.

The Christian tradition that John helped to shape had to devote considerable energy and ingenuity to domesticating Doubting Thomas's unsettling implications. To what extent was John taking account of proto-Gnostic currents of thought when he devised

Thomas? To what degree was the appeal of Gnosticism then strengthened by John's inclusion of Thomas within his Gospel? We do not know: but what is certain is that forms of belief that the early church fathers decried as Gnostic came to identify themselves with Doubting Thomas, and that the evolution of Christianity itself was deeply influenced by controversies over Thomas's nature and actions. To bring Thomas into the camp of religious orthodoxy, Christian exegesis of John's Gospel had to argue for centuries, against the clear evidence of John's text, that Thomas not only could have touched, but actually did touch, the risen Christ's material body; even the Protestant return to the letter of the holy text was not able to resolve this hermeneutic issue for all interpreters but led only to further schism and doubt. At stake in this millennial debate was not only the exact meaning of a few elliptical sentences in a single text, but also the precise way in which Jesus' resurrection, and our own, was to be envisioned—and beyond that, the fundamental relation between our material body and our personal identity. In the meantime, for their own reasons and in their own ways, visual artists had almost always been depicting Thomas in the very act of penetrating Jesus' wound with his finger; and in so doing they contributed decisively to the widespread conviction that this is what he really did.

Thus Thomas is a useful index for articulating a number of central themes in the history of Christianity over many centuries. Yet his interest is not limited to Christians and those who study their religion: he raises questions of doubt and faith that can legitimately claim the attention even of those for whom Christianity is not an issue.

"Skepticism" is an ancient word; but for the most part, until modern times the attitude it denotes was philosophically sporadic and culturally marginal. In the ancient world, skepticism was a respectable philosophical position during only three relatively brief periods, during the lifetime of its founder Pyrrhon of Elis (ca. 365–275 B.C.), during the middle phase of the Platonic Academy from the third to the first century B.C., and during the Pyrrhonist Revival starting in the first century B.C.; but even during its three short-lived flowerings it remained a minority position, derided by its opponents as inconsistent and impracticable (though even its enemies made good use of its objections in order to sharpen their own dogmatic arguments). And in the public mind, the philosopher tended to be associated not at all with skepticism, but with asceticism and beards, with deeply held convictions and oracular utterances.

It was with Descartes, whatever his links with late medieval Scholasticism, that a new form of radical doubt made a dramatic entrance onto the philosophic scene in the seventeenth century. If the business of philosophy is understood as that of constructing an edifice built out of knowledge we can be certain of, then our everyday experience that we cannot believe what others tell us as much as we can believe what we see for ourselves can take on enormous philosophical consequences. In his search for a secure starting point for his knowledge the philosopher will feel obliged to neglect the forms of hearsay provided by tradition (and even ultimately by his own senses, including that of sight) in favor of what he believes to be the unshakable certainty of self-knowledge. In the centuries since Descartes, the philosophical search for certainty has always been marked by a deeply skeptical cast: in the last four hundred years or so the various philosophical schools have subjected religion, politics, science, morality, sensory knowledge, and all other sources of authority, including philosophy itself, to obstinately skeptical interrogation. And during the same period whole institutions—science and the university above all—which are based upon skepticism and are structured in terms of procedures designed to enhance and formalize doubt have moved beyond their earlier sporadic beginnings to become the dominant features of modern Western society.

Many of us cannot live without doubt any longer and cannot even imagine what a nonskeptical life would be like. Yet living with doubt is not easy. For all our skepticism, we must take much for granted. Our language, our traditions, and our society mold us profoundly, long before we can even begin to articulate our doubts, and it is only on the basis of that original shaping that our doubts can become intelligible to ourselves and to other people. Our involvement with other people—above all in love, but beyond that in almost all our social interactions—constantly requires that we adopt forms of trust that cannot be rationally justified and that a thoroughgoing skepticism would not only question but destroy. Our complex lives are negotiated across very heterogeneous domains—family, friendship, work, science, politics, shopping, to name only a few—among which the degree of our belief in doubt and the ways in which that belief is activated vary widely; yet it is only rarely, if at all, that we pause to wonder how justified our different modes and degrees of skepticism really are. Hardly ever do we subject our will to doubt to truly searching doubt in any fundamental way. And finally the irreconcilable contrast between our mortality and our aspirations inevitably brings us into various kinds of self-contradiction that skepticism can easily unmask but that our continued life requires we maintain. We know that we shall die and that all we love will too; yet this knowledge and the doubts it might engender do not stop us from living, from producing, and from loving.

In a certain sense, we are all failed skeptics. For those of us who are Christians, Thomas is an emblematic figure: he has expressed a doubt from which even the most pious believers cannot be entirely free at every moment of their lives, yet he has himself overcome this doubt once and for all. But he is emblematic too for those of us who are not Christians: his doubts are our doubts and his inconsistencies are our inconsistencies. John could never have foreseen, and would most likely have repudiated, the world we live in; yet, by introducing Doubting Thomas into his Gospel, he has inserted into it a character with whom all modern readers can identify.

Thomas stands for us.

❧

Bibliographical Essays
Illustration Credits
Indexes

❦

Bibliographical Essays

Epigraph: Maurice Blanchot, *Thomas the Obscure*, new version, translated by Robert Lamberton (New York, 1973), 27–28.

Seeing and Believing

The fundamental philosophical account of the five senses remains Aristotle, *De anima* 2.7–11. The standard commentaries on this treatise in English are R. D. Hicks, ed., *Aristotle De Anima* (Cambridge, 1907; repr. Hildesheim–New York, 1990), and David Ross, ed., *Aristotle De Anima* (Oxford, 1961); for a more recent philosophical commentary, see D. W. Hamlyn, *Aristotle De Anima—Books II and III (with passages from Book I)*, updated edition by Christopher Shields (Oxford, 1993). A number of good recent collections of essays focus on philosophical aspects of Aristotle's text: see Martha C. Nussbaum and Amélie Oksenberg Rorty, eds., *Essays on Aristotle's De Anima* (Oxford, 1992); Michael Durrant, ed., *Aristotle's De Anima in Focus* (London, 1993); and Gilbert Romeyer Dherbey, ed., *Corps et âme: Sur le De Anima d'Aristote*, Etudes réunies par Cristina Viano (Paris, 1996). For a general philosophical account, see Daniel N. Robinson, *Aristotle's Psychology* (New York, 1989).

The social history of truth is an area of research upon which historians of science have recently been focusing within the context of a growing interest in the social dimensions of scientific epistemology. See, for example, Steven Shapin and Simon Schaffer, *Leviathan and the Air-Pump: Hobbes, Boyle, and the Experimental Life* (Princeton, N.J., 1985); Steven Shapin, *A Social History of Truth: Civility and Science in Seventeenth-Century England* (Chicago, 1994); Bruno Latour and Steve Woolgar, *Laboratory Life: The Social Construction of Scientific Facts* (Princeton, N.J., 1986); and Bruno Latour, *Pandora's Hope: Essays in the Reality of Science Studies* (Cambridge, Mass., 1999).

On the nature of belief, especially empirical belief as distinguished from religious faith, the wise and humane remarks of Bernard Williams, *Problems of the Self* (Cambridge, 1973), chap. 9 (136–151), remain fundamental.

The two interpretations of biblical narratives which, as far as I know, come closest to the methodology I have employed in the first chapters of this study are Frank Kermode, *The Genesis of Secrecy: On the Interpretation of Narrative* (Cambridge, Mass., 1979), and Jean Starobinski, *Trois fureurs: Essais* (Paris, 1974), 73–126 on Mark 5:1–20. I admire both works enormously, despite disagreement on various matters small and large, and I hope that their authors would not be too embarrassed to learn that it was they I had taken as my models. For other important literary studies of the Bible, see, for example, Erich Auerbach, *Mimesis: The Representation of Reality in Western Literature*, trans. Willard R. Trask (Princeton, N.J., 1953), 3–23; Jan P. Fokkelman, *Narrative Art in Genesis: Specimens of Stylistic and Structural Analysis* (Assen, 1975); Robert Alter, *The Art of Biblical Narrative* (New York, 1981); Northrop Frye, *The Great Code: The Bible and Literature* (New York, 1981); and M. Sternberg, *The Poetics of Biblical Narrative: Ideological Literature and the Drama of Reading* (Bloomington, Ind., 1985). For general discussion of literary critical approaches to the Bible, see William A. Beardslee, *Literary Criticism of the New Testament* (Philadelphia, 1969); S. D. Moore, *Literary Criticism and the Gospels: The Theoretical Challenge* (New Haven, Conn., 1989); Elizabeth Struthers Malbon and Edgar V. McKnight, eds., *The New Literary Criticism and the New Testament* (Sheffield, UK, 1994); and Jan P. Fokkelman, *Reading Biblical Narrative: An Introductory Guide*, trans. Ineke Smit (Louisville, Ky., 1999). There is a recent overview by Yairah Amit, *Reading Biblical Narratives: Literary Criticism and the Hebrew Bible* (Minneapolis, 2001).

On rhetorical approaches to the New Testament, see in general George A. Kennedy, *New Testament Interpretation through Rhetorical Criticism* (Chapel Hill, N.C., 1984), and Carl Joachim Classen, *Rhetorical Criticism of the New Testament* (Tübingen, 2000).

My hermeneutic use of the concept of narrative lacunae or gaps is much indebted to the work of Wolfgang Iser: see especially *The Implied Reader: Patterns of Communication in Prose Fiction from Bunyan to Beckett* (Baltimore, 1974) and *The Art of Reading: A Theory of Aesthetic Response* (Baltimore, 1978). And my understanding of the literary and rhetorical interpretation of narratives has been influenced above all by Gerard Genette: see especially *Discours du récit,* in *Figures III: Essais* (Paris, 1972), 65–283; an English translation is available as *Narrative Discourse,* trans. Jane E. Lewin (Ithaca, N.Y., 1980).

In a different field, that of Renaissance studies, Alastair Fowler, *Renaissance Realism: Narrative Images in Literature and Art* (Oxford, 2003), has recently raised the methodological objection that supplying hypothetical psychological motivations to fill perceived lacunae in texts means reading them anachronistically, on the basis of expectations derived from the experience of modern realistic fiction over the past several centuries. To be sure, it would obviously be mistaken to expect the degree of literary coherence and the kind of character portrayal from the Gospel accounts to which the great European novels have accustomed us. But one can perceive lacunae, and suggest minimal hypotheses to fill them, without committing oneself to expectations of that sort; and, as we shall see, the development of a large number of explicatory narratives on the basis of the Gospel of John proves that many readers already had exactly this response to that text in the first centuries A.D.

Before Thomas: The Synoptic Gospels

I have gratefully availed myself of most of the standard commentaries on the synoptic Gospels. The following ones I have found to be particularly helpful: Hugh Anderson, *The Gospel of Mark: The New Century Bible Commentary* (Grand Rapids, Mich., 1976); *The Gospel according to Luke: The Anchor Bible,* a new translation with introduction and commentary by Joseph A. Fitzmyer, S.J., two vols. (Garden City, N.J., 1981–85); *Matthew: The Anchor Bible,* a new translation with an introduction and notes by W. F. Albright and C. S. Mann (Garden City, N.J., 1971).

Authoritative guides to the many thorny textual problems of the New Testament are to be found in Bruce M. Metzger, *A Textual Commentary on the Greek New Testament,* corrected ed. (London, 1975), and *The Text of the New Testament: Its Transmission, Corruption, and Restoration,* 2nd ed. (New York, 1968). The reader should also consult Vincent Taylor, *The Formation of the Gospel Tradition* (London, 1953). A general account of the development of the New Testament is provided by Hans von Campenhausen, *The Formation of the Christian Bible,* trans. John Austin Baker (London, 1972).

An easily accessible popular presentation of the accounts of Jesus' resurrection, written by one of the greatest experts in this field, is Raymond E.

Brown, *A Risen Christ in Eastertime: Essays on the Gospel Narratives of the Resurrection* (Collegeville, Minn., 1991). A recent, massive exploration of the New Testament resurrection accounts against the background of ancient views of life after death is N. T. Wright, *The Resurrection of the Son of God: Christian Origins and the Question of God*, vol. 3 (London, 2003).

The scene in the synoptic Gospels of the three women at the empty tomb is the subject of a fascinating semiotic interpretation by Louis Marin, "Les femmes au tombeau: Essai d'analyse structurale d'un texte évangélique," in Marin, *Sémiotique de la passion: Topiques et figures* (Paris, 1971), 221–231; English translation available in *The Semiotics of the Passion Narrative: Topics and Figures*, trans. A. M. Johnson, Jr. (Pittsburgh, 1980). Other important studies of this episode in the synoptic Gospels include the following: A. R. C. Leaney, "The Resurrection Narratives in Luke (xxiv. 12–53)," *New Testament Studies* 2 (1955–56): 110–114; Charles H. Dodd, "The Appearance of the Risen Christ: An Essay in Form-Criticism of the Gospels," in D. E. Nineham, ed., *Studies in the Gospels: Essays in Memory of R. H. Lightfoot* (Oxford, 1955), 9–35; Hans Grass, *Ostergeschehen und Osterberichte*, 3rd ed. (Göttingen, 1964); Augustin George, "Les récits d'apparitions aux Onze à partir de Luc 24, 36–53," in Paul de Surgy et al., eds., *La résurrection du Christ et l'exégèse moderne*, Lectio Divina 50 (Paris, 1969), 75–104; Frans Neirynck, "Les femmes au tombeau: Étude de la rédaction Matthéenne," *New Testament Studies* 15 (1969): 168–190; John E. Alsup, *The Post-Resurrection Appearance Stories of the Gospel Tradition: A History of Tradition Analysis with Text-Synopsis*, Calwer theologische Monographien 5 (Stuttgart, 1975). A useful collection of essays on the subject with an extensive bibliography is to be found in Paul Hoffmann, ed., *Zur neutestamentlichen Überlieferung von der Auferstehung Jesu*, Wege der Forschung 522 (Darmstadt, 1988).

The conclusion of the Gospel of Mark has been studied from different points of view by Joseph Hug, *La finale de l'Evangile de Marc (Mc 16, 9–20)* (Paris, 1978), and Paul L. Danove, *The End of Mark's Story: A Methodological Study* (Leiden, 1993). The theory that, for the community for which this Gospel was composed, the story of the Resurrection was too important to be put into writing, in which form it could fall into the wrong hands, and hence was committed only to oral communication, is particularly associated with William Wrede, *Das Messiasgeheimnis in den Evangelien: Zugleich ein Beitrag zum Verständnis des Markusevangeliums* (Göttingen, 1901; repr., 1969), translated by J. C. G. Greig as *The Messianic Secret* (Cambridge, 1971); cf. also Vincent Taylor, *The Gospel according to St. Mark* (London, 1952), 122ff.

On the legal status of women in Palestine at the time of the New Testament as well as other aspects of the social context of the Gospels, see Ekkehard W. Stegemann and Wolfgang Stegemann, *Urchristliche Sozialgeschichte: Die Anfänge im Judentum und die Christusgemeinden in der mediterranen Welt*, 2nd ed. (Stuttgart, 1997); and Kenneth C. Hanson and Douglas E. Oakman, *Palestine in the Time of Jesus: Social Structures and Social Conflicts* (Minneapolis, 1998), with extensive bibliography; also John M. Court and Kathleen Court, *The New Testament World* (Cambridge, 1990), and Bruce J. Malina, *The New Testament World: Insights from Cultural Anthropology*, rev. ed. (Atlanta, 1993).

Believing and Touching: The Gospel of John

The fundamental English-language commentary on the Gospel of John is Raymond E. Brown, *The Gospel according to John: A New Translation with Introduction and Commentary*, The Anchor Bible, 2 vols. (New York, 1966–70); see also his "The Resurrection in John 20—A Series of Diverse Reactions," *Worship* 64 (1990): 194–206. But I have also benefited from many other contemporary exegetical works, especially Sir Edwyn Hoskyns, *The Fourth Gospel*, rev. ed., ed. Francis Noel Davey (London, 1947); Barnabas Lindars, *The New Century Bible Commentary: The Gospel of John* (Grand Rapids, Mich., 1972); Rudolf Schnackenburg, *Das Johannesevangelium*, pt. 3 (Freiburg, 1976); M. de Jonge, ed., *L'Evangile de Jean: Sources, rédaction, théologie*, Bibliotheca Ephemeridum theologicarum Lovaniensium 44 (Louvain, 1977); John Ashton, *Understanding the Fourth Gospel* (Oxford, 1991); C. K. Barrett, *The Gospel according to St. John: An Introduction with Commentary and Notes on the Greek Text*, 2nd ed. (Philadelphia, 1978); Attilio Gangemi, *I Racconti post-pasquali nel Vangelo di S. Giovanni*, vols. 1–3 (Acireale, 1989–93); and Thomas L. Brodie, *The Gospel according to John: A Literary and Theological Commentary* (New York, 1993). I have also consulted with profit C. H. Dodd, *The Interpretation of the Fourth Gospel* (Cambridge, 1953) and *Historical Tradition in the Fourth Gospel* (Cambridge, 1963). Even in David Friedrich Strauß, *Das Leben Jesu für das deutsche Volk bearbeitet*, 3rd ed. (Leipzig, 1874), 604–611, there is still much to learn. Through the kind offices of Adolf Martin Ritter (Heidelberg) I was able to read through the relevant sections of Hartwig Thyen's forthcoming important commentary on the Gospel of John, which emphasizes the intertextual links between John and the Synoptics; my thanks to both.

The author of the Gospel of John does not identify himself explicitly with the beloved disciple John, and I keep the two separate in my own treatment.

See Burton L. Mack, *Who Wrote the New Testament? The Making of the Christian Myth* (San Francisco, 1995), 218–22; and Harold W. Attridge, "The Restless Quest for the Beloved Disciple," in David H. Warren, Ann Graham Brock, and David W. Pao, ed., *Early Christian Voices: In Texts, Traditions, and Symbols: Essays in Honor of François Bovon*, Biblical Interpretation Series 66 (Boston, 2003), 71–80.

The question of the precise relation between John's account of the Passion and Resurrection and those in the synoptic Gospels remains fundamental and unresolved. Frans Neirynck, "John and the Synoptics: The Empty Tomb Stories," *New Testament Studies* 30 (1984): 161–187, argues forcefully that John had no other sources available to him for his account than the three Synoptics. On the contrary, D. Moody Smith, "John and the Synoptics: Historical Tradition and the Passion Narrative," in James H. Charlesworth and Michael A. Daise, eds., *Light in a Spotless Mirror: Reflections on Wisdom Traditions in Judaism and Early Christianity* (Harrisburg, Pa., 2003), 77–91, has stressed the possible historicity of John's account.

Important literary critical commentaries on John include A. Stock, *Call to Discipleship: A Literary Study of Mark's Gospel* (Wilmington, Del., 1982); R. A. Culpepper, *Anatomy of the Fourth Gospel: A Study in Literary Design* (Philadelphia, 1983); and Robert Kysar, *John's Story of Jesus* (Philadelphia, 1984). For literary approaches to John 20, see also especially B. Lindars, "The Composition of John xx," *New Testament Studies* 7 (1960–61): 142–147, who argues that John invented the story of Thomas in order to dramatize the theme of doubt found in the synoptic Gospels; also Ignace de la Potterie, "Genèse de la foi pascale d'après Jn. 20," *New Testament Studies* 30 (1984): 26–49; Dorothy Lee, "Partnership in Easter Faith: The Role of Mary Magdalene and Thomas in John 20," *Journal for the Study of the New Testament* 50 (1995): 37–49; and William Bonney, *Caused to Believe: The Doubting Thomas Story as the Climax of John's Christological Narrative* (Leiden, 2002), on John 20, especially 131–173. For other literary critical analyses of various parts of the Gospel of John, see also Rudolf Schnackenburg, "Strukturanalyse von Joh. 17," *Biblische Zeitschrift* 17 (1973): 67–78, 196–202; J. L. Resseguie, "John 9: A Literary-Critical Analysis," in K. R. R. Gros Louis, ed., *Literary Interpretations of Biblical Narratives II* (Nashville, Tenn., 1982), 295–320; J. D. Crossan, "It Is Written: A Structuralist Analysis of John 6," *Semeia* 26 (1983): 3–21; M. Rissi, "Der Aufbau des vierten Evangeliums," *New Testament Studies* 29 (1983): 48–54; Robert Kysar, "Johannine Metaphor—Meaning and Function: A Literary Case Study of John 10:1–18," *Semeia* 53 (1991): 81–111; J. Warren Holleran,

"Seeing the Light: A Narrative Reading of John 9," *Ephemerides Theologicae Lovanienses* 69 (1993): 5–26, 354–382; and Mark W. G. Stibbe, ed., *The Gospel of John as Literature: An Anthology of Twentieth-Century Perspectives* (Leiden, 1993). A number of recent investigations of irony in the Gospel of John have raised interesting issues of literary criticism: H. Clavier, "L'ironie dans le Quatrième Evangile," *Studia Evangelica* 1 (1959): 261–276; George W. MacRae, "Theology and Irony in the Fourth Gospel," in R. J. Clifford and George W. MacRae, eds., *The Word in the World: Essays in Honor of Frederick L. Moriarty* (Cambridge, Mass., 1973), 83–96; D. W. Wead, "Johannine Irony as a Key to the Author-Audience Relationship in John's Gospel," in Fred O. Francis, ed., *American Academy of Religion: Section on Biblical Literature, 1974* (Missoula, Mont., 1974), 33–50; and P. D. Duke, *Irony in the Fourth Gospel* (Atlanta, 1985).

Various kinds of rhetorical approaches to this Gospel are to be found in P. P. A. Kotzé, "John and Reader's Response," *Neotestamentica* 19 (1985): 50–63; J. A. Staley, *The Print's First Kiss: A Rhetorical Investigation of the Implied Reader in the Fourth Gospel* (Atlanta, 1988); D. Culbertson, "Are You Also Deceived? Reforming the Reader in John 7," *Proceedings, Eastern Great Lakes and Midwest Biblical Societies* 9 (1989): 148–160; and Lauren L. Johns and Douglas B. Miller, "The Signs as Witness in the Fourth Gospel: Reexamining the Evidence," *Catholic Biblical Quarterly* 56 (1994): 519–535.

On the relation between belief and knowledge in John's thought, see J. Gaffney, "Believing and Knowing in the Fourth Gospel," *Theological Studies* 26 (1965): 215–241; on the importance of vision, G. L. Phillips, "Faith and Vision in the Fourth Gospel," in F. L. Cross, ed., *Studies in the Fourth Gospel* (London, 1957), 83–96, Patrick Grant, "John: Seeing and Believing," in *Reading the New Testament* (Grand Rapids, Mich., 1989), 59–77, and Craig Koester, "Hearing, Seeing, and Believing in the Gospel of John," *Biblica* 70 (1989): 327–348; on the relation between faith and miracles, M.-É. Boismard, "Rapports entre foi et miracles dans l'Evangile de Jean," *Ephemerides Theologicae Lovanienses* 58 (1982): 357–364. The semantics of πιστεύω in the New Testament are studied by Rudolf Bultmann, "πιστεύω," in Gerhard Kittel and G. W. Bromley, eds., *Theological Dictionary of the New Testament*, vol. 6 (Grand Rapids, Mich., 1974), 174–228; and J. E. Botha, "The Meanings of *pisteuo* in the Greek New Testament: A Semantic-Lexicographical Study," *Neotestamentica* 21 (1987): 225–240.

For a suggestive, if somewhat idiosyncratic, philosophical and psychoanalytical interpretation of John's account of the encounter between Mary

Magdalene and Jesus, see Jean-Luc Nancy, *Noli me tangere: Essai sur la levée du corps* (Paris, 2003), esp. 21–42, 47–53, 60–68, 71–79, 84–89.

Why did Jesus tell Mary not to touch him? Jos. Maiworm, " 'Noli me tangere!' Beitrag zur Exegese von Jo 20,17" *Theologie und Glaube* 30 (1938): 540–546, criticizes twelve different explanations and then offers his own (none of these coincides with the one proposed here); Manuel Miguens, "Nota esegetica: Juan 20, 17," *Studii Biblici Franciscani Liber Annuus* 7 (1956–57): 221–231, examines a variety of patristic and modern approaches to this question, reaching from St. Cyril of Alexandria to the twentieth century, and concludes that Jesus means that Mary should not delay him on his way to ascending to the Father.

In any case, the question of the exact meaning of Jesus' prohibition to Mary cannot be resolved by grammatical considerations alone. In the language of the New Testament, the verb form in the Greek original, Μή μου ἅπτου ("Do not touch me" 20:17), a present tense imperative (and not an aorist), is semantically ambiguous: while it can certainly be used in order to interrupt an action which is already in progress, it can also be used to block an attempt to perform that action. Cf. James Hope Moulton, *A Grammar of New Testament Greek*, 3 vols. (Edinburgh, 1930–63) 1:122–126, 3.74–78; Friedrich Blass-Albert Debrunner, *Grammatik des neutestamentlichen Griechisch*, ed. Friedrich Rehkopf, 16th ed. (Göttingen, 1984), §336, 274–275, esp. 275n4 "(was schon geschehen oder versucht ist)" ("what has already happened or been attempted"). In the Latin Vulgate, the manuscript tradition is split at this point between *tenere* ("hold") and *tangere* ("touch"), evidence that already in late antiquity there was considerable uncertainty regarding the exact meaning of Jesus' prohibition.

For a stimulating and provocative account of the role played by disgust in individual and social life, see William I. Miller, *The Anatomy of Disgust* (Cambridge, Mass., 1997); on wounds, cf., for example, 53. For a historical and philosophical approach to disgust and its role in European aesthetics and art, see Winfried Menninghaus, *Ekel: Theorie und Geschichte einer starken Empfindung* (Frankfurt, 1999); for the complexities of disgust in Roman culture, Robert A. Kaster, "The Dynamics of *Fastidium* and the Ideology of Disgust," *Transactions and Proceedings of the American Philological Association* 131 (2001): 143–189.

I borrow the term "hyperbolic doubt" from Descartes' *Meditations on First Philosophy*, though of course his own usage is quite different from mine.

Early attempts to identify Nathanael equated him with Bartholomew, who is paired with Philip at Mark 3:18, Luke 6:14, and Matthew 10:3; cf. U.

Holzmeister, "Nathanael fuitne idem ac S. Bartholomaeus Apostolus?" *Biblica* 21 (1940): 28–39. This identification seems to be entirely arbitrary, but it may be worth noting that at Acts 1:13 it is Thomas who is paired with Philip; perhaps this may be taken as another faint trace of the recognition of some affinity between Nathanael and Thomas.

For the general preference in the Hebrew Bible for faith based upon hearing God's word over the demand for the sight of miracles, cf. H. H. Wolff, *Anthropologie des Alten Testaments* (Munich, 1973), 115ff.

I gratefully borrow the terms "epistemic" and "nonepistemic" belief from Arnold Davidson, who has suggested them to me orally. They reflect the views of Ludwig Wittgenstein on the differences between religious faith and other kinds of belief, cf. especially his *Culture and Value*, ed. G. H. von Wright and Heikki Nyman, trans. Peter Winch (Chicago, 1980); *Lectures and Conversations on Aesthetics, Psychology, and Religion*, ed. Cyril Barrett (Berkeley, 1966), 53–72; and Rush Rhees, ed., *Recollections of Wittgenstein* (Oxford, 1984), 76–171.

On John 21, see S. S. Smalley, "The Sign in John XXI," *New Testament Studies* 20 (1974): 275–288, who argues for its authenticity; and P. S. Minear, "The Original Function of John 21," *Journal of Biblical Literature* 102 (1983): 85–98.

Sources and Reflections

Twins have long been a favorite subject for anthropology and history of religion. Important general works in this area include Hermann Usener, "Göttliche Synonyme" and "Zwillingsbildung," in *Kleine Schriften* 4 (Leipzig, 1913), 259–306 and 334–356; Julius von Negelein, "Die abergläubische Bedeutung der Zwillingsgeburt," *Archiv für Religionswissenschaft* 5 (1902): 271–273; P. Saintyves, "Les jumeaux dans l'ethnographie et la mythologie," *Revue Anthropologique* 35 (1925): 262–267; E. Sidney Hartland, "Twins," in James Hastings, ed., *Encyclopaedia of Religion and Ethics*, vol. 12 (Edinburgh, 1980), 491–500; Leo Sternberg, "Der antike Zwillingskult im Lichte der Ethnologie," *Zeitschrift für Ethnologie* 61 (1929): 152–200; Alexander Haggerty Krappe, "Zum antiken Zwillingsmythus im Lichte der Ethnologie," *Zeitschrift für Ethnologie* 66 (1934): 187–191; Alfred Métraux, "Twin Heroes in South American Mythology," *Journal of American Folklore* 59 (1946): 114–123; Claude Lévi-Strauss, *Histoire de Lynx* (Paris, 1991), chap. 5, "La sentence fatidique," 79–92.

An extremely rich, if sometimes rather nebulous account of twins in the religions of the Ancient Near East (including the Hebrew Bible and Thomas) is provided by Raymond Kuntzmann, *Le symbolisme des jumeaux au Proche-Orient ancien: Naissance, fonction, et évolution d'un symbole* (Paris, 1983).

Various kinds of twins play an important role in Christian legend: see J. Rendel Harris, *The Dioscuri in the Christian Legends* (London, 1903), *The Cult of the Heavenly Twins* (Cambridge, 1906), *The Twelve Apostles* (Cambridge, 1927), and *The Piety of the Heavenly Twins*, Woodbrooke Essays 14 (Cambridge, 1928).

For twins in ancient Greece, see, for example, S. Eitrem, *Die göttlichen Zwillinge bei den Griechen* (Christiania, 1902); Jean-Pierre Vernant, "Figuration de l'invisible et catégorie psychologique du double: Le colossos," in Vernant, *Mythe et pensée chez les Grecs* (Paris, 1974), 2:65–78; Claudie Voisenat, "La rivalité, la séparation et la mort: Destinées gemellaires dans la mythologie grecque," *L'Homme* 28 (1988): 88–103; Françoise Frontisi-Ducroux, "Les Grecs, le double, et les jumeaux," *Topique* 50 (1992): 239–262; Véronique Dasen, "Les jumeaux dans l'imaginaire funeraire grec," in Geneviève Hoffmann, ed., *Les pierres de l'offrande* (Zurich, 2001), 72–89.

For Roman twins, the reader may consult Ekkehard Stärk, *Die* Menaechmi *des Plautus und kein griechisches Original* (Tübingen, 1989), esp. 147–152; and Francesca Mencacci, *I fratelli amici: La rappresentazione dei gemelli nella cultura romana* (Venice, 1996).

On Celtic and Germanic twins, see Alexander Haggerty Krappe, "Les dieux jumeaux dans la religion germanique," *Acta Philologica Scandinavica* 6 (1936): 1–25; Donald Ward, *The Divine Twins: An Indoeuropean Myth in Germanic Tradition* (Berkeley, 1968); S. O'Brien, "Dioscuric Elements in Celtic and Germanic Mythology," *Journal of Indoeuropean Studies* 10 (1982): 117–135.

On twins in the Middle Ages, see J. M. M. H. Thijssen, "Twins as Monsters: Albertus Magnus's Theory of the Generation of Twins and Its Philosophical Context," *Bulletin of the History of Medicine* 61 (1987): 237–246.

For a sociological perspective, see Laura Makarius-Levi, "Les jumeaux: De l'ambivalence au dualisme," *L'Année Sociologique* 18 (1967): 373–390. For a psychological one, René Zazzo, *Les jumeaux, le couple, et la personne* (Paris, 1960) and *Le paradoxe des jumeaux* (Paris, 1984); L. Valente Torre, ed., *I gemelli: Il vissuto del doppio* (Florence, 1989).

There is an extensive medical literature regarding the risks involved in twin births. Recent studies in highly industrialized Western countries with modern medical systems all tend to confirm that the perinatal mortality rate of twins is three to four times higher than for single births, and that second twins have a somewhat and, in some studies, a considerably lower chance of survival than do first twins; recent studies suggest that even when the perinatal mortality of the second twin is not appreciably higher than that of the first twin, s/he more often has a lower Apgar score and is otherwise disadvantaged with respect to the first one. See, for example, Jose C. Scerbo, Pawan Rattan, and Joan E. Drukker, "Twins and Other Multiple Gestations," in Robert A. Knuppel and Joan E. Drukker, eds., *High-Risk Pregnancy: A Team Approach* (Philadelphia, 1986), 335–361; Ralph C. Benson, "Multiple Pregnancy," in Martin L. Pernoll, ed., *Current Obstetric and Gynecologic Diagnosis and Treatment*, 7th ed. (Norwalk, Conn., 1991), 352–363; Louis Keith and Emile Papiernik, eds., *Multiple Gestation: Clinical Obstetrics and Gynecology* 41:1 (March 1998): 1–139. On the other disadvantages for the second twin besides increased mortality, see T. K. Eskes et al., "The Second Twin," *European Journal of Obstetrics, Gynecology, and Reproductive Biology* 19 (1985): 159–166; B. K. Young et al., "Differences in Twins: The Importance of Birth Order," *American Journal of Obstetrics and Gynecology* 151 (1985): 915–921; R. Nakano and H. Takemura, "Birth Order in Delivery of Twins," *Gynecologic and Obstetric Investigation* 25 (1988): 217–222.

Obviously no statistics are available for twin births in Palestine in New Testament times. But it seems more than likely that the relatively unfavorable outcomes found in these modern European and American studies for twins as compared with single births, and for second twins as compared with first twins, must have been greatly amplified in conditions of inadequate hygiene, primitive medicine, and much higher normal infant mortality. This hypothesis finds strong support in the results of research on twin mortality throughout the modern preindustrial world. See, for example, Richard L. Naeye, "Twins: Causes of Perinatal Death in Twelve United States Cities and One African City," *American Journal of Obstetrics and Gynecology* 131 (1978): 267–272 (comparison with Ethiopia); O. Fakeye, "Twin Birth Weight Discordancy in Nigeria," *International Journal of Gynaecology and Obstetrics* 24 (1986): 235–238 and "Perinatal Factors in Twin Mortality in Nigeria," *International Journal of Gynaecology and Obstetrics* 24 (1986): 309–314; C .A. Crowther, "Perinatal Mortality in Twin Pregnancy: A Review of 799 Twin Pregnancies," *South African Medical Journal J* 71 (1987): 73–74 (Harare, Zimbabwe); A. Bugalho, F. Strolego, and G. Carlomango, "Outcomes of Twin Pregnancies at the Hospital Central of Maputo: Retrospective Study of 315 Consecutive Twin Deliveries, January 1–September 30, 1987," *International Journal of Gynaecology and Obstetrics* 29 (1989): 297–300 (Maputo, Mozambique); A. Dolo, N. G. Diall, and F. S. Diabate, "A propos de 507 grossesses et accouchements gémellaires dans le district de Bamako," *Dakar Médical* 35 (1990): 25–31 (Mali); K. Coard et al., "Perinatal mortality in Jamaica 1986–1987," *Acta Paediatrica Scandinavica* 80 (1991): 749–755; R. Rachdi et al., "Problèmes posés par l'accouchement de la grossesse gémellaire," *Revue Française de Gynécologie et d'Obstétrique* 87 (1992): 295–298 (Tunisia); L. Kouam and J. Kamdom-Moyo, "Les facteurs de risque fœtal dans les accouchements gémellaires: Une analyse critique de 265 cas," *Revue Française de Gynécologie et d'Obstétrique* 90:3 (March 1995): 155–162 (Yaoundé, Cameroon; my thanks for the authors' courteous assistance); M. Nkata, "Perinatal Mortality in Twin Deliveries in a General Hospital in Zambia," *Journal of Tropical Pediatrics* 45 (1999): 365–367; J. F. Meye et al., "Prognosis of Twin Deliveries in an African Setting," *Santé: Cahiers d'études et de recherches francophones* 11 (2001): 91–94 (Libreville, Gabon).

Narrative Developments: The Apocrypha and Beyond

There can be little doubt that the Midrashic interpretation of the Jewish Bible provides an important hermeneutic parallel and cultural context for understanding the development of Apocryphal narratives out of the New Testament. The standard older collection of the Midrash in English is Louis Ginzberg, *The Legends of the Jews*, 7 vols. (Philadelphia, 1909); an abridged version is *Legends of the Jews* (New York, 1961). But see now also James L. Kugel, *Traditions of the Bible: A Guide to the Bible as It Was at the Start of the Common Era* (Cambridge, Mass., 1998); a more popular version is *The Bible as It Was* (Cambridge, Mass., 1997). In general on this whole subject see Michael Fishbane, *Biblical Interpretation in Ancient Israel* (New York, 1985), and now especially his *Biblical Myth and Rabbinic Mythmaking* (Oxford, 2003).

The English-speaking reader who wishes a reliable and authoritative collection of the New Testament Apocrypha is well served by two recent anthologies: *New Testament Apocrypha*, rev. ed., ed. Wilhelm Schneemelcher, Engl. trans. R. McL. Wilson, 2 vols. (Cambridge, 1991–92); and *The Apocryphal New Testament: A Collection of Apocryphal Christian Literature in an English Translation Based on M. R. James*, ed. J. K. Elliott (Oxford, 1993). Both collections include very helpful introductions and up-to-date bibliographies to all the texts they present, to which I refer the reader for generous and circumspect guides to the vast and highly controversial secondary scholarship. My references to the New Testament Apocrypha are keyed to these volumes: unless otherwise indicated, I quote from the translation in Elliott's edition.

The Nag Hammadi texts are conveniently collected in James M. Robinson, ed., *The Nag Hammadi Library in English* (San Francisco, 1981). A generous collection of Gnostic sources is provided by Werner Foester, ed., *Gnosis: A Selection of Texts*, 2 vols., trans. R. McL. Wilson (Oxford, 1974). Among the many important works of scholarship on Gnosticism, at least the following monographic accounts must be mentioned, if only to indicate the variety of approaches and positions: Hans Jonas, *Gnosis und spätantiker Geist*, 2 vols. (Göttingen, 1934–54; 3rd ed., 1964–93) and *The Gnostic Religion: The Message of the Alien God and the Beginnings of Christianity* (Boston, 1958; 3rd ed., 1963); Gilles Quispel, *Gnosis als Weltreligion* (Zurich, 1951); Robert M. Grant, *Gnosticism and Early Christianity*, rev. ed. (New York, 1966); Hermann Langerbeck, *Aufsätze zur Gnosis*, ed. Hermann Dörries (Göttingen, 1967); R. McL. Wilson, *Gnosis and the New Testament* (Oxford, 1968); Edwin M. Yamauchi, *Pre-Christian Gnosticism: A Survey of the Proposed Evidences* (Grand Rapids, Mich., 1973; 2nd ed., 1983); Kurt Rudolph, *Gnosis: The Nature and History of Gnosticism*, trans. R. McL. Wilson (San Francisco, 1983); Walter Schmithals, *Neues Testament und Gnosis* (Darmstadt, 1984); Charles W. Hedrick and Robert Hodgson, Jr., ed., *Nag Hammadi, Gnosticism, and Early Christianity* (Peabody, Mass., 1986); Gilles Quispel, "Gnosticism: Gnosticism from Its Origins to the Middle Ages," in Mircea Eliade, ed., *The Encyclopedia of Religion* (New York, 1987), 5:566–574; Elaine Pagels, *Adam, Eve, and the Serpent* (New York, 1988); Giovanni Filoramo, *A History of Gnosticism*, trans. Anthony Alcock (Oxford, 1990); Birger A. Pearson, *Gnosticism, Judaism, and Egyptian Christianity* (Minneapolis, 1990); Simone Pétrement, *A Separate God: The Christian Origins of Gnosticism*, trans. Carol Harrison (San Francisco, 1990); Pheme Perkins, *Gnosticism and the New Testament* (Minneapolis, 1993); Stuart Holroyd, *The Elements of Gnosticism* (Shaftesbury, Dorset, UK, 1994); and Christoph Markschies, *Die Gnosis* (Munich, 2001). Some particularly useful collections of essays are K. W. Troeger, *Gnosis und Neues Testament: Studien aus Religionswissenschaft und Theologie* (Berlin, 1973); Kurt Rudolph, ed., *Gnosis und Gnostizismus*, Wege der Forschung 262 (Darmstadt, 1975); Martin Krause, ed., *Gnosis and Gnosticism: Papers Read at the Seventh International Conference on Patristic Studies (Oxford, September 8th–13th 1975)* (Leiden, 1977); and Bentley Layton, ed., *The Rediscovery of Gnosticism: Proceedings of the International Conference on Gnosticism at Yale, New Haven, Connecticut, March 28–31, 1978*, 2 vols. (Leiden, 1980–81).

For a different view of the relation between the Gospel of Thomas and possible Christian sources, see Ron Cameron, "Ancient Myths and Modern

Theories of the Gospel of Thomas and Christian Origins," *Method and Theory in the Study of Religion* 11 (1999): 236–257.

The intricate question of the relation between the Gospel of John and Gnostic modes of thought has been much studied. For very different views on this subject see, for example, Rudolph Bultmann, *Das Evangelium des Johannes*, 10th ed. (Göttingen, 1941), translated into English as *The Gospel of John: A Commentary*, trans. G. R. Beasley-Murray, ed. R. W. N. Hoare and J. K. Riches (Oxford, 1971); Elaine Pagels, *The Johannine Gospel in Gnostic Exegesis: Heracleon's Commentary on John* (Nashville, Tenn., 1973); Peter Hofrichter, *Im Anfang war der "Johannesprolog": Das urchristliche Logosbekenntnis, die Basis neutestamentlicher und gnostischer Theologie* (Regensburg, 1986); Helmut Koester, "The History-of-Religions School, Gnosis, and the Gospel of John," *Studia Theologica* 40 (1986): 115–136; Alastair H. B. Logan, "John and the Gnostics: The Significance of the Apocryphon of John for the Debate about the Origins of the Johannine Literature," *Journal for the Study of the New Testament* 43 (1991): 41–69.

Michael Allen Williams, *Rethinking "Gnosticism": An Argument for Dismantling a Dubious Category* (Princeton, 1996) has furnished provocative arguments for questioning the usefulness of the concept of "Gnosticism," as well as sophisticated surveys of both the historical issues involved and the history of scholarship on them. See too, in a similar if not quite identical vein, Karen L. King, *What Is Gnosticism?* (Cambridge, Mass., 2003).

Just as I was putting the finishing touches on this study, Elaine Pagels, *Beyond Belief: The Secret Gospel of Thomas* (New York, 2003), was published. In this deeply personal book, especially in Chapter 2, 30–73, as well as in an earlier scholarly article of hers, "Exegesis of Genesis 1 in the Gospels of Thomas and John," *Journal of Biblical Literature* 118 (1999): 477–496, upon which that chapter is based, Pagels presents a view of the Gospel of Thomas and of its relation to the Gospel of John that is very much at variance with the one for which I argue here. Although the constraints of these bibliographical essays mean that I cannot do full justice here to her arguments and ideas, the general importance of her earlier work on various aspects of Gnosticism and the considerable differences between her views and mine require that I indicate to the reader at least briefly what those differences are. Pagels believes (1) that the Gospel of Thomas is earlier than or at least contemporary with the Gospel of John; (2) that the author of the Gospel of John is attempting to refute the author of the Gospel of Thomas; and (3) that Thomas's vision of those capable of salvation is universally inclusive whereas John's is highly restrictive. But (1) she offers no evidence whatsoever in support of her claim that the Gospel of Thomas was composed as early as the first century A.D., whereas the large majority of scholarly opinion dates the text to sometime around the middle of the second century; hence I see no reason to abandon my view that the Gospel of Thomas was written some significant time, perhaps about half a century, after the Gospel of John. Of course, individual sayings in the Gospel of Thomas certainly go back to the first century A.D.; but to conclude from that fact that the text as a whole was composed that early, or that, whenever it was composed, it faithfully reflects as a whole the situation of the first century A.D., is a non sequitur. (2) Not a single one of the passages which Pagels analyzes requires that we understand John to be refuting texts found in the Gospel of Thomas; at most the two Gospels present two different views on a number of issues, but there is no reason at all to presume that John was familiar with those specific teachings that are found now in the Gospel of Thomas, nor that he identified them with Thomas or with Thomas Christians (whom Pagels supposes, without any evidence at all, to have existed already in the first century A.D.), nor finally that his intention was to refute them. The differences can just as easily be explained as simple doctrinal divergences, or else as attempts by the author of the Gospel of Thomas to refute the teachings of the Gospel of John—indeed, given the relative chronology of the two works, the latter hypothesis is certainly preferable. (3) Pagels herself is obliged to admit that "both John and Thomas include some sayings suggesting that those who come to know God are very few" (p. 46); in fact her claim that John is exclusive while Thomas is inclusive does not stand up to comparison with the evidence. John emphasizes belief, not knowledge, and nowhere suggests that such belief is something that not all human beings are capable of attaining; the fact that many have not yet attained belief in Jesus does not prevent John from hoping that his Gospel will persuade many more people to believe in Jesus, and there is no reason to suppose that John did not hope that all people might someday achieve this belief. The Gospel of Thomas, in contrast, emphasizes knowledge, not belief, and is full of suggestions that the number of people who are capable of attaining and understanding this knowledge is very small indeed. To support her position, Pagels must systematically distort the meaning of passages she quotes from the Gospel of Thomas, by suggesting that when the author refers to those who are capable of being saved, he means thereby all human beings; what he means is evidently not all mankind but rather those relatively few specific individuals whom he is addressing and who constitute, in his eyes and in their own, a tiny saved elite. It is difficult to imagine how Pagels could consider someone to be an advocate of a doctrine of universal salvation who reports Jesus as saying, "I shall choose you, one from a thousand, and two from ten thousand, and they shall stand as a single one" (§23) and "Blessed are the solitary and the chosen for you will find the kingdom" (§49) and "I tell my mysteries to those who are worthy of my mysteries" (§62) and "Many are standing at the door but the solitary are the ones who will enter the bridal chamber" (§75) and "The kingdom is like a shepherd who had a hundred sheep. One of them, the largest, went astray. He left the ninety-nine and searched for that one until he found it. After he had labored he said to the sheep, 'I love you more than the ninety-nine'" (§107).

Edessa, early a focal point for the cult of Thomas, is the subject of an important study: Steven K. Ross, *Roman Edessa: Politics and Culture on the Eastern Fringes of the Roman Empire, 114–242 CE* (London, 2001). Earlier works on the city include A. F. J. Klijn, *Edessa die Stadt des Apostels Thomas* (Neukirchen, 1965).

The attempt to explain the origin and history of the Thomas Christians in India has produced an enormous amount of scholarship of varying quality. A small selection of the more interesting accounts might include J. Dahlmann, *Die Thomas-Legende und die ältesten historischen Beziehungen des Christentums zum fernen Osten im Lichte der indischen Altertumskunde* (Freiburg, 1912); Leslie Brown, *The Indian Christians of St. Thomas: An Account of the Ancient Syrian Church of Malabar* (Cambridge, 1956; 2nd ed., 1982); Albrecht Dihle, "Neues zur Thomastradition," *Jahrbuch für Antike und Christentum* 6 (1963): 54–70, and "Indien," in *Reallexikon für Antike und Christentum*, vol. 18 (Stuttgart 1996), 1–56, esp. 36–55; E. R. Hamlye, "L'apôtre saint Thomas en Inde," *Orient Syrien* 8 (1963): 413–424; A. Mathias Mundadan, *History of Christianity in India*, vol. 1: *From the Beginning up to the Middle of the Sixteenth Century (up to 1542)* (Bangalore, 1984) and *Indian Christians: Search for Identity and Struggle for Autonomy* (Bangalore, 1984); Stephen Neill, *A History of Christianity in India: The Beginnings to AD 1707* (Cambridge, 1984).

For the *Culex* in the Appendix Vergiliana as a forgery intended to satisfy curiosity about the poetic productions of the young Virgil, see my article "The 'Virgilian' Culex," in M. Whitby, P. Hardie, and M. Whitby, eds., *Homo Viator: Classical Essays for John Bramble* (Bristol, 1987), 199–209. I hope to return to this and related texts in the future.

The question of the relation between Philostratus' account of Apollonius of Tyana and the New Testament accounts of Jesus has been an unsolved problem for historical scholarship at least since D. Baur, "Apollonius von Tyana und Christus, oder das Verhältniß des Pythagoreismus zum Christentum: Ein Beitrag zur Religionsgeschichte der ersten Jahrhunderte nach Christus," *Tübinger Zeitschrift für Theologie* 4 (1832): 3–235. G. Petzke, *Die Traditionen über Apollonios von Tyana und das Neue Testament* (Leiden, 1970), provides a recent survey of the issues and texts.

For early accounts of scenes of attempted, and successful, viewing and touching of the stigmata of Saint Francis of Assisi, see especially *Analecta Franciscana, Tomus X: Legendae S. Francisci Assisiensis saeculis XIII et XIV conscriptae,* ed. PP. Collegii S. Bonaventurae (Quaracchi, 1936–41), Fasc. I: Fr. Thomas de Celano, *Vita prima S. Francisci*, pars II, caput iii.95, 73; caput ix.113, 88–89; Fasc. II: Fr. Thomas de Celano, *Vita secunda S. Francisci*, pars II, caput xcviii–ci, 208–210; Fasc. III: Fr. Thomas de Celano, *Tractatus de miraculis S. Francisci Assisiensis,* caput ii.4–5, 274–275; Fasc. IV: Fr. Iulianus de Spira, *Vita S. Francisci,* caput xi.63, 364; *Legenda choralis umbra* 2, 544; Fasc. V: S. Bonaventura, *Legenda maior S. Francisci,* caput xiii.8, 618–619; *Quaedam de Miraculis ipsius post mortem ostensis,* caput i.2–3, 627–628; Iacobus de Voragine, *Vita S. Francisci* 23, 686; *Legenda Monacensis S. Francisci,* caput xxx.95, 718; also, for example, Guido Davico Bonino, ed., *I fioretti di San Francesco* (Turin, 1964), 194–196, 200, 211–212.

I cite "Marienkind" from *Kinder- und Hausmärchen gesammelt durch die Brüder Grimm* (Darmstadt, 1978), 46–50. The story figures as number 710 in Antti Aarne-Stith Thompson, *The Types of the Folktale: A Classification and Bibliography,* 2nd revision, 2nd ed. (Helsinki, 1973), 246–247. For parallels and variants, see Johannes Bolte and George Polívka, *Anmerkungen zu den Kinder- und Hausmärchen der Brüder Grimm,* vol. 1 (Leipzig, 1913; repr. Hildesheim, 1992), 13–21; Walter Scherf, *Das Märchenlexikon* (Munich, 1995), 2:847–853; and Daniel Drascek, "Marienkind," in *Enzyklopädie des Märchens,* vol. 9 (Berlin, 1999), 336–342 (the latter two articles with further bibliography). On "Marienkind" and related issues I have learned much from Almut-Barbara Renger, *Zwischen Märchen und Mythos: Die Abenteuer des Odysseus und andere Geschichten von Homer bis Walter Benjamin: Eine gattungstheoretische Studie,* diss. Heidelberg 2001. The earliest extant version of the fable was published under the title "La facce de crapa" in Gian Alesio Abattutis [i.e., Giambattista Basile], *Lo cunto de li cunti o vero lo trattenemiento de peccerille* (Naples, 1634): see

Giambattista Basile, *Lo cunto de li cunti*, ed. Michele Rak (Milan, 1986), 166–179; an English translation is available in *The Pentamerone of Giambattista Basile*, trans. from the Italian of Benedetto Croce and ed. N. M. Penzer (London, 1932), 1:75–85.

Exegetical Reactions: From the Church Fathers to the Counter-Reformation

For the theory of textual exegesis, Hans-Georg Gadamer, *Wahrheit und Methode: Grundzüge einer philosophischen Hermeneutik* (Tübingen, 1960), now available in an expanded edition in *Gesammelte Werke*, vols. 1 and 2 (Tübingen, 1986); English translation by Garret Barden and William G. Doerpel, *Truth and Method*, 2nd rev. ed. (New York, 1993), remains fundamental. See also Emilio Betti, *Teoria generale della interpretazione*, 2 vols. (Milan, 1955), German translation by the author, *Allgemeine Auslegungslehre als Methodik der Geisteswissenschaften* (Tübingen, 1967); and *Die Hermeneutik als allgemeine Methode der Geisteswissenschaften* (Tübingen, 1962). A useful introductory anthology is provided by David E. Klemm, ed., *Hermeneutical Inquiry*, 2 vols. (Atlanta, 1986).

The anecdote about Gulliver is in Jonathan Swift, *Gulliver's Travels*, part III, chapter 8, at the beginning.

An extremely helpful survey of virtually all the exegetical material concerning Thomas, from Irenaeus to the Reformers, is provided by a German dissertation: Ulrich Pflugk, *Die Geschichte vom ungläubigen Thomas (Johannes 20,24–29) in der Auslegung der Kirche von den Anfängen bis zur Mitte des sechzehnten Jahrhunderts*, diss. Hamburg 1965. Although I disagree with some of Pflugk's larger and smaller conclusions and have corrected a small number of his omissions and errors, I acknowledge gratefully the enormous benefit I have derived from his Herculean labors.

There do not seem to be any significant differences between the Orthodox and the Catholic churches in their interpretation of Doubting Thomas: see in general above all Martin Jugie, *Theologia dogmatica Christianorum orientalium ab ecclesia Catholica dissidentium*, vols. 1–5 (Paris, 1926–35).

I am much indebted to a splendid study of the theological traditions regarding the nature of the resurrected body: Caroline Walker Bynum, *The Resurrection of the Body in Western Christianity, 200–1336* (New York, 1995); for her stimulating discussion of the metaphors in 1 Corinthians 15, see 3–6; the passage quoted from her is on 6. See also on this subject M. E. Dahl, *The Res-*

urrection of the Body, Studies in Biblical Theology 36 (London, 1962); and J. A. Schep, *The Nature of the Resurrection Body: A Study of the Biblical Data* (Grand Rapids, Mich., 1964).

For the wider context of early Christian views on the body, and not merely on sexuality in particular, Peter Brown, *The Body and Society: Men, Women, and Sexual Renunciation in Early Christianity* (New York, 1988) remains a learned and humane guide. On the indispensability of a body for the concept of personal identity, there is much to learn from Bernard Williams, *Problems of the Self* (Cambridge, 1973), 1–18, 19–25, 64–81; on some puzzles involving resurrection, 92–94.

The interpretation of Paul's First Epistle to the Corinthians, and especially the identification of the exact targets of his polemics, remains highly controversial. Guidance may be found in Hans Lietzmann, *Handbuch zum Neuen Testament 9: An die Korinther I/II*, 4th ed., supplemented by W. G. Kümmel (Tübingen, 1949); Margaret E. Thrall, *The Cambridge Bible Commentary on the New English Bible: I and II Corinthians* (Cambridge, 1965); Hans Conzelmann, *1 Corinthians: A Commentary on the First Epistle to the Corinthians*, translated by James W. Leitch, bibliography and references by James W. Dunkly, edited by George W. MacRae, S.J. (Philadelphia, 1975); and William F. Orr and James Arthur Walther, *The Anchor Bible: I Corinthians, A New Translation, Introduction, with a Study of the Life of Paul, Notes, and Commentary* (Garden City, N.J., 1976).

There is an excellent comprehensive account of the history of biblical exegesis: Henning Graf Reventlow, *Epochen der Bibelauslegung*, vols. 1–4 (Munich, 1990–2001). An indispensable guide to the vast medieval material is Fridericus Stegmüller, *Repertorium Biblicum Medii Aevi*, vols. 1–11 (Madrid, 1940–80). Introductory surveys include Robert McQueen Grant, *The Bible in the Church: A Short History of Interpretation* (New York, 1948), and, with David Tracy, *A Short History of the Interpretation of the Bible*, 2nd ed. (Philadelphia, 1984); Rolf Schäfer, *Die Bibelauslegung in der Geschichte der Kirche* (Gütersloh, 1980); Rudolf Smend, *Epochen der Bibelkritik* (Munich, 1991); Bertrand de Margerie, *Introduction to the History of Exegesis*, vols. 1–3 (Petersham, UK, 1991); Pierre Gibert, *Petite histoire de l'éxègese biblique: De la lecture allégorique à l'éxègese critique* (Paris, 1997).

For the early stages of biblical interpretation in Alexandria, principally in Philo, Valentinus, and Clement of Alexandria, see David Dawson, *Allegorical Readers and Cultural Revision in Ancient Alexandria* (Berkeley, 1992). On Origen as a biblical interpreter, Henri de Lubac, *Histoire et esprit: l'intelligence de l'Écriture d'après Origène* (Paris, 1950), remains fundamental; for a useful recent collection of essays, see Gilles Dorival and Alain Le Boulluec, eds., *Origeniana sexta: Origène et la Bible* = *Origen and the Bible*, Bibliotheca Ephemidarum theologicarum Lovaniensium 118 (Louvain, 1995). For biblical exegesis in antiquity, see Hans Rost, *Die Bibel in den ersten Jahrhunderten*, Beiträge zur Kulturgeschichte der Bibel 2 (Westheim bei Augsburg, 1946); and now the collective volume of Johannes van Oort and Ulrich Wickert, eds., *Christliche Exegese zwischen Nicaea und Chalcedon*, Studien der Patristischen Arbeitsgemeinschaft (Kampen, 1992).

For interpretation of the Bible in the Middle Ages, see Hans Rost, *Die Bibel im Mittelalter: Beiträge zur Geschichte und Bibliographie der Bibel* (Augsburg, 1939); Ceslas Spicq, *Esquisse d'une histoire de l'éxègese latine au moyen âge* (Paris, 1944); Beryl Smalley, *The Study of the Bible in the Middle Ages*, 3rd ed. (Oxford, 1983). On the relation between faith and rationality in medieval exegesis in general, and not just in the cases of Tertullian and Origen, there are important observations in Ulrich Wickert, "Glauben und Denken bei Tertullian und Origenes," *Zeitschrift für Theologie und Kirche* 62 (1965): 153–177.

I cite the pre-Reformation commentators from the most recent critical edition available, or, where these are not available, from *PG* or *PL* (see the list of abbreviations at the beginning of this volume). The passage from Asterius referred to is at *Asterii Sophistae Commentariorum in psalmos quae supersunt* (Oslo, 1956), p. 158.

The reformers and Erasmus are cited from the following editions: Georg Buchwald, *Ungedruckte Predigten Johann Bugenhagens aus den Jahren 1524 bis 1529: Zumeist aus Handschriften der Großherzoglichen Universitätsbibliothek zu Jena zum erstenmal veröffentlicht*, Quellen und Darstellungen aus der Geschichte des Reformationsjahrhunderts 13 (Leipzig, 1910); *Ioannis Calvini In Novum Testamentum Commentarii*, ed. A. Tholuck, vol. 3: *In Evangelium Joannis Commentarii* (Berlin, 1833), 368–371; Desiderius Erasmus, *Paraphrasis in Evangelium Joannis* = *Desiderii Erasmi Opera Omnia* (Lugduni Batavorum, 1706; repr. London, 1962), vol. 7, and *Apologia respondens ad ea quae Iacobus Lopis Stunica taxaverat in prima duntaxat Novi Testamenti aeditione*, ed. H. J. de Jonge = *Opera Omnia* IX.2 (Amsterdam, 1983); Martin Luther, *Werke: Kritische Gesamtausgabe* (Weimar, 1883ff.); *Philippi Melanthonis Enarratio in Evangelium Ioannis* = *Opera quae supersunt omnia*, ed. Carolus Gottlieb Bretschneider, *Corpus Reformatorum* 15 (Halle, 1848); Wolfgang Musculus, *Commentarii in Evangelium Joannis* (Basel, 1545); Erasmus Sarcerius, *In evangelia festivalia postilla, ad methodi formam expedita* (Marburg, 1544), 18–24; Johann Spangenberch, *Postilla düdesch aver dat gantze jar* (Magdeburg, 1549). On Musculus in particular, but also on the wider context of his contemporaries, see especially Craig S. Farmer, *The Gospel of John in the Sixteenth Century: The Johannine Exegesis of Wolfgang Musculus* (Oxford, 1997). My Chicago students Rodrigo Sanchez and Aaron Tugendhaft helped me obtain copies respectively of Sarcerius and Spangenberg from Wolfenbüttel, and of Musculus from Freiburg: my thanks to both.

On Luther as an interpreter, see Jaroslav Jan Pelikan, *Luther the Expositor: Introduction to the Reformer's Exegetical Writings* (St. Louis, 1959); and Siegfried Raeder, "Luther als Ausleger und Übersetzer der Heiligen Schrift," in Helmar Junghans, ed., *Leben und Werk Martin Luthers von 1526 bis 1546: Festgabe zu seinem 500. Geburtstag* (Göttingen, 1983), 1:253–278, 2:800–805.

The Counter-Reformation commentators are cited according to the following editions: *Ioannis Maldonati Commentarii in quatuor Evangelistas, Tomus II: in Lucam et Ioannem* (Mussiponti, 1597); Fr. Cajetanus Potesta de Panormo, *Evangelica historia, seu quatuor evangelia in unum redacta* (Panormi, 1726; first published 1550); *Franciscae Riberae Villacastinensis In sanctum Iesu-Christi Evangelium secundum Ioannem Commentarii* (Lugduni, 1623); *Alfonsi Salmeronis Toletani Commentarii in Evangelicam historiam & in Acta Apostolorum, Tomus Undecimus: Qui de Resurrectione, et Ascensione Domini inscribitur* (Coloniae Agrippinae, 1604); Fr. *Toleti Cordubensis In Sacrosanctum Ioannis Evangelium Commentarii* (Brixiae, 1603). For Alfonso Salmerón, a fairly recent biography and evaluation is William V. Bangert, *Claude Jay and Alfonso Salmeron: Two Early Jesuits* (Chicago, 1985). Melchor Cano's method of *loci theologici* has been studied within the context of the history of theology: see Albert Lang, *Die Loci Theologici des Melchior Cano und die Methode des dogmatischen Beweises: Ein Beitrag zur theologischen Methodologie und ihrer Geschichte*, Münchener Studien zur historischen Theologie 6 (Munich, 1925; repr. Hildesheim, 1974), and Bernhard Körner, *Melchior Cano, De locis theologicis: Ein Beitrag zur theologischen Erkenntnislehre* (Graz, 1994). My thanks to Dr. Rosa Maria Piccione (Jena) for making it possible for me to examine these Counter-Reformation commentaries in the library of the Pontifical Gregorian University in Rome.

San Carlo Borromeo is cited from *Homélies et discours de Saint Charles Borromée*, traduits en français par MM. les abbés Lecomte et Venault: Avent et Carême (Paris, 1901), 344–360: Cinquième homélie sur la passion de Notre-Seigneur, prononcée dans la Métropole de Milan, le 23 Mars 1584. On the sacred eloquence of San Carlo Borromeo and its religious and institutional contexts, see especially Marc Fumaroli, *L'âge de l'éloquence: Rhétorique et «res literaria» de la Renaissance au seuil de l'époque classique* (Geneva, 1980; Paris, 1994), 116–152 (I cite from the second edition).

Pictorial Versions: Thomas in Sacred Images

For the various and complex ways and degrees in which medieval art succeeds in communicating with viewers of various degrees of literacy, see especially Michael Camille, "Seeing and Reading: Some Visual Implications of Medieval Literacy and Illiteracy," *Art History* 8 (1985): 26–49. On aspects of literacy in the ancient world, see William V. Harris, *Ancient Literacy* (Cambridge, Mass., 1989); in the Middle Ages, Franz H. Bäuml, "Varieties and Consequences of Medieval Literacy and Illiteracy," *Speculum* 55 (1980): 237–265. On the use of religious painting for propagandistic purposes, especially in contrast with sculpture, see Lucien Febvre, "Iconographie et évangélisation chrétienne," in *Pour une Histoire à part entière* (Paris, 1962), 795–819; on the interrelation between image and word in Christian preaching, see now Lina Bolzoni, *La rete delle immagini: Predicazione in volgare dalle origini a Bernardino da Siena* (Turin, 2002); and for a small but useful collection of medieval statements of the doctrine of "muta praedicatio" from Gregory the Great to Villon, L. Gougaud, "Muta praedicatio," *Revue Bénédictine* 42 (1930): 168–171, here 168–170.

The only monographic treatment of the theme of Doubting Thomas in art history is Sabine Schunk-Heller, *Die Darstellung des ungläubigen Thomas in der italienischen Kunst bis um 1500 unter Berücksichtigung der lukanischen Ostentatio Vulnerum*, Beiträge zur Kunstwissenschaft 59 (Munich, 1995); this work must be used with considerable caution, but nonetheless I have gratefully benefited from its presentation of the evidence.

For articles on Thomas in encyclopaedic surveys of Christian iconography, see Louis Réau, *Iconographie de l'art Chrétien*, vol. 2: *Iconographie de la Bible, II: Nouveau Testament* (Paris, 1957; repr. Neudeln, 1977), 568–570, and vol. 3: *Iconographie des Saints, III: P–Z, Répertoire* (Paris, 1959; repr. Millwood, N.Y., 1983), 1266–72; Gertrud Schiller, *Ikonographie der christlichen Kunst*, vol. 3: *Die Auferstehung und Erhöhung Christi* (Gütersloh, 1971), 108–114, 446–455 (illus. 341–369); M. Lechner, "Thomas Apostel," in *Lexikon der christlichen Ikonographie*, begründet von Engelbert Kirschbaum, herausgegeben von Wolfgang Braunfels, vol. 8: *Ikonographie der Heiligen, Meletius bis Zweiundvierzig Märtyrer. Register* (Rome, 1976), 467–475; George Kaftal, *Saints in Italian Art:*

Iconography of the Saints in the Painting of North East Italy (Florence, 1978), 968–972 (Nr. 293), *Iconography of the Saints in the Painting of North West Italy* (Florence, 1985), 637–640 (Nr. 223), *Iconography of the Saints in Tuscan Painting* (Florence, 1986), 970–978 (Nr. 296), and *Iconography of the Saints in Central and South Italian Painting* (Florence, 1986), 1080–88 (Nr. 384).

Hints toward a sexual interpretation of Doubting Thomas's penetration of Jesus' wound with his finger are provided, perhaps unsurprisingly, by Meyer Schapiro, "From Mozarabic to Romanesque in Silos," in his *Romanesque Art: Selected Papers* (New York, 1977), 87–88n123. Suggestive remarks, along somewhat similar lines, on pictorial representations of the body in general, especially of the body in pain, can be found in James Elkins, *Pictures of the Body: Pain and Metamorphosis* (Stanford, 1999).

My use of the term "syntagmatic" to describe the way in which the specific location of representations of Doubting Thomas with respect to neighboring ones within pictorial cycles of the Resurrection helps to identify its meaning and "paradigmatic" to refer to the relations of similarity and dissimilarity between images of Doubting Thomas and other images such as "Noli me tangere" is derived from Roman Jakobson, "Two Aspects of Language and Two Types of Aphasic Disturbances," in Linda R. Waugh and Monique Monville-Burston, ed., *Roman Jakobson: On Language* (Cambridge, Mass., 1990), 115–133.

For a suggestive, if somewhat idiosyncratic, philosophical and psychoanalytical interpretation of the pictorial theme of the encounter between Mary Magdalene and Jesus, see Jean-Luc Nancy, *Noli me tangere: Essai sur la levée du corps* (Paris, 2003), esp. 42–46, 55–60, 68–69, 81–84. For a somewhat more conventional art historical account of representations of this episode, together with various literary and theological reflections, the reader is referred to Marianne Alphand, Daniel Arasse, and Guy Lafon, *L'Apparition à Marie-Madeleine* (Paris, 2001).

Medieval cycles representing Thomas's missionary activity in India, especially those produced in various media in thirteenth-century France, are the subject of a forthcoming doctoral dissertation by Margarete Zink at the University of Freiburg in Breisgau; I thank her for her helpful correspondence and discussion with me on this subject.

On representations of Doubting Thomas in late antiquity, see especially Santi Muratori, "La più antica rappresentazione della incredulità di san Tommaso," *Nuovo Bulletino di Archeologia Cristiana* 17 (1911): 39–58.

The attribution of the Doubting Thomas in S. Maria del Fiore to Bicci di

Lorenzo and its dating to 1439 are now confirmed by Michael J. Amy, "The
Revised Attributions and Dates of Two 15th Century Mural Cycles for the
Cathedral of Florence," *Mitteilungen des Kunsthistorischen Institutes in Florenz* 42
(1998): 176–189.

For Verrocchio's double statue of Jesus and Thomas in Orsanmichele, see
Loretta Dolcini, ed., *Il Maestro di Leonardo: Il restauro dell'incredulità di san Tommaso
di Andrea del Verrocchio* (Milan, 1992), esp. Andrew Butterfield, "L'Incredulità di
San Tommaso di Andrea del Verrocchio," 61–87; Kristen van Ausdall, "The
'Corpus Verum': Orsanmichele, Tabernacles, and Verrocchio's 'Incredulity of
Thomas,'" in S. Bule, ed., *Verrocchio and Late Quattrocento Italian Sculpture* (Flor-
ence, 1992), 33–49; Herbert Beck, Maraike Bückling, and Edgar Lein, eds.,
Die Christus-Thomas-Gruppe von Andrea del Verrocchio (Frankfurt, 1996); and Andrew Butterfield, *The Sculpture of Andrea del Verrocchio* (New Haven, Conn.,
1998), 57–80.

The development of the half-figure in Renaissance religious painting is
the subject of an important study by Sixten Ringbom, *Icon to Narrative:
The Rise of the Dramatic Close-Up in Fifteenth-Century Devotional Painting*, 2nd ed.
(Doornspijk, 1984); on the Stein triptych, 205–209, fig. 194 (Doubting
Thomas is the third figure from the left in the third row from the top).

On painting as a rhetorical medium in the period after the Council of
Trent, see in general Marc Fumaroli, *L'École de silence: Le sentiment des images au
XVIIe siècle* (Paris, 1994).

The literature about Caravaggio is already enormous and seems, especially in recent years, when he has achieved extraordinary popularity, to
increase by the hour. Still fundamental are the works of Roberto Longhi:
see especially his *Studi Caravaggeschi*, 2 vols. = *Opere Complete*, vol. 11.1–2 (Milan, 1999–2000). Fundamental, too, is Walter Friedländer, *Caravaggio Studies*
(Princeton, 1955; 2nd ed., New York, 1969), on Caravaggio's *Doubting
Thomas*, especially 161–163 with fig. 89 (A. Dürer, *Doubting Thomas*, from the
Small Passion). Howard Hibbard, *Caravaggio*, 2nd ed. (Boulder, 1985) presents
a balanced biography and sound brief accounts of the paintings, together
with a helpful appendix reprinting, in the original languages and English
translation, the early biographies of the painter; on *Doubting Thomas*, 167–
168, 311. Another well-illustrated and helpful general work is Catherine
Puglisi, *Caravaggio* (London, 1998); on *Doubting Thomas*, 209–219. Other recent general studies include John Gash, *Caravaggio*, 2nd ed. (London, 1980);
Alfred Moir, *Caravaggio* (London, 1989); Mina Gregori, *Caravaggio* (Milan,
1994); Marco Bona Castellotti, *Il paradosso di Caravaggio* (Milan, 1998); and

Helen Langdon, *Caravaggio: A Life* (New York, 1998), on *Doubting Thomas* 235–237. The curious reader might also wish to consult such other works as Jutta Held, *Caravaggio: Politik und Martyrium der Körper* (Berlin, 1996), on *Doubting Thomas* 63–65; Leo Bersani and Ulysse Dutoit, *Caravaggio's Secrets* (Cambridge, Mass., 1998); Mieke Bal, *Quoting Caravaggio: Contemporary Art, Preposterous History* (Chicago, 1999), on *Doubting Thomas* 31–44; Graham L. Hammill, *Sexuality and Form: Caravaggio, Marlowe, and Bacon* (Chicago, 2000); Peter Robb, *M: The Man Who Became Caravaggio* (London, 2000), on *Doubting Thomas* 207–208; and now a novel, Atle Næss, *Doubting Thomas: A Novel about Caravaggio,* trans. Anne Born (London, 2000), on *Doubting Thomas* 64–65, 145–146.

Among recent publications on Caravaggio, some of the most interesting have investigated in detail the painter's relations to his patrons and collectors. See, for example, Francesca Cappelletti and Laura Testi, *Il trattenimento di virtuosi: Le collezioni secentesche di quadri nei Palazzi Mattei di Roma* (Rome, 1994); Creighton E. Gilbert, *Caravaggio and His Two Cardinals* (University Park, Pa., 1995); *Caravaggio e la collezione Mattei* (Milan, 1995); Silvia Danesi Squarzina, "The Collections of Cardinal Benedetto Giustiniani," *Burlington Magazine* 139 (1997): 766–769 and 140 (1998): 102–118, and ed., *Caravaggio e i Giustiniani: Toccar con mano una collezione del Seicento* (Milan, 2001), on *Doubting Thomas* 278–281. A useful collection of documents regarding Roman art in its social and institutional context in this period is furnished by Morton Colp Abromson, *Painting in Rome during the Papacy of Clement VIII (1592–1605): A Documented Study* (New York, 1981).

Recent studies of the scholarly reception of Caravaggio include Margrit Brehm, *Der Fall Caravaggio: Eine Rezeptionsgeschichte* (Frankfurt, 1992); and André Berne-Joffroy, *Le dossier Caravage: Psychologie des attributions et psychologie de l'art* (Paris, 1999), on *Doubting Thomas* 209–211.

Among other recent studies on Caravaggio I have found most useful the following: Michael Fried, "Thoughts on Caravaggio," *Critical Inquiry* 24:1 (Autumn 1997): 13–56; Franco Mormando, ed., *Saints and Sinners: Caravaggio and the Baroque Image* (Chicago, 1998); Sergio Benedetti, *Caravaggio: The Master Revealed,* 2nd ed. (Dublin, 1999), on the Dublin *Arrest of Christ in the Garden;* Beverly Louise Brown, ed., *The Genius of Rome: 1592–1623* (London, 2001). On philosophical dimensions of Caravaggio's paintings, see Adrienne von Mattyasouszky-Lates, "Stoics and Libertines: Philosophical Themes in the Art of Caravaggio, Poussin, and Their Contemporaries" (diss. Columbia 1988), on *Doubting Thomas* 68–69. Ellen Spolsky, "Doubting Thomas and the

Senses of Knowing," *Common Knowledge* 3:2 (1994): 111–129, provides a sophisticated though not fully coherent interpretation of Caravaggio's painting that emphasizes issues of knowledge, skepticism, and sexuality; a revised version of the article appears in her *Satisfying Skepticism: Embodied Knowledge in the Early Modern World* (Aldershot, UK, 2001), chap. 2, 28–44. I acknowledge with gratitude the kindness of Nicola Suther, who brought to my attention her lecture on the painting, delivered at a conference in June 2000 and available on the Internet (http://www.fu-berlin.de/giove/giove-audio/suthor.html); and that of Eleftheria Diamantopoulos, who sent me her MA degree submission of January 2002 for Essex University, Department of Art History and Theory, entitled "Doubting Thomas: A Painting with a Meditative Focus."

Alfred Moir, *Caravaggio and His Copyists* (New York, 1976), 88–90, lists the following copies of Caravaggio's *Doubting Thomas:* three prints, two drawn copies, fourteen extant painted copies, and thirteen lost painted copies.

The Christian and skeptical readings of Caravaggio's painting mentioned in the text are derived respectively from Maurizio Calvesi, *Le realtà di Caravaggio* (Turin, 1990), 40, and Ferdinando Bologna, *L'incredulità del Caravaggio e l'esperienza delle «cose naturali»* (Turin, 1992), 168, 320.

On the iconography of the German tradition of Doubting Thomas within the context not only of art history but also of Christian mysticism, see Rolf Wallrath, "Der Thomas-Altar in Köln: Zur Ikonographie des Thomaswunders," *Wallraf-Richartz-Jahrbuch* 17 (1955): 165–180.

The passage from Sandrart on Caravaggio and Holbein occurs in Sandrart's biography of the latter artist and runs as follows: "Finally, to summarize his [Holbein's] renown: already during his lifetime he was esteemed so highly that the most distinguished Italians did not hesitate to take over many things from his inventions into their own works, especially Michelangelo Caravaggio, as where St. Matthew is called away from the tax-collection by Jesus, also the gambler who scrapes up the money from the table, and other things too . . ."("Schließlich sein Lob zusammen zu fassen / so ist er noch in seinen Leb-Zeiten in so hohem Wehrt gewesen / daß die fürnehmste Italiener keinen Scheu getragen / aus seinen Inventionen viel in ihre Werke zu bringen / sonderlich Michael Angelo Caravaggio, als da Mattheus von dem Zoll durch Christum beruffen wird / auch den Spieler / der das Geld vom Tisch abstreicht / und anders mehr . . ."): Joachim von Sandrart, *Teutsche Academie der Bau-, Bild- und Mahlereykünste*, Nürnberg 1675–1680, in ursprünglicher Form neu gedruckt mit einer Einleitung von Christian Klemm (Nördlingen, 1994), pt. 2, bk. 3, 1:252. On the relation between Holbein's works and Caravaggio's, see especially Bernd Wolfgang Lindemann, "Sandrart beim Wort genommen—Holbein und Caravaggio," in Frank Matthias Kammel and Carola Bettina Gries, eds., *Begegnungen mit alten Meistern: Altdeutsche Tafelmalerei auf dem Prüfstand*, Wissenschaftliche Beibände zum Anzeiger des Germanischen Nationalmuseums Band 17 (Nuremberg, 2000), 245–256.

I have consulted the following repertories of North European printed illustrations: F. W. H. Hollstein, *German Engravings, Etchings, and Woodcuts ca. 1400–1700*, vol. 1ff. (Amsterdam, 1954ff.); *The New Hollstein: German Engravings, Etchings, and Woodcuts 1400–1700* (Rotterdam, 1986ff.); F. W. H. Hollstein, *Dutch and Flemish Etchings, Engravings, and Woodcuts ca. 1450–1700*, vol. 1ff. (Amsterdam, 1949ff.); *The New Hollstein: Dutch and Flemish Etchings, Engravings, and Woodcuts, 1450–1700* (Rotterdam, 2000ff.); Walter L. Strauss, ed., *The Illustrated Bartsch*, vol. 1ff. (New York, 1978ff.). Other versions of Doubting Thomas in *The Illustrated Bartsch* that bear some degree of similarity to Caravaggio's composition include those by Albrecht Dürer, 10:550 (.527kk); Urs Graf, 13:81 (4-[31] [460]); Georg Pencz, 16:99 (48 [332]); Jost Amman, 20,1:334 (2.36 [366]); and anonymous artists of German single leaf woodcuts before 1500, 162:174–78 (16201.567-2 to .575).

On the question of the relation between Dürer's *Arrest of Christ in the Garden* in *The Small Passion* and Caravaggio's version of the same theme, see Kristen Herrmann Fiore, "Caravaggio's *Taking of Christ* and Dürer's woodcut of 1509," *Burlington Magazine* 137 (1995): 24–27.

For the facial expression indicative of astonishment, see especially Charles Darwin, *The Expression of the Emotions in Man and Animals*, definitive edition, ed. Paul Ekman (New York, 1998), 278–289.

On Caravaggio's influence on painters in the early seventeenth century, see Arthur von Schneider, *Caravaggio und die Niederländer*, 2nd ed. (Amsterdam, 1967); Alfred Moir, *The Italian Followers of Caravaggio*, 2 vols. (Cambridge, Mass., 1967); Benedict Nicolson, *The International Caravaggesque Movement: Lists of Pictures by Caravaggio and His Followers throughout Europe from 1590 to 1650* (Oxford, 1979), and *Caravaggism in Europe*, ed. L. Vertova, 3 vols., 2nd ed. (Turin, 1990).

Gianni Papi, "Il Maestro dell'Incredulità di San Tommaso," *Arte Cristiana* 85 (1997): 121–130, discusses nine paintings, including a *Doubting Thomas* in Palazzo Valentini in Rome, which he attributes to a follower of Caravaggio and of his less celebrated contemporary Bartolomeo Manfredi who was working in Rome between 1620 and 1640 and whom Papi tentatively identifies as Jean Ducamps.

On Rubens's *Doubting Thomas*, see David Freedberg, *Rubens: The Life of Christ after the Passion* (Oxford, 1984), 81–87.

A study of Delacroix' version of the theme that also makes important remarks on the iconography of Doubting Thomas as a whole is Gert Van Osten, "Zur Ikonographie des ungläubigen Thomas angesichts eines Gemäldes von Delacroix," *Wallraf-Richartz-Jahrbuch* 27 (1965): 371–388, especially 374–385 on the history of images of Doubting Thomas.

Finally, I am indebted in various ways to a number of friends and colleagues, most of them from Florence, for their advice and assistance concerning specific aspects of the Italian iconography of Doubting Thomas, including Andrea Baldinotti, Miklos Boskowitz, Mina Gregori, Martina Hansmann, Maurizio Marini, and Dino Savelli. My grateful thanks to them all.

The Holy Finger

The brochure describing the relics displayed in the Roman church of Santa Croce in Gerusalemme is D. Balduino Bedini, O.Cist., "Le Reliquie della Passione del Signore," 3rd ed., Rome, 1997.

More information about the cult of Saint Thomas in Ortona can be obtained from a local periodical, *La voce di San Tommaso: Periodico della Concattedrale di San Tommaso Apostolo;* the editorial office is the Curia Vescovile, Largo Riccardi, Ortona.

✿

Illustration Credits

18. Albrecht Dürer: Doubting Thomas, *Die kleine Passion* (Nürnberg, 1511). From Walter L. Strauss, ed., *The Illustrated Bartsch* (New York: Abaris Books, 1978ff.), vol. 10 (formerly vol. 7, part I), p. 144, fig. 49 (120).

19. Albrecht Dürer: Jesus taken captive in the garden, *Die kleine Passion* (Nürnberg, 1511). From Walter L. Strauss, ed., *The Illustrated Bartsch* (New York: Abaris Books, 1978ff.), vol. 10 (formerly vol. 7, part I), p. 122, fig. 27 (119).

20. Hans Schäufelein, Doubting Thomas, in Wolfgan von Män, *Das Leiden Jesu Christi vnnsers Erlösers* (Augsburg, 1525). From Walter L. Strauss, ed., *The Illustrated Bartsch* (New York: Abaris Books, 1978ff.), vol. 11, p. 234, fig. 34-26 (253).

21. Hans Schäufelein, The disrobing of Christ, in Wolfgan von Män, *Das Leiden Jesu Christi vnnsers Erlösers* (Augsburg, 1525). From Walter L. Strauss, ed., *The Illustrated Bartsch* (New York: Abaris Books, 1978ff.), vol. 11, p. 221, fig. 34-13 (253).

22. Charles Darwin, *The Expression of the Emotions in Man and Animals,* definitive edition, edited by Paul Ekman (1872; New York: Oxford University Press, 1998), 279, fig. 24. Ekman cites G.-B. Duchenne de Boulogne, *Mécanisme de la physionomie humaine* (1862), pl. 56, as the photograph's source. See also G.-B. Duchenne de Boulogne, *The Mechanism of Human Facial Expression*, edited and translated by R. Andrew Cuthbertson (1862; Cambridge: Cambridge University Press, 1990).

23. Royal Cabinet of Paintings, Mauritshuis, The Hague

24. Koninklijk Museum voor Schone Kunsten, Antwerp. Copyright IRPA-KIK, Brussels.

25. "The Incredulity of Saint Thomas" by Bernardo Strozzi, about 1620, oil on canvas. Purchased by the Peter Moores Foundation for display at Compton Verney, Warwickshire. © Compton Verney. Photograph Marcus Leith.

26. Caravaggio, Supper at Emmaus, © National Gallery, London.

27. Su concessione del Ministero per i Beni e le Attività Culturali.

28. Reproduction of Jesus taken captive in the garden, by Caravaggio, courtesy of the National Gallery of Ireland.

❧

General Index

Index Locorum

New Testament Apocrypha and Gnostic Writings